IMAGINING
—— THE ——
WORLD
—— INTO ——
EXISTENCE

"Normandi Ellis takes her reader on an extraordinary journey into the myths and magic of Ancient Egypt. And the journey is as beautiful, fragrant, and mysterious as Egypt itself."

TIMOTHY FREKE AND PETER GANDY, AUTHORS OF
THE HERMETICA AND *THE JESUS MYSTERIES*

"This remarkable book emulates Egypt itself; it fuses philosophy, religion, art, and science into a single inextricable Unity. Like an accomplished Egyptian temple or sculpture, it looks effortless yet is extremely subtle and complex. It resonates Egypt. It 'breathes' Egypt. It is almost like actually being there! Not many books do that."

JOHN ANTHONY WEST, AUTHOR OF *SERPENT IN THE SKY* AND
THE TRAVELER'S KEY TO ANCIENT EGYPT

"Bravo! At last, the book from Normandi Ellis we have all been waiting for! Her knowledge and direct connection to the myths, the glyphs, and the symbolism of ancient Egypt have given us the clearest statement ever of the cosmology and relevant truths written in the scrolls. This book is a must for anyone seriously interested in the magic of ancient Egypt. I'm awed and inspired by its brilliance!"

NICKI SCULLY, COAUTHOR OF SHAMANIC MYSTERIES OF EGYPT AND THE ANUBIS ORACLE

"Normandi Ellis's work of a lifetime began when she wrote *Awakening Osiris,* her ecstatic translation of the hieroglyphs found in the ancient Egyptian Book of the Dead. It culminates nearly 30 years hence in her newest book, *Imagining the World into Existence.* In 1988 she said: 'We make of ourselves what we imagine.' Now, in 2012, we see she has imagined well."

ALAN RICHARDSON, COAUTHOR OF THE INNER GUIDE TO EGYPT

IMAGINING
— THE —
WORLD
— INTO —
EXISTENCE

An Ancient Egyptian
Manual of Consciousness

NORMANDI ELLIS

Bear & Company
Rochester, Vermont • Toronto, Canada

Bear & Company
One Park Street
Rochester, Vermont 05767
www.BearandCompanyBooks.com

Text stock is SFI certified

Bear & Company is a division of Inner Traditions International

Library of Congress Cataloging-in-Publication Data
Ellis, Normandi.
  Imagining the world into existence : an ancient Egyptian manual of
consciousness / Normandi Ellis.
     p. cm.
  Includes bibliographical references and index.
  Summary: "Reveals the secret language and words of power that enabled the
ancient Egyptians to imagine the world into existence"—Provided by publisher.
  ISBN 978-1-59143-140-4 (pbk.) — ISBN 978-1-59143-891-5 (e-book)
  1. Egypt—Religion. 2. Creation. 3. Imagination—Religious aspects. 4.
Evolution—Religious aspects. I. Title.
  BL2441.3.E45 2012
  299'.3124—dc23

2012007687

Printed and bound in the United States by Lake Book Manufacturing, Inc.
The text stock is SFI certified. The Sustainable Forestry Initiative® program
promotes sustainable forest management.

10 9 8 7 6 5 4 3 2 1

Text design and layout by Virginia Scott Bowman
This book was typeset in Garamond Premier Pro and Gill Sans with Goudy and
Swiss used as display typefaces.

To send correspondence to the author of this book, mail a first-class letter to the
author c/o Inner Traditions • Bear & Company, One Park Street, Rochester, VT
05767, and we will forward the communication, or contact the author directly at
www.normandiellis.com.

Contents

PART THREE
The Secret of Coming into Light

Dog in the Night

*I can feel a dog's furry face as he pushes his wet nose
   under my hand.*
But this is a hospital
They wouldn't let a dog in here?
This late at night?
Should I buzz for the nurse?
I can't move my hand.
I must be dreaming.
No, I'm very much awake.
*And I can feel the dog's furry face as he pushes his wet
   nose under my hand.*

I stroke his head.
He wants to play.
How can I play with a dog . . . ?
*Now I am sitting up, something I haven't done for
   weeks.*
A black dog, so friendly, no collar, no leash.
He must have run away from somewhere.

He wants me to follow him.
But I can't . . . yes I can, I'm walking behind him.
"Come on doggie. I'll take you home."

But . . . no . . . he's taking me home.

Harold Moss (1937–2010),
Words from a Silent Man

Foreword

Quite simply, this is a masterpiece. It is the life work of the numinous poet, writer, and Egyptian scholar Normandi Ellis. To read this work is to be planted with the seed of once and future mysteries. It is to become alive to the depth and genius of ancient Egypt in ways that give us keys to the portals that reveal our own unique capacities. And it is to uncover and bring to light something that the ancient Egyptians knew and that this profound book reveals—the archetypal basis of our reality.

We think about Egypt. We are drawn into Egypt. Egypt is farmed in our souls. During all my years of working with the imagery of the inner life, the emblems and attributes of Egypt recur again and again. In dreams and reveries, the symbols of Egypt rise to the inner vision: we see scarabs and ankhs, winged disks of the Sun. We long for our pilgrimage to the foot of the Sphinx, as if it could speak our deepest knowing. We recognize and relish the images of pharaonic masks and animal-headed gods that reside in every major museum throughout the world. We imagine vividly that eternally green oasis of the Nile Valley split by the life-giving blue river. Egypt seizes the Western psyche and we feel a collective shock of recognition. She seems to promise, "Travel where you may, do whatever you must, you will never forget *me*." And indeed I have traveled . . .

In the predawn call of the muezzin, in the late afternoon playing of a flute in the marketplace, I have heard the music that ripples across the friezes in the tombs of ancient musicians. On the curved lips of merchants in the night bazaar, I've noted the same beatific smiles as those that appear on the granite faces of the kings in Karnak.

The same dawn that bespoke the moment of creation to the ancient priestess washes across the faces of countless Egyptians—the light-skinned young businessmen in Cairo crossing the street, the dark Nubian children of Aswan weaving garlands, the sun-bronzed Bedouin camel drivers walking through the smoke of campfires below the dusty yellow plateau of Giza, and the almond-eyed gatekeepers smoking cigarettes outside the temple of Edfu.

In the dark heart of the Great Pyramid, I've spent the night staring into the dark, hearing the echo of ancient cantors and feeling the timeless pulse of the universe. On the edges of the desert, at the foot of the pyramids, I have looked up and seen the vibrant stars that are the gods in hiding, the souls waiting to be born. As the wind blows across the desert sands, I can imagine the shushing sounds of the bare feet of dancing tribal women as they make supplications to their goddess.

From Aswan to Luxor, the Nile River is crisscrossed by a constant flotilla of luxury boats, small skiffs, ferries, and sleek white-sailed feluccas. Its markets throng with vendors selling African spices, metal works, replicas of ancient statues, and colorful, vibrant textiles. Its streets are congested with camels and garden-variety hucksters whispering, "Mummy beads, miss. Ancient Egyptian mummy beads." If you are lucky enough or look especially gullible, a *galabeya*-clad man will pull you to the side, look furtively up and down the street, and then take from some hidden pocket a noxious desiccated foot smelling of turpentine, saying, "Found in the tomb, by my grandfather. For you, my sister, only a thousand dollars." And when you try to hurry away, he runs after you, calling, "How much you want to pay?"

Egypt is not only a culture that existed in a certain time and place, with a certain history, geography, and economics. Egypt, as Normandi Ellis so brilliantly informs us, is also a state of being that exists eternally in archetypal realms. The historical Egypt was but a backdrop for the essential Egypt, the Egypt of the eternal return. In this view, Egypt did not *have* but rather *was* a quality of intelligence.

In ancient Egypt, at least for a period of time, something happened. The essence of possibility entered into historic time. And it is that primary essence that resonates through archetypal Egypt—through the Egypt of our psyches—representing the creative potency of universal form and power. It is that which unfolded into what we know as the historical, exoteric Egypt.

It is one of the themes of this book that this template of essential and archetypal reality, along with the concept of the gods and goddesses—the *neteru,* as the ancients called them—created the charge and possibility for the pattern that became ancient Egypt.

Part of ancient Egypt's power to enthrall lies in a great paradoxical mystery. How did it happen that in a two- to five-hundred-year period, somewhere between 3100 and 2600 BCE, an aboriginal people on the banks of a swampy delta recovered the land and invented an agronomy that has lasted for five thousand years? What leaps of imagination caused them to discover many of the fine points of astronomy, architecture, medicine, mathematics, and literature? What infusion of wisdom, intuition, or intelligence conceived the enormity of pyramids, their eternal presence, and also created the delicate balance of *ma'at,* a system of governance and law based on principles of cosmic truth?

What priests or kings divined in their hearts a consummate theology and symbology, an enormously artful and enduring culture, and a written language based on hieroglyphs? How could it be that in so short a time the Egyptian people's bodies, minds, and souls entered into a congruence that quickened a surge of creativity that, as far as we know, has not been rivaled since? In exploring this mystery, Normandi Ellis not only reveals the art and science that quickened and evolved the mind of ancient Egypt but gives us keys to discovering and manifesting the great creative principles that lie within us all. What emerges for the reader then is not only an ingenious and thrilling exposition on the underlying principles of the sacred psychology of ancient Egypt but what is perhaps one of the finest explorations of the nature and practice of the creative imagination.

THE NETER AS THE GOD IN NATURE

Of the forces contributing to the intense and complex growth of ancient Egyptian civilization one of the most vital was the notion of the living gods, or the concept of "neteru neteru." Egyptian gods and goddesses are the divine impulses that reveal themselves in the natural world and in the body.

NETER AS ARCHETYPE

The neteru operate on a psychological level, as well as a spiritual level; that is, they are not only the creators of patterns but the holders of patterns, the embodiment of an ancient consciousness. They served as dynamic archetypes and motivating principles to which the Egyptians consciously attuned themselves. Neteru presented themselves symbolically in animal and human forms, as well as with a combination of animal and human features. Their diverse outward appearances were not arbitrary fantasies but symbols based on careful consideration, deep meditation, and meticulous observation of the nature of reality.

The divine attributes of neteru are present and active in human life: the human being always contains the potential to be raised to the gods. Thus neteru serve as evolutionary principles of reality, engendering a higher development by functioning on a psychospiritual level in much the same way as DNA functions on an organic level. At any moment the possibility exists for us to make the next leap to a higher level of spiritual understanding and creative fulfillment. In essence, we are made of cosmic dust, of wavering particles of light, of the great expansive creative "Ahhh!" We are the latest product of the metabolism of the galaxy. We are the substance of gods. We are made from the body of gods, all the bits of humanity moving around like atoms in the body of the divine. As the ancients used to say, "The divine mother of the universe (Nut) has many souls."

NETER AS SCIENCE

For the ancient Egyptians, life was a dynamic interaction between essence and existence, between theocentric reality (divine centered) and anthropocentric reality (human centered). Man was a model of the universe, and the universe was a model of god. When he understood himself fully, he could also understand the universe: its laws of astronomy, astrology, proportion, mathematics, geography, measure, medicine, anatomy, rhythm, magic, art. All were linked in one dynamic scheme. One part could not be understood if separated from any other part.

Anthropocentric thinking and theocentric thinking were not opposed to each other at all but formed an essential bridge as a way of understanding the relationship of the self to the divine. As Rainer Maria Rilke has said, "Take your practiced powers and stretch them out until they span the chasm between two contradictions . . . for the god wants to know himself in you." This acceptance and application of the dual principles operating in the cosmos create the tension and energy necessary to project us toward great leaps of culture and development. The merger of human and "netered" knowing—a psychology unique to the Egyptians—helped create in a brief period, and literally from the mud, one of the most complex and brilliant civilizations that has ever existed.

We come to understand the dynamic vibration and effect of the creative principle in all things by discovering the interrelationships of the neteru. When we discuss the theory of spiraling black holes, or what preceded the big bang, for example, we can also understand the creation of the space-time continuum in relation to the Egyptian notion of divine creation. In the beginning, lying with primordial chaos (Atum), are the principles of darkness, inertia, the void, and hidden energy (the *ogdoad*). All of these are the precursors to the spontaneous explosion of light (the birth of Ra). In the end of days, so say the Egyptians, all of these return again to Atum, to chaos, to the swirling void, the inert, and the dark, as the circling serpent, Atum, swallows its tail.

Within their concept of neteru, the Egyptians wove a very conscious sacred science from physical, psychological, mythic, and spiritual threads. On the physical level the god or goddess embodied a planet, a plant, or, as we have seen, an organ of the body. The ancient Egyptian met the grain god Osiris in any wheat field.

On a psychological level the archetypal neter served as a great animating force whose actions mimicked one's own, giving one's life purpose, meaning, and even the momentum behind taking action and making choices. Whenever he fought an oppressor, the ancient Egyptian reenacted the battle of Horus and Seth.

On a mythic level, a god represented an entire story that illuminated the stages, sufferings, and ultimate ennoblement of existence. By recalling the sorrows of Isis, the birth of her child, her wanderings, and ultimate triumphs, the ancient Egyptian entered into a deeper pattern encoded in both psyche and spirit, which allowed for the unfolding of her imagination and a deeper connection to her own life.

Finally, on the integral or religious level, the neter was a great mediator between the Earth realm and the transcendent realm, helping to seed or crystallize within us higher patterns of existence in the way that spiritual yearning allows one to transcend the temporal and contact the divine in one's own nature. These patterns manifest in time and space in the devotee through the neter's communion and love. This integral spiritual level embraces and infuses with its qualities the other three levels.

Traces of this way of experiencing a netered world remain in the contemporary Egyptian's psyche. While leading a tour through Egypt some years ago, I performed an engagement ceremony for two of our Egyptian guides at sunset atop the Temple of Hathor, an Egyptian goddess of love. During the ceremony the planet Venus rose, and the young couple exclaimed, "Look! Hathor is rising and blessing our engagement!"

In *Imagining the World into Existence,* Normandi Ellis provides ways of moving from outmoded existence to an amplified life that is at once more cherished and more cherishing. It requires that we undertake the extraordinary task of releasing part of our current, local selves and of being reborn to our eternal selves. When we descend into the forgotten knowings of earlier or deeper phases of our existence, when we descend into the Egypt of ourselves, we may find hidden potentials, the unfulfilled and unfinished seedlings that, when attended to, can bring into being the green world within that can restore the wasteland without.

Ultimately then, this extraordinary work is a manual for the gardening of soul and world.

JEAN HOUSTON

Jean Houston, Ph.D., scholar, philosopher, and researcher in human capacities, is considered to be one of the foremost visionary thinkers and doers of our time. She is the founder of a program of cross-cultural mythic and spiritual studies, dedicated to empowering change agents and people around the world by teaching history, philosophy, the new physics, psychology, anthropology, myth, and the many dimensions of our human potential. She is also the founder of training programs in social artistry, which enables leaders to extend their own development so as to more adequately deal with the social challenges of today's world. The author of some twenty-six books, she has worked in over one hundred countries, holding conferences and training seminars with government leaders and educational and business institutions and organizations. As a consultant to the United Nations, she brings training to leaders in many countries, helping to produce new pioneers—social artists—working on the frontiers of the emerging global society while deepening their own cultural and artistic values. She keynotes many international conferences, consults widely with governments and heads of state, and also works at a grassroots level, helping to actualize the United Nations Millennium Development Goals. She has been acknowledged as one of the most innovative thinkers of our time; Buckminster Fuller called Jean Houston's mind a national treasure.

Acknowledgments

This work is a culmination of thirty years of experience, study, and thought that, by its nature, has been influenced by many individuals. If your name appears in my bibliography, it is certain that your life and work have been pivotal to my thinking. I especially want to thank Nicki Scully, John Anthony West, and Jean Houston for many years of friendship and support. It would have been a very different life without your presence in it. I thank Jon Graham, acquisitions editor at Inner Traditions, for seeing the merit in this project, and Ray Grasse, Alan Richardson, John Darnell, and Greg Reeder for their generous permission to quote and use their material.

Thanks to the artists and photographers who brought to life the images of Egypt—Karen Kaplan Klein, Jane Brantley, Cathleen Shattuck, Patricia Haynes, my daughter Alaina Schroth, and cover artist Lucie Lamy. For their close readings of the text, I offer special thanks to Anne Dillon, my editor at Inner Traditions, whose careful editing and coaxing elevated the work, and to David Hurt, my husband, who gave this work an in-depth reading above and beyond the duty of any spouse. I thank him especially for opening the way for this work to enter, for growing the garden, tending our home, and nobly embodying the Green Man, Osiris. I am deeply grateful to my many friends in Chesterfield, Indiana—and especially my mentors Reverand Glenda Cadarette and Reverand A. Win Srogi, who saw and encouraged the future potential of this work.

More than all of that, I must acknowledge the spiritual integrity and the heritage of Egypt's great metaphysicians, scribes, and master teachers, whose lives and work so influenced mine. And I am grateful to have been given this life to live, this book to write, and this Creator to serve.

Open Sesame!
Introduction to the Work

This book is a meditation on the spiritual nature of the creative process. It recalls through myths the many ways of creation. It examines how the divine creative impulse infuses humankind so that we may work as co-creators of our world. The ancient Egyptian priest called this inherent spiritual force *heka*—a word identified as magic, but it is magic as prayer and invocation aligned with the will of the Divine. This belief in the shared magical power of the spirit permeated Egyptian life, and it is the foundation of many world religions. The use of invocation as an agent of transformative energy deepens one's connection to the Divine. It is a powerful form of prayer.

Just as Akhenaten reached toward his god Aten, when I reach toward the Divine, the Divine reaches back. Studying the Egyptian mysteries provides us with a record of human longing for and reaching toward understanding our relationship to our Creator. Inscribed inside the sacred Egyptian temples and tombs, and written within the funerary scrolls and along the edges of shrines and coffins, we have a record of human spiritual longing. These books of prayer and sacred texts represent the oldest spiritual documents in the world.

If casual readers want to see these texts as gobbledygook, they will appear for them as gobbledygook. Rational thinking has never been the key to understanding the intricate mysteries of symbols. The maker of this world is as radiant and various as the natural world that reflects the Divine Creator, and there may be worlds beyond our ken that are also divinely created.

Hieroglyphic images work upon the psyche through symbol, association, metaphor, story, and sound. They require the spiritual aspirant to slow down, to meditate, to intuit, and to dream in order to understand a language in which God speaks through the eye, the ear, the heart, and the natural world. The ancient Egyptians said that their sacred texts were written in the god Thoth's own hand "with his own fingers." In much the same way, the thirteenth-century Jesuit mystic Meister Eckhart said, "Apprehend God in all things, for God is in all things. Every single creature is full of God and is a book about God."[1]

Swiss Egyptologist Eric Hornung believes the Egyptian mysteries were not gained by elaborate initiation rites but by reading and contemplating during one's lifetime the books that held "the 'mysterious' knowledge of the afterlife." Over time, these shamans and priests continued to write and develop an ever-richer literature. "No initiation was needed to do this," Hornung says.[2] One need only be literate and curious and spend time literally walking around inside the great books of the temple inscribed upon the walls. As they entered the book, the book entered them.

This book represents my thirty years of walking around inside the hieroglyphs.

It explores psychospiritual creative states of mind first articulated by the ancient Egyptians. What we know about religious doctrines, I believe, has come down to us from those enlightened beings of the distant past. Where did they come from? They seem to have sprung up overnight. Perhaps they were god-sent. Why are we still exploring their multimillennial-year-old culture? Because change is once again upon us; it is everywhere around us. I believe we have the opportunity to be again participants in our own becoming. We are seedlings in a new era.

Read some of the bibliography texts if you are interested in learning more and, of course, make a sojourn in Egypt. If that is not possible, make a trip into your own backyard to be with the sun, the wind, the green leaves, and the beetles.

ENTERING THE GARDEN

Two nights ago, as a full moon rose over the hills, I stood with my husband overlooking our garden. It was a verdant, abundant, and renewing world full of beans, corn, squash, tomatoes, and onions. The peas and lettuces had already come and gone, having given us the fruit of their leaves and vines, leaving us next year's seed. The month before, I had left my job. Now here I stood in my field of vegetables starting a new life and a new book. How appropriate, I thought, that on this evening I was beginning to write my "field guide" to the Egyptian mysteries of life and death. These mysteries belonged to the Egyptian god Osiris, who created the underworld and ruled over all fecund, green things that grew above ground.

In my youth, I had planted many seeds. The dreams I held then had now come to fruition. I have harvested many seeds from the many fruits of many labors. What has been growing in me now is a new way of caring for my body and soul. The idea of the seed, I realized, is vital to the Egyptian mysteries. That is why so many Arabic tales of magic begin with the words *open sesame*. Within the sesame seed—the smallest seed imaginable—lies the symbolic key that opens the door to spiritual growth.

Let us ask a simple blessing as we prepare to enter the mystery by simply saying the phrase *open sesame*.

PLANTING THE SEED

The hieroglyph for seed is *per-t*, ⬜ ◠ ⸫ ⸲. It contains three sound images—a house, an open mouth, and a loaf of bread, which is the phonetic *t* and gives a feminine quality to the word for seed. Two more hieroglyphs follow: three seeds and a plow. These two images more or less provide the context for the sound. In this case, we are talking about seed that is being planted into a furrow. This one word holds the secret of our entire study of the ancient Egyptian mysteries of Osiris.

The tiny sesame seed depicted here produces a plant five feet tall, about the same height as the average ancient Egyptian. The plant's bell-shaped flowers turn into pods containing hundreds of tiny seeds. By analogy, we might say that from one creation many creations are possible. The seeds were crushed in ancient times to create oil used in cooking and lighting oil lamps. (Sesame seed oil is used also to stimulate the production of testosterone.)

To plant the seed (a field is also called per-t, ⬜ ⬜ ◠◟) is to create new life, to engage in a cycle of unending generation. The seed offers unlimited supply; its potential represents the continuity of life. The male seed planted within the female body (called *per-it*) grows into a new human form. Our children inherit not only our land but also our DNA. A seed planted in one's mind and cultivated grows over time through action and contemplation into an outward visible form. The big bang was the ultimate bursting seedpod that created all matter and antimatter in the universe. All the atoms that originated with the big bang are the star seeds that became all the universes and everything in the cosmos.

The seed is the core of our existence. The seed may be a similar concept to the soul. As the German poet Rainer Maria Rilke says in "Buddha inside the Light":

> *The core of every core, the kernel of every kernel*
> *an almond! held in itself, deepening in sweetness:*
> *all of this, everything, right up to the stars,*
> *is the meat around your stone.*[3]

CRACKING THE SEED

In the ancient language, whatever multiplies and grows is indicated by the hieroglyph of the three seeds. The creative force is multiple and constantly unfolding. The universal god force is multiple—both male and female (*neteru*, ꜰꜰꜰ). Beauty is multiple (*nefert*, ꜰ◠◠ꜰ). Light itself is multiple (*khu*, 🦩⊙ᵇ); and magic, defined as "words of power" (*hekau*, ⚡⚒⚑ᵇ), is multiple. Abstract concepts whose definitions we take for granted are seen in the hieroglyphs as being multiple. Truth (*ma'at*, ⚖⚑ᵇ) is often more than one thing, and so it is written with the multiple sign of seeds.

The idea that truth is more than one thing expands our notion of reality. It prevents us from thinking only in sound bites, slogans, or tweets. It offers us layers of meaning. The word for truth, *ma'at*, also means "foundation." One may think either of the foundation of a house or of layers of soil that create a fertile environment for a seed. All that grows above the surface has its first seed and roots in this foundation. Over time, these multiple layers become bedrock—the foundation stone on which to build temples.

A seed shows us complex layers of meaning, which often include that which we cannot see at first glance. Look at the hieroglyph for light (khu) above and one will see a dark sun, or the veiled light, included with the crowned ibis. The meaning of a seed is not known simply by looking at the seed. The true power of a tiny seed is that it must be exposed to sunlight even before it is planted in the dark. It must be allowed to break down and then to regenerate, taking its sustenance from the dark, unknowable realm beneath the ground, and in time, as if by magic, the seedling pushes through the earth. Imagine that this early exposure to the light somehow programs the seed to seek the source of light as it develops.

It is by this same process of using both the conscious and the unconscious mind—that is, knowledge that is outwardly visible and inwardly felt—that the secrets of ancient Egypt have been revealed. These secrets or mysteries (*seshet*, ⚬▢⚬⚑ᵇ) are processed first through the unconscious. The true meaning of seed is alive beneath the surface of things—for all that grows from seed has roots below the soil as well as flowers above the surface.

The magician, priest, and the modern-day alchemist recognize that the sacred language of prayer, invocation, and affirmation initiates changes within us and in the outer world. These words of power, or heka, are seed thoughts of reality. Invocation and affirmation reinforce the idea that as living members of the body of the Divine, we cocreate the world in which we live. The simple phrase *open sesame* works as an agricultural model, as a sexual metaphor, and as a symbol for all things that grow.

The seeds contained in the word *hekau*, 𓏏𓇳𓏤 (meaning both magic and words of power), set forth the idea that everything we say, how we think of it, and how we say it casts a kind of magical spell of consciousness over our world. Another way of understanding this is to recall the biblical verse: "As you sow, so shall you reap." Pay attention to what you plant in thought, word, and deed. Prepare yourself as fertile soil so that when the time is right you will see your desires bear fruit.

PREPARING THE GROUND

The word *per* (𓉐𓂋) not only means "field" or "ground"; it also depicts a container and its symbol is a house. *Per ankh* means "the house of life" and refers to a temple library and the many incantations written on papyrus scrolls and stored there. *Per ur* means "the great house" or the home of the gods. The temple sanctuary, or holy of holies, is called *per ur*. It rests in the center of the god's or goddess's temple, and the golden shrine placed there contains the statue of the divine being. Or it may refer to the sky, which is altogether another kind of great house where gods and goddesses dwell. In the modern church, this per ur functions as the altar, which contains the host and chalice, containers of the body and blood of the divine son.

A human being is also a container for the Divine. The living pharaoh housed the Divine within his person. This living word of God, the *per áa* (𓉐𓂋𓂝) was the earthly, fleshy residence of the god Horus. At death that divinity is not lost. The succeeding pharaoh becomes the living and reigning Horus, but the deceased and mummified pharaoh becomes the manifestation of Osiris, lord of the dead. After his passage through the underworld, the resurrected pharaoh reemerges as the golden, rising sun god Re. Still a container for the divine light of God, the pharaoh has simply changed form, as if one were pouring honey from one jar to another.

How this transformation occurs is the essential secret of the Osirian Mysteries that seed the many ancient wisdom texts and books of the afterlife. The mystery of the magical rebirth of Osiris as the god of light is contained in the ancient text known as the Secret of Osiris Becoming Re, which appears on one of the shrines of Tutankhamun. Even our English word *mystery* refers to the *myst-Re,* that is, to the giving birth (*myst*) to Re, the eternal solar god linked to Horus. The dead pharaoh, wrapped in his mummy cloths, was buried like a seed in a mound of earth (whether in a pyramid or within a cave carved into the side of a mountain). He was deposited into the many layers of his tomb, which included his shrines and sarcophagi. Then he was placed beneath his pyramid or inside his tomb and sealed within. In Tutankhamun's tomb, archaeologists found a mummy effigy containing germinated wheat. Recently wheat seeds were found in Saqqara inside the Step Pyramid of Djoser, Egypt's oldest pyramid. They were radiocarbon-dated to the date of the pyramid's construction nearly five thousand years ago.

A pyramid, *per-áa-met,* is a house of endings and beginnings (□ ◇ ⇔ ⌐). *Met,* which is indicated by the phallus, means "seed" and "birth." *Met* can also be written as 🜍, which means "to die"; the image appears to be blood spurting from a head wound. Both words link to the vulture goddess Mut, who feeds upon the corpse that signifies the past but lays the egg of new beginnings.

COMING FORTH BY DAY

On the Giza Plateau the three pyramids of the Old Kingdom pharaohs Khufu, Khafre, and Menkare lie like a row of three planted seeds. The symbolism of burying a king inside a mound of earth was linked with the idea of burying seed in the ground, and now the empty sarcophagi lie open like burst seedpods. These three pyramid seeds reflect the three stars aligned in the belt of Orion, the constellation that is the celestial body of the god Osiris.

The deceased pharaoh, like the god Osiris, has gone home, having vanished into the star-spangled belly of his mother, the sky goddess Nut. As Southern ministers are wont to say: "He has been called home." Being called back or called forth is another meaning of the word *per-t*. In particular, it means to come forth at the sound of one's voice. The soul of the recently dead travel through the twelve portals of the underworld, which represent the twelve hours of night. On this perilous trip, one needs the proper words of power to cross to the other side unharmed.

In a similar manner, the living initiate into the Egyptian mysteries undergoes a death-in-life transformation. He understands the mysteries by having read and understood the lessons contained in what we call the Egyptian Book of the Dead. The ancient Egyptians called it the Book of Coming Forth by Day, the Book of Coming into Light, or the Secret of Osiris Becoming Re. A seedling that lies buried in the ground is called by spirit to live again and rise up toward the light.

According to certain mystical traditions, the initiate must stand at one point before a particular stone block that hides the entryway into the initiation chambers inside the Great Pyramid. What stands between him and an understanding of the meaning of life and death is a magically sealed door that only he can open when he calls out the correct words. The words he speaks will indicate that he has understood the lessons of life, death, and transformation into rebirth. When he calls correctly, spirit will come forth to meet him at the sound of his true voice.

The initiate cries, "Open sesame."

And so the mystery continues to evolve. As above, so below. The ground on which we walk—and wherein we do all our birthing, living, and dying—is but a mirror of the celestial creation story that unfurls in a starry scroll in the night sky above us. Now let us begin to unfold the many layers of this most sacred story.

PART ONE

In the Beginning

Cosmogenesis
Stories of How the World Began

Mysterious, mysterious is the Opener of the mysterious neterworld, the unveiler of the darkness, he who chases away clouds, who bursts forth as a shooting star.[1]

LITANY OF RE

First, there was nothing. Nothing. Nothing. Nothing.

It is hard to imagine this nothingness. It is not even empty space, for space is something begging definition. It is not darkness, for darkness exists in opposition to light. There is nothing before it. There is only perhaps a point in the midst of that which cannot be known, and then what happens? Bam! The universe flings itself into existence with ever-expanding sparks of light, like fireworks exploding in the sky, like petals of chrysanthemums unfolding.

Light exists because its energy pushes against the darkness. Space exists, created by the vibration of energy moving out from each side, above and below. Time rides through space on the back of light. There was nothing, and then there was everything.

Where did it come from, when did it happen, and why did it happen? We don't know. Creation of the universe is by definition *super-*natural because, before the universe existed, there was no nature and no natural world to explain its appearance. How something like a universe emerges out of nothingness has long been the mystery, the ineffable secret of life and death. Physical sciences attempt to explain this, calling forth the metaphor of the seed in which the whole essence of the plant's life cycle exists before the seed takes root in the earth. But even that original seed comes from something. It may come from a divine source.

THE UNITY AND
MIND OF THE ONE GOD

The creative intelligence that made this world and all the other worlds and universes, seen and unseen, drew that substance from within. The breath of God exhales the molecules that are part of its creative body. That includes you and me, and everything else. The emptiness and the fullness we may define as God. What is breathed out may be seen as divine sparks, the seeds of God's spiritual nature in which we all partake. Perhaps these light particles are atoms or seed forms that emanate from the divine creative impulse that ancient Egyptians would have called Atum. The seeds that emerge from Atum were described as Re, or light. In their book *The Hermetica,* Timothy Freke and Peter Gandy explore the concept of Atum. "Atum is whole and constant. In himself he is motionless, yet he is self-moving. He is immaculate, incorruptible and everlasting. He is the supreme Absolute Reality. He is filled with ideas which are imperceptible to the senses, and with all-embracing Knowledge. Atum is Primal Mind."[2]

How nothing generates everything is a religious conundrum. The mind of God conceives us and, apparently, continues operation through the individual sparks within our minds. Consciousness becomes cosmos. Every creative principle that flows from that point on is known as natural law.

Every sacred tradition, to my knowledge, offers a story of creation that tells us how we humans and our world were made and for what purposes. Each sacred scripture offers a language of unity. One God makes the universe, which creates the many fires in the one nature of being. From the various traditions, we read:

> Allah is the one light that illuminates heaven and earth. (Islam)
> Truth is one and the learned call it by many names. (Hindu)
> There is only one God; all the "gods" are but his ministering angels
> who are his manifestations. (Shinto)
> Every object in the world has a spirit and that spirit is wakan. . . .
> The word *Wakan Tanka* means all of the wakan beings because
> they are all as if one. (Lakota)[3]

Most of our life is nonphysical. That might be hard to believe looking at the world through physical eyes inside physical bodies, as the majority of life happens inside our heads or far outside it. Thought is not our brain; it is the electrical zap—a small light sparkle—that happens between neurons inside the gray matter of the cerebellum. Whatever that electrical zap is contains the seed thought that may result in action or awareness—anything from "I think I'll plant beans today" to "You know, those twelve yellow flame symbols on the tower tarot card might also be god seeds falling from the sky to Earth."

Even at that, to be understood, thought is converted into image. Humans live in a physical universe, and so we must use the language of that physical universe in any attempt to explain how creativity starts and creation begins. The closest means to approach the ineffable mystery is through a symbol, which may be another way of explaining how and why ancient Egyptians used hieroglyphs as the sacred language of the Divine.

The people of Egypt found the Creator's signature in every living thing. The many ways in which God was perceived did not conflict with but rather supplemented each other. The God who made us must be various and have many aspects. That God must be as unique as we are; that God also must be a unified being, as all human races are a unified community.

ATUM: THE SUPREME BEING

To show the many ways of making that arise from the mind of God, the ancient Egyptians offered more than one creation story. The word *mes* or *mys* implies actual birth and the *mys*tery of rebirth. One of the oldest spiritual texts, the Secret of Osiris Becoming Re, explores ever-changing states of being and becoming, teasing out the luminous connections between birth, death, and rebirth. The text details the ascension of Osiris into heaven and his appearance in the night sky as a being of light, Orion. This recurrence of the risen Osiris as a light in the sky is a cyclical event that assures us of our own return to the god spark from which we came. The mystery of death is woven into the mystery of birth. Celestial generation becomes the archetypal creative pattern that sets up regenesis.

How does a thing come into being? We can see it, we can dream it, we can shape it with our hands, we can unite with our mate, we can speak about our ideas, and we can plant a seed that grows through nature's magical processes. Each of these is part of a natural process of creation in a physical universe—but what creates the physical universe?

The Book of Knowing the Creation of Re and the Overthrow of Chaos (also known as the Bremner-Rhind Papyrus) shows us the ultimate unnamed God of creation who is later called Atum. Atum's story is the most ancient creation myth; it arises from Heliopolis, the city of light. The god Atum is the alpha and omega of the Egyptian pantheon. He is the original light vibration emerging from the void. Atum explains how the universe originated from his own body. "In the beginning I became the becoming, being what I created."[4]

Atum tells us that at first there was nothing and then he existed. Rising up out of the inertness and the watery abyss, he created an opposite—the primeval mound. How did he do this? "I came into being in my heart," he says. "I saw it all before my eyes. I made every form before sneezing Shu and spitting forth Tefnut."

Everything existed as a seed of itself before Atum brought it forth.

In his mind and in his desire, life already existed before the physical act of making his creations. In the creation story of Atum, everything hinges on the word *kheper* and the variant connections to the repeated image of the hieroglyphic dung beetle Khepera, 𓆣, which is the sign for potentiality, being, becoming, making, doing, creating, beginning, and so on. (Please see plate 7 of the color insert.)

Thus a process of unfoldment occurs in which time and space begin.

STORIES OF THE FIRST TIME

The first creation must occur somewhere, and that place the ancient Egyptians called the *Nun,* a watery abyss that one may imagine as a vast body of vapor or swirling cosmic dust. From this dark, chaotic emptiness, matter formed; or another way of saying this is that from the great deep, a mound of earth arose. Any celestial event has an earthly counterpart, says the Hermetica, an ancient wisdom text said to record a dialogue between the Old Kingdom scribe Imhotep and the god Thoth (Hermes Trismegistus). "Egypt is made in the image of heaven. It is the projection below of the order of things above."[5]

In the physical world, Egyptian stories of the beginning of time and space focus on a great flood that is mirrored in the annual flooding of the Nile that begins the Egyptian calendar. The first day of the new year is known as Zep Tepi—which means "the First Time." The First Time symbolizes how the Creator arose from the watery abyss, or the Nun, and stood on the primeval hill. Every year, the story recurs when the all-encompassing floodwaters of the Nile fill the land. As the flood recedes, a mound of fertilized earth emerges, like the mound on which the god Atum first stood.

Every year at the same time, the world is made anew just as it was made on the first day at the beginning of time. This rejuvenation extends not only to the fields and crops but also to all the kingdoms of the natural world. Every major city in ancient Egypt had its own version of the creation story—Heliopolis, Memphis, Abydos, Hermopolis, and so on.

These many sacred, complementary creation stories were inscribed on the temple walls of Egypt. Each story told how the divine being of that particular place made the worlds of gods and humans. The story of the Nile's regeneration is the story of our regeneration. Alan Richardson has called it "a ribbon of inner consciousness . . . that rises from the lost and forgotten areas of the unconscious mind and flows onward to those curious areas where the human touches the divine. The Nile lies hidden within us all."[6]

Each version of the creation story is considered a true story, just as there is more than one creation story told in Genesis. The ways of divine creation are as various as earthly and human creations, and yet all stem from what Emory J. Michael defines as the "Law of Seed"[7] and the indwelling presence of our God who made us. This law of seed means that we, too, create our world through thought, word, and deed. All of life is a state of consciousness filled with the particularities of the divine powers and impulses that created the universe.

The essences of the natural world are used to symbolize the divine energies that flow all about us—seen and unseen. What we call god or goddess the ancient Egyptians called *neter,* the Coptic Egyptians called *netcher,* and the Greeks called nature. For example, Shu is the neter of wind, of breath, of invisibility. Neith is the *netert* of the principle of unification through the weaving and merging of opposites. The maternal, divine impulse of Neith brings the spiritual into form by creating a net of mental, astral, and physical energies. Isis is the netert of birthing, nurturing, and protecting. The god Horus is the archetypal hero, the warrior, the child who grows wise and leads his people. As these divine energies (or god seeds) move through us, they could be seen in Jungian terms as archetypes.

For our purposes, I will examine five myths from five Egyptian cities that demonstrate five ways of creation.

NEITH WEAVES THE WORLD INTO BEING

Gods and goddesses have many names and forms. The first hieroglyph to indicate a divine being was *n-t*, ⌇ ◠⅂. The hieroglyph even looks like the primordial water and the mound of earth beginning to emerge from it. *Nt* is the hieroglyphic precursor to the word *neter*, and this original name for Neith meant "the goddess." In the creation story of the city of Sais, Neith existed before anything else. Her divine, fertile body was the emptiness in which lay unlimited potentiality. Identified as the cosmic, watery abyss from which light first arose, her cult festival was called the Feast of Light and reminded one of how at winter solstice the light returns from the darkest part of the year. At the water's edge, celebrants floated lit candles to replicate the story of light emerging from the waters. The festival reappears in the Christian tradition as Little Christmas, which occurs in early January.

Here we see Neith, the weaver goddess who embodied the primordial waters, as she appeared in the New Kingdom tomb of Ramses III.

Neith, we are told, wove a net—like her name N-t—and cast it into the primordial waters of herself, the Nun or nothingness. Waves of energy moved across these waters, weaving together a pattern like strands of DNA. From her deepest desires at the depths, or the Nun, of her being, the goddess drew forth the first divine beings. This self-generated mother of all gave birth to both that which is above and that which is below, namely the sun god Re and the crocodile god Sobek.

Again reaching into the murky waters, she drew forth all creatures of the deep, the hippopotami, fish, and frogs. She brought forth all fowl and birds. She pulled from her depths the trees, grass, rocks, and clouds. She fished out of the abyss men and women and all other living creatures—serpents, lions, gazelles, jackals, and elephants. What was of light and what was of darkness, she wove together. The oppositions created a whole cloth and web of being.

She weaves life around us in twisting fibers and circular patterns. The planets spin in spiraling universes. All the atoms in every form spin. Clouds and oceans move about the face of Earth. The breath in our bodies and all of our thoughts and desires circulate inside and around us. Our physical, astral, ethereal, and mental bodies weave together and make us human. Each of us circles each other, creating communities, making connections. The sun rises and sets; we live and we die—all these activities belong to a goddess who knits life in her womb and who, in the end, has woven the mummy cloth that binds us in a transformative cocoon as we shift from one plane of existence into the next. Neith guards the soul as it moves into a realm that is invisible. The departed spirit is not dead; it is transforming, its essence returning to the restful inertia from which it came and awaiting a surge of new energy that moves it forward into the next realm.

Neith is the oldest divine being: her name reaches back to the predynastic culture. Often called the grandmother of the other gods and goddesses, Neith is guardian of the mysteries. Her energies are serpentine and undulating, progressing as she slips quickly side to side, back and forth. She is the reason that the hieroglyphic sign for a goddess (any goddess) is a cobra.

A second creation story about Neith depicts her as the original, androgynous serpent lying in the abyss. She has seen the world and herself made anew and destroyed and remade by cosmic floods, over and over, time and again. Each cataclysm spawns a new generation. Unless one dies to the old, one cannot awaken to the new. The priests of her sacred temple in Esna called her "the mother and father of all things."[8] She is the vessel of both birth and of death. She is mother and warrior; she gives and she takes.

Neith rules both heaven and Earth. In the great glittering waters of our galaxy, N-t becomes the sky goddess Nut. She is both the brilliant, white light of stars that form the body of the Milky Way and the celestial energies of the stupendous big bang that seeded all things in our universe. Each star is the soul of one of her children who has been born and died, who is currently alive on Earth, or who is awaiting rebirth. When the candle flames float upon the dark waters of the earthly Nile during the evening ritual of the Feast of Light, they reflect the millions of stars aflame in the night sky. As above, so below, and each human being is a conduit between the worlds through which that divine light energy passes.

The Creatrix wore upon her head the sign of a shuttlecock to remind us how she draws the threads of life across the sky above and through the waters beneath, how she pulls together the positive and negative energies. Neith wears an emerald green dress reminiscent of the waters that surrounded her sacred delta city, Sais. In fact, Neith was linked to the nearby Mediterranean Sea and sometimes was called the Great Green. Her dress is woven in a diamond pattern in which the warp and weft are clearly seen, almost as if they were serpent scales, and each center is sprinkled with glittering stars reminiscent of the night sky.

The consciousness Neith represents is that which is intuitive and follows the spiritual path of the merger of oppositions. The creative energy of Neith exudes the sensory pleasures of good things to eat, enchanting songs and aromas, and the fecund, sensual Garden of Eden. Neith holds the keys to time, moving fluidly between the temporal realm and eternity. Hers is a distinctly feminine myth of creation in which the Goddess reaches into her depths to birth that which comes from within, and she sustains its life with her own divine essence.

KHNUM SCULPTS THE HUMAN AND HIS *BA*

In the middle of the Nile at the first cataract lies an island whose gray, granite boulders resemble elephants (*hebu*). From his temple on Elephantine Island, the ram-headed god Khnum controls the river's flood. His horizontal horns appear to flow from the sides of his head, almost as if they were ripples of moving water. From the mud left by the receding water, the potter god sculpts all living forms on his potter's wheel. He shapes all creatures, all people, even the other worlds. Lord of creation, Khnum made heaven, Earth, and Duat (what is under Earth), as well as the water and the moon. Khnum was the father of fathers and the mother of mothers.

Khnum creates Queen Hatshepsut and her ka double. This illustration of making humans from clay is seen at Deir el Bahari and Luxor Temple.

All of Khnum's creations share his creative power. Animals create their offspring, humans mold their clay pots, the river fertilizes the field, and the field nurtures the seeds it contains. All of these carry the same creative impulse as Khnum because they come from Khnum's spirit. The ram-headed god also shaped the soul or *ba*—so named after the bleating sound that a ram makes. In other words, we are the little sheep, the flock of the ram god, Khnum. Gods and goddesses, as well as living creatures, have a ba. Even the stars in heaven and the rocks of Earth have bas. The ba of Khnum operates as a trinity of divine beings—the sun god Re in heaven, the Earth god Geb, and Osiris, lord of the underworld.

Near Khnum's temple at Elephantine, archaeologists found the remains of a Hebrew temple and city. There the god Yahweh was worshipped as Creator by the Hebrews. Khnum and Yahweh each sculpted humans from clay. They share a similar story. "Then God said, 'Let us make man in *our* image, after *our* likeness; and let them have dominion over the fish of the sea, and over the birds of the air, and over the cattle, and over all the earth, and over every creeping thing that creeps upon the earth.' So God created man [*bara*] in his own image, in the image of God he created him; male and female he created them" (Genesis 1:26–28).

The humans, *bara,* that Re (Ra) creates are the manifestations of his divine soul, his ba. The ba of Re is the light that the Divine Creator has put in every human vessel. This spiritual light comes from a divine source. The ba is an eternal soul. It does not die but returns to its origin, then it may reincarnate into whatever form it desires or has prepared for itself. One customary burial ritual of Egyptians, Greeks, and Romans was to carry a clay pot to the burial site and break it upon the ground. The act symbolizes the release of the spirit that once was held inside this human vessel. The broken pot returns its clay to the earth. The Genesis 3:19 quotation repeats the idea. "For dust thou art, and unto dust shalt thou return." Seeing the heaps of potsherds piled up in predynastic cemeteries shows me how old this burial rite is. Death releases the soul contained in a human vessel. (Please see plate 10 of the color insert.)

Legend says that the Nile arises from a cavern beneath the island. The flow of water is controlled by Khnum and the goddesses Anket and Satis. In the dog days of summer, before the flood, a bright star (Sirius) rises and signals renewal. The star is linked to Isis and also to Satis, whose name means "enough" or "abundance." At the same site that the priests of Khnum recited their prayers and extolled the world of his creation, the rabbis in their temples recalled the creation of the world in similar fashion:

> At the time when the Lord God made the earth and the heavens, while as yet there was no field shrub on earth and no grass of the field had sprouted, for the Lord God had sent no rain upon the earth and there was no man to till the soil, but a stream was welling up out of the earth and was watering all the surface of the ground— the Lord God formed man out of the clay of the ground and blew into his nostrils the breath of life, and so man became a living being. (Genesis 2:4–7)

Khnum's creative act comes from deep within himself, from an almost unconscious place. He takes the darkest muck, the detritus of millions of life-forms, and gives it new form. He breathes life into matter. Even this beautiful beginning requires a sacrifice, however, and whether or not we like it, we are part of that bargain. A vessel must die to release its ba. Perhaps all that we do is for this higher purpose, which requires us to shift forms and consciousness eternally.

Satis stands with Anket, goddess of the bow and arrow. Satis brings life, while Anket holds the instrument of death. The ba vessel created by the ram god Khnum contains its sacrificial lamb, so to speak. How does one reconcile the opposing angels, the forces of life and death, that stand beside Khnum as he spins the karmic wheel on which we are made? Contemplation of the bow and arrow that Anket holds may contain the answer.

The poet John Keats described the act of creation as "negative capability," which he defined as "when man is capable of being in uncertainties, mysteries, [and] doubts, without any irritable reaching after fact and reason."[9] This intentional open-mindedness recognizes that both seemingly opposed arguments can be true. I imagine this poetic tension as similar to a string drawn between two ends of a bow. From that central tension, the arrow of intention might fly. The human creative urge uses opposition as an expression of a divine creative urge. This is the mystery of Gnosticism, the acceptance of two forms within one body of flesh and spirit. That is the heart of the mystery.

Khnum's artistic expression draws his own hidden essence outward into form. We might imagine Khnum sitting beneath his island in his darkened cavern at the center of the universe. He makes himself even as he makes us. Onto his turning wheel, he throws a lump of clay. The vibrations of the wheel and the movement of his hands call forth a shape that already exists, a shape that will contain the divine spiritual tincture of God the Creator. Says Khnum, "It is for my conscience to guide my hand, my deed to create myself. I am myself perceiving myself—making, making, making . . ."[10]

PTAH OPENS HIS MOUTH AND LIGHT EMERGES

The New and Old Testaments and the Egyptian myth of Ptah refer to the creation of the material world through work on the mental plane. Thought finds its form on Earth. The Gospel of John 1:1 declares, "In the beginning was the Word, and the Word was with God and the Word was God." The story of Genesis 1:2–3 recalls the same event, by saying, "And the Spirit of God was hovering over the face of the waters. Then God said, 'Let there be light'; and there was light."

In Memphis, the ancient Egyptian god Ptah opened his mouth and light sprang from his lips. The sacred text found on the Shabaka Stone tells us that Ptah created the world with the sound and light of his voice vibrating across the waters. The Shabaka Stone (an ancient stele unfortunately used as a millstone by farmers who could not read the hieroglyphs) suggests that Atum made the world, but prior to that, Ptah spoke the magical words of truth (*heka* and *ma'at*) across the water of nothingness. According to the legend, the light from Ptah's lips allowed Atum to see himself for the first time. In that way, he saw that he was a god, and only after Ptah created the light was he visible even to himself.[11] In other words, the solar god Atum made the world, but first, Ptah had to make Atum visible. Ptah preceded Atum. Thought preceded action.

As the world's first architect, Ptah was the god of Egyptian stonemasons, craftsmen, scribes, and priests. They were seen as the metaphysicians who crafted, invoked, and operated the sacred energies within the temple. The generation of ideas, the enunciation of truth, and the energy to create order from chaos are the gifts of Ptah. The emblems of the Freemasons—the craftsman's square and compass—were the hieroglyphs of Ptah's name. The all-seeing eye that appears above the pyramid on the back of the American dollar is another Masonic idea. If one can envision a better world, if one sees it and acts upon it, that world already exists.

Like Khnum, Ptah, the other craftsman god, possesses a potter's wheel. On it, he shapes the egg of the world. Although Ptah is inert, bound in mummy cloth, his hands reach through the void into the air; thus he shapes the cosmos from the beginning. Ptah's cosmic egg contains a goose that emerges full grown and squawking. Ptah names him the Great Cackler. This goose is sometimes given the name of the hidden god Amun and sometimes the Earth god Geb. When Ptah speaks the sun into being, the egg of light that is created separates heaven and Earth.

Ptah stands upon a solid foundation, the plinth of truth. He wears a gleaming sky blue crown that represents his supreme power—the power of the universal mind to create. Through thought alone, Ptah reaches into the unseen spirit realm and draws down through himself the energy to create. The energies of the chakras (the sacred centers of the body) are indicated on the scepter he holds. This staff of life aligns heart and the solar plexus chakras, signifying united desire and will. The mind of God manifests through the use of ma'at, a feminine principle of unified desire and action. Ma'at is called "the heart and tongue of Ptah."[12]

Ptah spoke Atum (or Amun Re) into being. He also spoke all of the other divine archetypes into existence, calling them by name and attri-

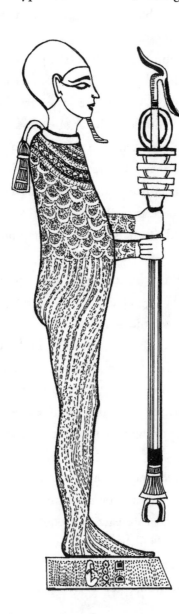

Ptah, who stands upon the sure foundation of the world, created the world by speaking the Word into being.

bute. In a way, Ptah acts like Adam naming the plants, animals, and things of the world. Because he speaks every neter and every creature into existence, all share the divine spark of Ptah through the power of their name vibration.

"Say my name that I may live," the spirits call to those on this side of life. A name recalls a legacy and aligns us to our higher purpose. The Egyptians understood that their names aligned them with the energies of the divine being for whom they were named. Ramses (or Ra-moses) pulled in the solar, masculine power of the sun. That name identified him as a child (moses) of the sun god. Tutankh*aten* (the living image of Aten) was the original name of the son of the Akhenaten, the first monotheistic pharaoh. When his father Akhenaten died, the priests of Amun—who had not been happy with the previous king's decision to leave the great Temple of Amun at Karnak—brought the boy king back to Thebes. They changed his name to Tutankh*amun,* to realign his energy with the worship of the ram god.

The priests of Ptah surely knew about name vibration and numerology. Names offered protection, and certain intimate names were only spoken between parent and child, husband and wife, or devotee and deity. Knowing a secret name and the sacred breath of its vowels heightened the vibration. If one knew a man's, or even a god's, secret name, one acquired a kind of power over him. The shamans of Ptah possessed that kind of power and guarded it.

The spoken name (the *ren*), or the logos, was more powerful than the written name. A large part of the name vibration flowed out with the sound of the voice. Thoughts are things, and invocation (or thoughts spoken aloud) became the first creative act. What we say matters, but how we say it, how often we say it, and how we align our intention with those words creates the kind of world in which we live. The hieroglyph for Ptah's name (□ ◠ 𓈖 𓂋) shows a pair of lips spurting liquid. His name sounded something like *p-tooh*. The hieroglyph for ren (𓂋𓈖) shows an open mouth above a wave of water.

Old Kingdom priests of Ptah built temples at Memphis, the nome, and Saqqara, the necropolis to the west. Ptah, the creator, was also a magician, much like Thoth, god of wisdom. His priests and those of Sekhmet, Ptah's consort, were viewed as shamans. They seemed able to manifest things out of thin air through mind and willpower. Their healings appeared to be spontaneous. Some priests had the power to raise the dead—a talent in great demand in the cities of the dead. Before burial, priests also performed an Opening of the Mouth ritual, which allowed the spirit to be nourished and to speak in the realm of the dead. Perhaps the ritual set up a clear, mediumistic channel for the spirits of the living to communicate with the dead and to assure their loved ones that life and consciousness continue after apparent death.

THOTH STIRS THE CAULDRON

Life began as a bubbling cosmic soup that Thoth, the god of wisdom, stirred with his magic wand or caduceus. (Please see plate 17 of the color insert.) On this caduceus are two serpents entwined, symbols of the unity needed to uplift the shadowy depths of the unconscious mind. Thoth peered into the emptiness and called forth all light. The god often appears with an ibis head, for when the bird is seen fishing along the Nile banks, it lifts one wing to create a shadow on the water. It stands very still and peers into this shadow in order to see clearly the fish lying in the deeper part of the river. Its contemplative pose and keen sight (or insight) resembles that of the Egyptian god of wisdom. Thoth wears a feathered crown of light on his head.

As a hieroglyph, the crowned ibis, 🦆, symbolizes shining intelligence or *akhu,* the highest spiritual essence that is of the mind of God. To see into the natural laws of God requires silence, meditation, and observation. What lurks in the depths is seen more easily within the shadow of its wing. The combination of darkness and light allows the ibis to find just the right fish, frog, or water snake, to snatch it quickly with his beak, and to bring it up into the light.

*Thoth, the creator god of Heliopolis, plays a prominent
role in the Temple of Abydos built by Seti I.*

The priests in Khemennu, Thoth's sacred city, said that he used the
power of his mind to peer into the Nun and see its potentiality. From
the dark abyss, the hidden ones emerged. Inside this vortex of energy,
Thoth saw four pairs of opposites, twin souls swimming in the murky
water. Eight creatures twisted about to embrace each other. They were
the nascent principles of time and space swirled together like the energy
of galaxies.

The females took the shapes of serpents and the males, frogs. Nun
and Naunet ruled the cosmic waters or primordial deep from which
matter would emerge. Heh and Hauhet became misty, endless time;
while Kek and Kauket reigned over the darkness. To Amun and
Amentet belonged the energy of the whirlwinds, the void, and whatever was hidden, unfathomable, and unknowable. (Please see plate 20
of the color insert for a depiction of Amun.) In the creation account
of the Old Testament, four similar aspects appear: "And the earth was

without form and void; and darkness was upon the face of the deep. And the Spirit of God [wind] moved upon the face of the waters" (Genesis 1:2).

These eight beings, like strands of DNA, twisted and linked to form life inside the cosmic egg. At the right moment, Thoth spoke the words of power (heka), breathing out the breath of life, and the egg cracked open, spewing stars, solar systems, and planets and life upon those planets. Perhaps the priests of Thoth imagined the magic of the big bang that created all matter in our universe. Perhaps the priests understood the law of vibration in all things as answering to the sound of Thoth's voice through music and color and the speed of atoms whirling. Perhaps they understood how fractals, the spiraling action of energy moving out into form, are the essence of our lives. Says the god of Petamon in the Coffin Texts, "First I was one, then I was two, then I was four, then I was eight. Then I was one again."[13]

The Shu Texts, written by the priests of Thoth in Khemennu before the Middle Kingdom, says that the great soul of light burst forth "in the infinity, the nothingness, the nowhere and the dark." Something happened, and the primeval waters pushed up the mound of earth on which the great soul emerged from his egg, like the Great Cackler seen in Ptah's myth. This primeval mound was planet Earth's first fertile black land, what the ancients called Khem. It arose from its submerged state in the vast floodwaters of the abyss (Nun). Upon this very mound of earth, the priests say they built the city of Khemennu.

The mix of dissimilar elements to create life points to the magical lore of alchemy. The word al-Khemi comes from the Arabic language, meaning "of the Land of Khem." Thoth observes that the known world begins in energies that may indicate a chemical and mathematical structure to the universe. The story of world creation may also mimic the creation of the human form inside the mother. One can imagine the movements of the eight divine creatures (ogdoad) in the cosmic soup, twining and merging with each other, like a chain of DNA combining or like cells dividing.

Thoth shaped the universe by using ma'at, the principles of order, truth, and justice. These reveal themselves in the physical world as geometry, higher math, and physics. A messenger from the divine mind, he invented the hieroglyphs (*medju neter,* or words of God). In this way, he translated divine truth into concepts we could grasp. He created symbol as the form that most easily provided number, name, story, law, and humor. His creation of the universe and his knowledge of time, space, being, and nothingness made him the first master teacher of the first known university.

Through his mystery texts, Thoth taught humankind the laws of being, creating, and becoming as it was accomplished by the god. In essence, he created an operations manual for cocreation of our world. The forty-two books he wrote—"with his own fingers"—include texts of psychospiritual exploration that appear in the Book of the Dead, or the Book of Coming into Light. For thousands of years, these books were copied and preserved by priest-scribes dedicated to the work of Thoth. "Hail Thoth, architect of Truth," they prayed before beginning to write, "give me words of power that I might write the story of my own becoming!"[14]

Thoth was patron of all books and libraries, including the great house of life in Alexandria and Egypt's first library erected in Khemennu. The Greeks called him Hermes Trismegistus and credited him with writing the spiritual wisdom found in the Emerald Tablets, the source of hermetic wisdom. That original text vanished, but Greek translations of it were handed down. Its oft-quoted maxim "as above, so below" demonstrates the way in which Thoth was said to mediate the upper and lower worlds, the inner world and the outer world, balancing the needs of the ba and *ka* (the soul and its desire nature) with the understanding of the *akh,* or higher mind.

In the realm of the departed, Thoth holds a reed stylus and writes on a scroll. He tallies figures; he records the soul's history and the deceased's deeds. As keeper of the akashic records, he works with the god Anubis as they measure and weigh the heart after death upon the scales of truth.

He has at his disposal the soul's long history. His record becomes the deceased's fate at judgment.

Thoth kept the stellar, solar, and lunar calendars of Egypt as well. With Seshet, the architect goddess, he aligned the temples to the stars and all of Egypt with the cycles of time. He tracked the rising and falling of the constellations and the shifting of the pole stars and used sacred geometry to orient the building of the pyramids and the temples.

Thoth was intimately connected with the physical realm and had control over every spiritual body—the shadow, the will, the name, the desire nature, the seat of consciousness, the higher mind, and the soul. He worked with physical bodies as well as astral ones. Greek physicians later displayed the intertwined snakes on the caduceus of Thoth as an indication of their role as healer. Of all the creation gods, Thoth seems to have kept a more direct connection to the daily affairs of humanity.

ATUM IS THE CREATIVE LIGHT FORCE

The creation god of Heliopolis was probably the most widely known. The stories of Atum evolving into the world, becoming the phoenix, and creating nine great gods and goddesses of Egypt began in Heliopolis. Sadly there are no temples to visit here. His sacred city has been absorbed by modern Cairo; only one ithyphallic obelisk remains in a city of once shining electrum-tipped obelisks.

Atum is the *materia prima* of every Egyptian myth. His priests say that he emerged into being out of the nothingness, the Nun. How he did this is a conundrum. Lucie Lamy has said, "The great mystery is the passage from the invisible into the visible, to be realized by the Power which from the One will call forth the Many."[15] The priests of Heliopolis will tell us three versions of the Atum story because no one version seems complete.

For Atum, "to be or not to be" really is the question. He is the god of the beginning and of the end. He creates time and yet he exists outside time. He is the "nothingness" from which everything came and into which everything one day will return. His name means "the completion," implying that from any beginning, an ending comes, and conversely, from all endings some new thing manifests.

Imagine, if you will, a formless essence exists in the center of a foggy, nondescript world. Imagine sitting in this watery world where everything below is flooded and everything above is fogged. You can't see any horizon, so you can't get your bearings, and you don't know where you are. Suddenly the sun rises, separating the upper and lower worlds, parting heaven from Earth. Rays of light, like seeds, fly out from the nothingness, and in a flash, we see the light strike objects, bringing out the particularities of each—a rock, or a blue heron, or a human being. Imagine that the sun is like the pupil of an eye resting between its two eyelids, gazing at the world before it. In this way, the sun god Re is born. Like Ptah, whose creation of Earth is similar, Atum sees that the light is himself. "He saw that he was god and only after Atum created Re was he visible even to himself."

Here first consciousness arises.

One account tells us that out of the nothingness of Atum a mound of earth rises. On this egg of earth sits a *bennu* bird, a phoenix, a shining form that is the soul of Atum. Legends suggest that on this same hill in Heliopolis a sun temple was built, and the phoenix came to rest there on its *ben-ben* stone. The sacred mound is drawn as a short, truncated obelisk that contains the solar spirit or ka of the sun. It resembles the Step Pyramid of Djoser more than it does the Great Pyramid of Giza. This ben-ben stone where the sun is born becomes the funeral pyre of the phoenix, who ritually incinerates himself every five hundred years, then arises from the ashes. The self-immolation of the phoenix marks the cycles of cosmic regeneration and renewal.

The word *ben-ben* means several things, including "not-not," a double negative. *Ben* refers to the idea of ascension, of rebirth in a new form, of rising again. Death and life coexist within the body of Atum, and the Litany of Re invokes his twin souls, saying, "The soul of Osiris is in Re, and the soul of Re is in Osiris. The word *ben-ben* offers a dual

By and large, Atum was the invisible power of God and did not have a physical human form until the New Kingdom. The bennu bird or phoenix was used to express Atum's omnipotent power of creation, death, and rebirth.

meaning: first, of conception, and second, of regenesis, which is intricately tied to the idea of a unified state of being and nonbeing, of life and death and life reborn again.

We learn more about Atum through the answer to the well-known riddle of the Sphinx. The Sphinx, of course, guards the pyramids and the land of the dead. He sits in Giza on the western bank of the Nile facing old Heliopolis and guards the entrance into the land of the dead. The enigmatic Sphinx contains the mysteries of creation, death, and regeneration. He holds his stoic, eternal gaze, facing east, waiting for the rising sun. When the Sphinx asks Oedipus, the traveler, "What walks on four legs at dawn, two legs at noon, and three legs at eventide?" Oedipus answers, "Man." Man crawls on all four limbs at birth, walks upright when he is grown, and leans upon his cane when he is old.

That is a partial answer.

Pharaoh Tuthmosis IV actually carved the answer to the riddle on the stele that lies between the paws of the Sphinx. The Sphinx addresses the young boy who would be king, saying, "'Behold me. Look at me, thou, my son Tuthmosis. I am your father Horemkhu, Kheper, Re, Atum."[16] Horemkhu means "the Shining Rays of Intelligence of Horus," and these shining rays are composed of three divinities: Kheper, Re, and Atum.

The three light essences to which he refers are: the growing, ever-brightening, evolving (Khepera) rays of sunrise; the strong rays (Re) at noon; and the ebbing and depleting solar energy at sunset, or day's end (Atum). We humans have inherited the same celestial ray energy that has cracked open the keys to the universe. Like the sun in its daily cycle, we are strong and grow weak; we rest and are renewed. Our life, which appears to end one day, is revitalized again after death.

"I am the Alpha and the Omega," says the god of John in Revelations 22:13.

"I am the beginning and the end," says the god of Jacob in Isaiah 44:6.

The Egyptian god Atum embodies that same concept. In the dark, watery Nun, the beginning and the end are all contained within the seed, within the nucleus of the smallest atom from which all life begins. The hidden god Atum (atom, as the Greek philosopher and scientist Lucretius [99–55 BCE] called "the first seeds")[17] was a speck of potentiality. The idea of himself somehow came into form in the same way that the dung beetle Khepera (meaning "to create") pushes a ball of dung along the riverbank. In the beginning of time, this creative energy pushes the first rays of sunlight out of the watery abyss. The story of the dung beetle Khepera clarifies the alchemical creation tale. This beetle lays her eggs in cow dung that she then rolls into a ball. That image of creation appears in nearly every Egyptian temple carved onto the wall behind the holy shrine of the god or goddess. Khepera, the scarab, models the kind of creation that begins in the lowest, most base matter, a dung ball. In twenty-eight days, the dried dung ball suddenly cracks open and out flies the golden, winged beetles, appearing to generate spontaneously.

In truth, it is the process of living transformation. It takes one life-form and turns it into another; it is similar to the alchemist's desire to turn lead (base matter) into gold. Through the process of our spiritual development, we, too, can turn the base matter of our life, its dark and difficult passages, into light and thus be reborn. The flesh is but the container for the spirit in the way that an alchemist's *athanor* contains the elixir. The athanor is a sacred vessel, but the point of the alchemical process is the creation of the elixir.

Atum Creates through Sexual Mystery

The oldest story, found in the Pyramid Texts, says that Atum, the all, comes into being by himself "in his name of Kheperi"; in other words, he becomes because becoming is his nature. The priests of Heliopolis told the conception of the universe as a sexual mystery. Atum, the Great He/She, became his own enjoyment. With phallus in hand, he creates the first seeds of life. He spews forth, or spits out, the twins Shu and Tefnut, who became the dry wind and the moisture.[18]

Two feminine beings within the Nun assist in the creation of Shu and Tefnut. They are Iaauas and Nebethetept, two early forms of the sisters Isis and Nephthys, sisters to the god Osiris. As part of the Osirian Mysteries, Osiris dies and is united with Atum while his two sisters become the mothers of his two children, Horus and Anubis. The names of the two beings within the Nun, Iaauas and Nebethetept, mean She Who Comes Mightily and Lady of Offerings. On this earth plane, when the pharaoh embodies the divine gods Atum and Re, his consort becomes known as the Hand of God. The feminine hand receives and holds the masculine seed, forming it into life. In the Atum myth, the male and female aspects of the god are not separate.

I have often wondered if the story of Shu and Tefnut could find resonance in the big bang theory. Imagine that after Atum explodes into being, there are sudden, whirling solar winds and gaseous dust particles that cluster into the forms of planets. Perhaps Shu is the vibration that keeps the planets spinning in space and that holds together the atoms of our cells and of our planet. Perhaps the moist and fiery Tefnut is the solar light, the god spark through which everything operates in the universe as a part of everything else.

When Atum expels Shu and Tefnut, differentiation begins. The two shared one soul. In essence, these opposed pairs create the balance that is ma'at. We like to think truth comes to us only clothed in white, but that is not always the case. Light comes with shadow. Creation, we have seen, comes from the unity of opposites. And it is with opposing pairs that Atum continues his creation.

After Atum creates Nut, the water of heaven, and Geb, god of Earth, a long courtship ensues. Heaven longs for Earth, and Earth eternally longs for the sky. For myself, I think of the story of Nut and Geb's desire as the innate spiritual impulse—God leans toward us as we reach up toward the Divine. From this great love comes five children. Two brothers embody the processes of growth and dissolution, Osiris and Seth, and two sisters, Isis and Nephthys, create communion by societal connections in the outer world and intuitive connections in the inner world. In brief, I think of these neteru of Egypt as both divine embodiments of God and as processes through which the soul moves to integrate and understand spiritual archetypes.

Atum becomes the Re-Kheperi principle and this principle is the third son, the so-called elder Horus, the hawk, who stays close to his mother Nut. Yet Horus also is called the twice born because his soul is finally born on Earth as Horus the Younger, child of Osiris and Isis. It is through this Horus that the pharaoh comes to reign as the embodiment of the divine child of the neteru. Horus moves the cosmos from stasis to the next cycle of creation.

Atum calls and names each child as it comes forth. All have an individual consciousness that is a part of Atum's divine knowing. They are the first neteru, or the first natural laws of the universe, each having a function that works smoothly alongside all the other functions. "None of these (divine beings) are separate from him," say Pyramid Texts 2051–53. Each has a memory of its making, and when its function is complete, the individual neter reunites with the source. Through the Great Ennead (the nine beings), many more life-forms come into existence, including humankind. The Great Ennead sometimes shifts participants, but most often they include Nut, Shu, Geb, Tefnut, Isis, Osiris, Seth, Nephthys, and Horus.

The seed of Atum contained his nine souls, and within Atum exists the entire DNA of our cosmos, the akashic records of the universe. Each part contains the seed divinity of the whole, in the same way that each of our cells contains an exact replica of our DNA. From the one, many emerge. The Ennead sets the pattern.

Creation by the Numbers

Another way of creation known to the ancient Egyptian priests was creation through mathematics. When the one god (Atum) becomes nine gods (the Ennead) before the creation of the world, the numerical pattern 1 to 9 is established. After 9, the numbers jump into the next generation of numerals 10 to 99, and so on. The ancient Egyptians viewed the number 1 as the most powerful mathematical force in the hierarchy because 1 is considered the whole. The number one is a unity—whole and complete in itself; yet it contains all subsequent numbers. Two is one split in half.

In the Litany of Re, the stanzas are numbered, and whenever the numerical equivalent stanza begins as 1, as in stanzas, 10, 100, and 1,000, a creation myth is retold. Where the number 9 appears, as in 99 and 999, the narrative addresses the totality of the creation that began as 1. In this way, creation can always begin again; it simply begins on a slightly different plane.[19]

Thus the solar god Horus the Elder retains the numerical quality of a number 1 god, but as Horus the Younger, he becomes a number 10 god. In this way, the first son of a god becomes the first divine king on Earth. In the predynastic mists of time, those rulers who come after him are called the mythic Shemsu-Hor, or the followers of Horus. Each human being contains all of the neteru essences within himself. Our human body is a vessel for the Divine. In the next chapter, we will look at its nine divine bodies. The Litany of Re says that "[all of the king's] members are gods. He is a god completely. There is not a member in him without a god. The gods have become his members. The king is the coming into being of forms, Lord of Spirits."[20]

If this is so, then human beings are divine beings, and every creature is filled with God. Every part of a human is part of Atum. As the god of Genesis tells his people, "We made them in our own image" (Genesis 1:26). As individuals we know that we are a part of everything that is God. In these creation stories we observed how in the emptiness, the divine mind spoke and created an other with which to commune. God is consciousness attempting to know itself. If we live inside the mind of the Divine, then we must be its developing consciousness.

WHY SHOULD THESE STORIES MATTER?

These multiple creation stories are not competing tales. Each complementary narrative provides a clue about our own creative process. It points us toward an understanding of the ways in which we can become cocreators with God of the world in which we live. From these myths, we can glean a few concepts.

Formed of the divine body itself, we carry the genetic codes of its creativity in our very cells. Therefore, by degree, what we make of our lives also becomes a part of the living mind of God. We create through our thoughts, deeds, words, and intentions, which arise from the depths of our own being and move outward into the world. This awareness is the essence of magic.

By our creative acts we, like Atum, come to know ourselves. As the sun reflects its creator's light, so does the art reflect the artist.

The potter's essence appears in the form of her pot, the school reflects the philosophies of the teachers, and the fruits of the field reflect the farmer. In other words, by their works, ye shall know them. It is by that reflection that Atum comes to know himself.

The power of conscious creation lies in one's ability to hold the tension between opposing desires or thoughts. Life is not a straight line. It is a tide that goes in and goes out. We walk because we have learned to balance the oppositions of right and left appendages. Change and motion are perhaps the only true constants in the universe.

The creative patterns that support all life already lie in the unconscious, often hidden and mysterious to us. These patterns of evolution, symbolized by the frogs and serpents in Thoth's stew or as the parts of the whole of Atum, are a reminder that life is about transformation. In the way that tadpoles turn into frogs and snakes shed skins, our lives should reflect the creative process. Life is about adaptability.

There is no one right way to imagine the world we want to live in. Diversity is a part of the pattern. Dissolution and decay are a part of the pattern. We all are not required to live or to think in the exact same ways. We are best served, however, when we accept the fact that differing ways of life from ours are as valid as our way. All are part of a divine pattern. Historical researcher Edward Malkowski has said, "Only by knowing the numerous qualities of God does one know god. So the more one learns of those qualities, or neteru, the closer one gets to man's divine origin."[21] Each creative act contains its own outcome and is the seed of further creation. Diversity and growth are necessary for us to have a more complete idea of our spiritual evolution.

Energy can never be destroyed. It simply changes form. The essential energy of life and creativity is eternal. As cocreators of the world, we must consciously (with our minds and hearts and words and acts) reflect the shape of the world we want to live in.

Many philosophers and metaphysicians speak of 2012 as a time of radical shift. Rest assured the world is not ending. We live in a millennial Zep Tepi—a time of changing consciousness that floods Earth and from which we will arise anew like a phoenix on its primeval mound. In a larger sense, we might see ourselves as living at a point of great regenesis. Know that we will be best served when we learn to truly live from our creative core. Imagine that the space between your every breath is that moment of Zep Tepi. Every heartbeat can be that new beginning.

Creation
and Evolving States
of Consciousness

Creation stories remind us that in the beginning the Divine Creator had a plan. In the Judeo-Christian tradition, that plan has been depicted as the Garden of Eden. The rest of the story tells us how close to or how far from we may find ourselves to that place of perfection. For the ancient Egyptians, humans originated when God's plan for heaven and Earth was set in motion. The foundation of every temple and the purpose of every life was to live in accordance with and as an embodiment of that cosmic pattern. Every pharaoh agreed to uphold the laws of order, or *ma'at*.

On the walls of his temple in Abydos, the pharaoh Seti I cups a small image of the goddess Ma'at in the palm of his hand. Tenderly he holds her, for that is the only way to hold "truth"—with a light touch. We learn more when our hearts are at ease with the divine plan than by gripping tightly what we think is truth. We cannot bring balance to our world if we cling to ideas of who is right or wrong. Seti I smiles with a slight, knowing upturn to his lips as he offers ma'at to the larger, seated goddess Ma'at. The "feather of truth," which she wears on her head, seems to emerge, as Rosemary Clark suggests, from "the fissure of two lateral lobes of the brain. She is thus associated with the combined use of intellect and intuition."[1]

In a gesture of gratitude, Nineteenth Dynasty pharaoh Seti I offers ma'at to Ma'at at the Temple of Abydos.

MA'AT AND THE HARMONY OF LIFE

To offer ma'at to Ma'at meant to take a responsibility for overseeing and maintaining justice, truth, and balance during one's life. At death the preserved universe was handed back to the Creator. Typically the pharaoh affirms something along these lines: "This is what you gave to me, and I give it back to you. Having cared for it, I have not changed it one whit." Sages, like the anonymous scribe who penned "The Eloquent Peasant" during the Middle Kingdom, encouraged all people to "Speak *ma'at*. Do *ma'at,* for She is mighty."[2]

In secular human terms, this means developing a conscience, or, more precisely, developing a consciousness. When Jesus said, "The Father and I are one" (John 10:30), he saw himself as the divine son of God, made of God's own essence, so that every part of him was a part of the Divine. For a pharaoh, the living son of a god and goddess, this same idea meant embodying the highest wisdom possible. It especially meant creating the world in which we live and aligning the human will with the will of the divine. Following the laws of ma'at kept Egypt vital, filled with the same magical abundance as it held at the beginning of time. To keep the world as fresh as Zep Tepi, life on Earth had to adhere carefully to divine laws. The goal of the living was to find harmony and balance in thought, word, and deed.

At death one would find out how well that balance had been maintained. In the afterlife truth prevailed. In the Halls of Osiris in the neterworld, the heart of the deceased was placed on the scales of ma'at and weighed against the balance of her white feather. For Egyptians, the heart held all memory and thought. The seat of consciousness dwelled there. If the balance of ma'at was attained in life, then the soul passed through the gateway into the realm of the gods.

WORKING WITH LAYERS OF MEANING

Everything in Egypt is built in layers. Its fertile soil was laid down over the aeons by the silt deposits of the Nile flood. Over time, the pebbles and sand hardened into stone whose quartzite crystals respond to sound vibrations. Earth itself holds a charge that responds to subtle vibrations. Consciousness is layered. In Duat, the Halls of Ma'at hold a charge created by the countless thoughts we have about the realm of the dead and what happens to us at death. Our energies respond to the divine world, and it responds to us. The temples of stone, which house the divine energy of the gods on Earth, were built along these same cosmic principles.

Humans, too, are made in layers—bones, nerves, veins and arteries, and skin. Beyond material form, we are created with subtler layers of emotions, sensory impressions, and thoughts. Even our words have levels of meaning. All these less tactile ways of being in the world not only have an effect on the physical form but also urge the heart toward enlightenment. Even our spiritual bodies exist in layers of consciousness.

What do we mean when we speak of the soul, the spirit, or the higher self? Are these three the same or do they differ slightly? The ancient Egyptians defined them as *ba, ka,* and *khu* (or *akh*), respectively. Once again we are exploring the layers of our spiritual dimensions that are built upon the bedrock of our experiences. The core of all of consciousness is the god spark resident within each of us. Becoming aware of it automatically increases your affinity for the divine experience.

The whole idea of enlightenment is to raise our vibrations—a New Agey term, I know, but if we examine it for a moment, perhaps it will make sense. A physical vibration is dense and coalesced into matter that is easy to identify. Atoms vibrate at differing rates of speed. The lower the vibration, the denser the matter. A higher vibration of light or sound may be less perceptible to the human eye or ear, but it exists all the same. Some people are more able to hear it or sense it than others. The task of "raising our consciousness" means to train ourselves (all aspects of the self) to perceive that which exists on a higher level than the ordinary view of our lives. Through raising consciousness, we become more aware of how our thoughts and feelings are affecting our environment. Eventually we may become aware that when we have more spiritual motives or reach toward a higher spiritual understanding, the burdens of the world become lighter and are more easily carried. We ourselves are raising our vibration, becoming lighter, and in that way, the spiritual realm is able to work through us. God does not have to hit us with a bolt of lightning to make us understand. We can hear the voice of the Divine whispering—alive in the air all around us.

To increase our awareness and experience of these progressively lighter and subtler vibrations, one does not need to give up the world. Rather, one must strive to see that God is alive within the world all around us. To perceive the finer and subtler layers of divinity, one must know that God as God appears cloaked in matter. I have explored the idea of the spiritual bodies at length in my book *Dreams of Isis.* The gloss below refers to that depth work but provides only what we will need to familiarize ourselves with the subtle, etheric layers of the body as discussed in the rest of this book.

THE NINE BODIES OF THE EGYPTIAN TRADITION

To the Egyptians, *aufu* means the physical body, which is also a container for the full life experience. All of the nine spiritual bodies identified as part of the living organism grow continually in the aufu. The many forms of light and illumination that comprise the body of Re were called the Aufu Re. All things that had names were his divine aspects; they were "the god's members," "his flesh," "his aufu." Aufu Re and the lord of Duat, Osiris, were equal. In the tenth division of the Book of What Is in Duat, it identifies the unification of spirit cloaked in matter.

The *khaibit,* often called the shadow, was not known in the Jungian sense as a disavowed, psychological shadow. It operated more as an instinct or an animating principle that kept one rooted in the world. The khaibit is not often mentioned in the ancient texts, but when it is, it operates more or less like a shade or ghost that may check in on loved ones who still live on Earth.

Ren and the *sekhem* will be explored in later chapters on magic. In brief, the ren represents the power of the name and one's language. Sound and soul vibrations attach to a name, and with repetition, words gain power. The sekhem is the vital force that enlivens the entire universe. When the personal will is linked with the divine will, energy becomes amplified. Sekhem literally means "the powers," and it can be felt physically as a channel of energy running through the body. Sekhem energy is the life force that travels between gods and humans. At times, others can feel sekhem as a presence or a force field.

The four subtler, spiritual bodies engaged in the task of growing consciousness were the *ab* (the heart), the *ka* (spirit double), the *ba* (soul), and the *khu* (higher self or divine intelligence). The integration of all of these higher spiritual states resulted in the creation of the *sahu,* or the light body.

The khaibit, *sometimes seen as the shadow or the specter of the individual, emerges from the tomb.*

DEVELOPING STATES OF CONSCIOUSNESS

Called the seat of consciousness, the heart, or ab, receives most of the attention in matters of life and death. The heart's task was to live in concert with the principle of ma'at (truth). A similar Oriental ideal would be learning to follow the tao. The ancient Egyptians articulated their moral precepts in a code of ethics known as the Negative Confession. The Negative Confession functioned as a statement of purity before Osiris, judge of the dead, as well as a code by which to live. In essence, one pledges to honor the Divine in all things, including the Divine in other human beings. For an Egyptian to say that she was "pure of heart" meant that she had constantly plumbed the depths of herself to make the unknown known. Her life goal was to exorcise any ill will, ask forgiveness, make amends, and wean herself from false ambitions, greed, lust, or anger. With every breath, she tried to manifest the greater will of the Divine and align the desires of her heart.

Sixth Dynasty sage Ptah-hotep wrote, "A man's heart is his life, prosperity and health."[3] In other words, what we carry in the heart becomes our destiny. Whether our actions reveal lightness or hardness of heart determines the fate of our soul. The heart retains a lifetime of memories, thoughts, feelings, actions, words, and intentions.

In the Halls of Osiris we stand in the presence of the lord of death and renewal, the judge of souls. This is the god most intimate with the mysterious ways of all our dying and becoming. The heart was placed on the scales of truth (ma'at) and weighed before Osiris to find its state and to determine the fate of the individual. In the Papyrus of Nu, the soul who stands in judgment before Osiris proclaims, "This is my heart. It weeps before Osiris. . . . I have given it unto him. I have dedicated the thought of this heart to him."[4] The heart symbolized life, the rhythmic pulse of the universe, and the desire that leads to transformation. When an ancient Egyptian died, the heart stayed within his body. Over the mummy's chest a winged scarab beetle, the emblem of rebirth, guarded the heart.

This lump of flesh we inhabit walks, breathes, and wants food, and love is its animating principle, the ka. The ka hieroglyph depicted upraised arms, a pose that suggests humans moved by spirit and reaching out toward God, or a priest elevating a host, or a mother uplifting a child to be kissed by the sun. All organisms have ka energies; it is not limited to animals and plants. Inanimate objects can be vitalized with ka energy that may be attached to it through ceremonial practices. For example, the bread and wine in a religious service is the living body of the divine being to whom it has been consecrated. Objects such as magical wands, holy water, and statues of the divine presence are animated by intention and attention. Ka is an energetic force holding and binding spiritual energy to the form. Ka is not eternal simply because it is a spiritual body. Nonliving ka receptacles need to be continually used in a ritual manner or rededicated at regular intervals. In essence, when we devote our energy to something, our energy remains with it.

"The *ka* of Re becomes a millionfold," says Coffin Text 261.[5] All that we create, love, and cherish belongs to our ka natures. Osiris was said to have fourteen kas, each one attached to a part of his severed body. His kas represent the creative power of food, the property of green growing things, intellectual power, mental penetration, radiance, venerability, spirituality, and magic. A god's transformations and his kas are many. As an etheric double, the ka energy may be the agent that creates the auric field that clairvoyants see.

After death, ka energy can attach to particular places or objects so that an energetic field of the deceased person's vitality can be felt. This energy can be invoked to bring forward the spiritual entity during offerings made at the tomb, or the ka may cross time and space to come forth when it is called. The ka does not come unbidden as a ghost might come. Ka links us to our ancestors. African tribes kept the spirits of their ancestors close to guard, protect, comfort, and assure future prosperity. The ka of ancestral ancient Egyptian kings grew to become powerful daimons who protected not only one tribe or city but also the entire Near East. Together they acted as a kind of collective energy field.

The hawk form of the Egyptian ba soul fluttered in heaven and on Earth, speaking in twittering words. It survives by staying close to the ka in the afterlife, but it is the body's direct connection to experience. In the cenotaph of Seti I at Abydos, one finds an oval in which three birds sit. They have "faces like men, but their nature is that of birds. One of them speaks to the other with words of weeping. Now after they come to eat vegetables and green stuff in Egypt they flutter under the rays of heaven and then their shapes become bird-like."[6]

The ba may be the conscience, or moral sense, that directs the ka's actions. In the anagrammatic way of many Egyptian hieroglyphs, ab

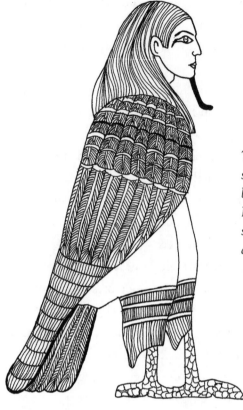

The ba *was an eternal soul depicted by a hawk's body and a human head. It had the capacity to soar at will both on Earth and into heaven.*

and ba, or the heart and the soul, are intimately connected. The ab contains the record of life actions, and the ba is the soul containing many lifetimes of records. Whereas the ba is a human-headed hawk, the god Horus is a hawk-headed human. Both humans and gods have bas. The ba of a god is its power manifest in all things. The Earth god Geb and his green growing body are the ba soul of Atum. Earth is the soul record of the divine. In the Book of the Dead when Atum appears as the Great Cackler, he says, "I am the Soul, the creation of the primeval waters . . . my nest was unseen, my egg was unbroken."[7]

The ba may occupy whatever form it likes. At death the ba soul goes with us. It may enter eternal life and commune with divine souls, or it may return to Earth in another incarnation. The ba connects us to the absolute. It is not changeable in the way that ka is changeable. It is as steady as ma'at. Ba is now as it was from the beginning. "My *ba* is the *ba* of the gods," says the Book of the Dead, "the *ba* of eternity, the *ba* in the body."[8]

Throughout life, the ba has been attached to the awakened heart. At death it is freed. "The Chapter of Becoming a Divine Hawk" in the Book of the Dead offers a mysterious spell that describes how the ancient record of the soul is released at death.

> You shall change into a living *ba* and take shape as a heron, or swallow, as a falcon, or a bittern, whatever pleases you. You shall cross in the ferryboat and not turn back. You shall sail on the waters of the flood, and your life shall start afresh. Your *ba* shall not depart from your corpse and your *ba* shall become divine with the blessed dead. The perfect *ba*s will speak to you and you will be their equal, receiving what is given on earth. . . . Your own true heart will be with thee; yea, you shall have your former heart. You shall go up to the sky and shall penetrate the neterworld in all the forms you like.[9]

SPIRITUAL ATTAINMENT

Gods and humans possessed two kinds of souls—a ba and a khu. The ba had its primary connection with the earth soul, while khu was a heavenly soul. The *baui,* or twin souls of Atum, were Re and Osiris. A mortal might gain these double souls through using words of power and ceremonial magic, an understanding acquired through studying the sacred texts of the afterlife.

The *bennu* (𓅣), or phoenix, we recall was a primeval form of Atum. This messenger of the god lived on the Island of Flame. It existed as a being of fire before anything else existed, and it consumed itself and returned to fire. Says the bennu in Chapter 83 of the Book of Coming into Light, "I am the seed corn of every god. I am Yesterday. . . . I am Horus, the god who gives light by means of his body. I come as day. I

The khu *or* akh *was the other immortal body and
was considered the divine spark of god.*

appear in the steps of the gods. I am Khonsu (the moon) who proceeds
through the universe."[10]

In human terms, this flame sparks from the mind of God to our
mind and then into form. The khu is to humans what bennu is to
Atum. Developing the khu created eternal contact with the divine
mind. It is not mind as we ordinarily think of it. It is mind as a statement of allness.

This is not a normal state of awareness. It develops over time
through meditation, through clairsentience, through ritual or magic.
Khu is our highest self, which draws from the inexhaustible splendor
and abundance of the universal mind to provide us with all that the
heart, body, and soul need. Khu is the goal, but it is not easily attained.
Usually such a true enlightened state is reached in this lifetime only
by master teachers, perhaps by the lamas of Tibet or the metaphysical
ascended masters or the Ishim of the Cabbalists. The Christians might

call these light workers the community of saints. These glorified souls work for the benefit of humankind rather than for personal means.

An imperishable body and the idealized state of being, khu was one's link to the Imperishable Stars that circle the North Pole and never set. The hieroglyph for khu was the golden crested ibis, with its shining feathers streaming from its crown around its body. Thoth, the high creative intelligence of the cosmos, was portrayed as a crested ibis. A priest or priestess may act as guide to the khu, but in this realm the neteru themselves—Thoth, Atum, Ptah, and so on—are the teachers. Signs, symbols, and synchronicities are part of their lesson plans.

Sahu is the light being that returns to Light. The sahu keeps an individual's essence or blueprint throughout its incarnations. An eternal body, the sahu accompanies a human being in the endless cycle of birth, death, transformation, and rebirth. In each incarnation, it carries the soul's suitcase packed with the projected personality, the memories, and the spiritual aims and purposes.

Thoth's magical words of power, combined with the prayers of high priests during the seventy-two-day burial rites, eased the transition from corporeal body into incorruptible sahu. The burial rite did not grow the sahu, but it allowed the soul to pass straightway from the tomb into the eternal realm. The shamanic traditions that use altered states (known as death-in-life experiences) engage the sahu body. The flight of the light body allows the shaman to journey beyond the boundaries of time and space to gain precognition of future events, dialogue with spirit beings, meet ancestors, and receive transfers of wisdom.

The sahu integrates the wisdom gained through all these spiritual bodies. The alchemists often depicted this being of light as a star being. Leonardo da Vinci drew this as a human pentagram standing with arms outstretched inside a circle. This emblem reveals a perfected man who contains within himself the god seed. After death, Osiris—Egypt's Green Man—became the constellation Orion and was called Sahu. To become like the stars was to have acquired the body of light. Through dedicated effort, the material realm has been elevated to higher and higher levels by raising one's consciousness. As the Pyramid Texts tell us, when a man partakes of the wisdom of gods and gains knowledge of his own existence, then he knows that life is eternal and he himself is "everlasting in any *sahu* he pleases himself to make."[11]

That talent came through the practice of *sekhem qet sahu*. Literally the phrase means "power that has built up an eternal body over time." Yogis use their kundalini energy to create the body of light. Over time, daily practice develops spiritual power and builds higher levels of awareness. It is not an act that can be short-circuited. Sahu wasn't built in a day. It is the last evidence of physical form and the first evidence of eternity.

Creating enlightened awareness inside the human vessel is the alchemical great work. If, indeed, we want to change things, we must begin that change in ourselves. We must become the container for transformation. We are the alchemist. We are the philosopher's stone. If a million people changed themselves, the world around all of us would change. We are the magnum opus, the work itself. As our vision evolves, the magnum opus evolves, and the magnum opus eventually will create a new magnum opus. There are worlds we have yet to see that we are building already through our daily actions, thoughts, and longing.

The judgment scenes that greet us in the halls of Ma'at show the culmination of life patterns that we have created. With time and committed work, we can gain true wisdom. If we want to align ourselves with the divine will, we must find a way to learn what is required of us.

The sacred writings of ancient Egypt were called the Baou Re, or the Souls of the God of Light.[12] The longer an individual works them, studies them, prays them, and investigates them, the more meaning they accrue. The magic of resurrection and rebirth begins first on this side of the tomb. The Secret of Osiris Becoming Re is the work required to make the unconscious conscious and to make the invisible manifest.

The Magic of Magic
Words of Power

In the antechamber of the Pyramid of Unas at Saqqara, I inhale the wonder of this place. In solitude, I gaze at the first known ancient Egyptian hieroglyphic text. The intention of its magical incantatory prose was spiritual transformation—the union of the king's soul with the gods Atum and Re. Row upon row, these precise glyphs recount the world's first religious yearnings and affirmations. There are no painted illustrations here. Instead, the hieroglyphs themselves seem to come alive. Gazing at the phonetic hieroglyph for *m,* I can see the texture of each of the owl's feathers. The arms of each *ka* (hieroglyph for spirit) reach toward the heavens in a gesture familiar to any who have attended charismatic prayer services.

Above me, the vaulted ceiling glimmers with a thousand bright imperishable stars, each hand carved and as individual as the human souls these stars represent. The eternal souls, children of the goddess Nut, shimmer inside her body, the dark blue sky. The empty black basalt sarcophagus of the last pharaoh of the Fifth Dynasty sits empty in the eastern room, attesting to a resurrection in a blaze of light. The walls of the narrow corridor leading in to the tomb (and out of the sky mother's womb) bear birthing texts on both sides. Here are the stories of divine generation and regeneration. Isis gives birth to Horus, the falcon, and Neith gives birth to Sobek, the crocodile.

Because humankind is the result of a divine process of manifestation, we and all things of the natural world share in the spiritual essence and immanence of that Creator. In early creation myths, we saw how the one became the many, begetting gods and goddesses, all the elements of the cosmos and all living things. At the beginning of space and time, Atum in Heliopolis (or Ptah in Memphis) opened his mouth and light sprang from his lips in the form of the sun god Re. Yet before there was anything that resembled Re, the god of light, there was the idea of Re that existed in the heart of God. The Shabaka Stone of the Memphite school of theology tells us that Re comes forth from the heart and tongue of Ptah.

> There originated in the heart and on the tongue of Ptah (some-thing) in the image of Atum. Great and exalted is Ptah who bequeathed his power to all the gods through his heart and on his tongue. It happened that heart and tongue prevailed over all other members. Consider Ptah as the heart in every body and the tongue in every mouth of all gods, people, beasts, crawling creatures and whatever else lives, while he thinks as the heart and commands with the tongue everything he wishes. Every divine word came into being through that which was thought by the heart and commanded by the tongue.[1]

In Utterance 570 of the Pyramid Texts, Unas announces, "Hear it, O Re, this word which I say to you. Your nature is in me, O Re, and your nature is nourished in me, O Re."[2]

Unas knows that the holy words he speaks are heard by Re because Re's nature is a part of his own constitution and Unas honors and nourishes that spiritual light. Ptah, the divine source, lives in every-thing and in every beat of the heart and in the thoughts of all creatures. Everything in the universe originates in and radiates out from the central point of light that is God. All of nature duplicates this pattern in which the center billows out—the rose unfolds from its secret center; the sun radiates its heat and light from a central core. And every center is connected to every other center, one source: the stars and their planets move in circling fashion from that central point of the big bang; the cells in our bodies grow from a central embryo. The Flower of Life that mysteriously appears on the pylon of the Osirion in Abydos is a geometric matrix imprinted there long ago to remind us that the life pulse manifests from the center.

Therefore when God used the force of magic to create the world and to fashion humankind, that magic swelled and blossomed from a central core outward and is inherent in all of creation. That magic still reverberates throughout the universe. The energy through which the Divine made humankind—"in our own image"—engendered the magic in each of us. Said Egyptologist Christian Jacq, "The supernatural force which maintains life is not beyond the comprehension of human intelligence. It dwells in the heart of man's being, in his inner temple."[3] Because like attracts like, we respond to the creative transformative power of the Divine, and the neteru, those divine god beings of the ancient Egyptians, respond to the magic within us.

Having completed his shamanic initiation in Saqqara—having died and been reborn—the pharaoh commands the same creative power that the god from primeval times possessed. On the wall of the antechamber inside his pyramid, the pharaoh sees the inscriptions that are the magical utterance. Utterance 472 says, "The sky trembles. The earth quakes before him. The Magician is Pepi. Pepi possesses magic."[4]

THE MAGICAL GOD OF PRIESTS AND KINGS

While Atum still floated in the waters of the Nun, before he even spoke, he was the unseen, nonexistent one with all of the potency and potentiality of everything that was yet to come. At his most inexhaustible, at the peak of his power, Atum's potentiality was the might of Heka, whom the Book of Coming into Light says existed before Atum. It was the impulse or the first thought of being. It was the spirit of Atum at the moment of his coming into being.

Therefore Heka is older and greater than all the gods that flow out of the unified body of Atum. Spell 261 of the Coffin Texts assures us of our magical inheritance. "To me belonged the universe before you gods had come into being. You have come afterwards because I am Heka."[5]

In other words, the magic—the heart and tongue that creates the utterance and the words of power—is older and mightier than the gods themselves. Because all of life issues from the seed thought of God and because everything flows out from the central god force of the universe, we have at our source Heka. Magic is a part of the constitution of our being, and so it is that we may truly claim a heritage as cocreators of our world.

In writing about the oldest magical tradition, the Pyramid Texts, French Egyptologist Christian Jacq had this to say about magic spells: "When the gods speak, they tear open the emptiness and open the way to the forces of life. That is why the magician repeats the words of gods. . . . The words and spells used by the magician are not a matter of chance; they are inspired by sacred legends, deeds from divine ages, which are repeated in the world of men. A magic spell is only effective in so far as it has its roots in the earliest antiquity, or more precisely, in the origin of life."[6]

The Middle Kingdom Coffin Texts affirm that "[m]y soul is God. I am the creator of the Word."[7] For more than two thousand years, the affirmation has been repeated—inscribed on tomb walls, on coffins, and on funerary scrolls. The eternal soul of the deceased is one with the god source. "God is my name," say the Coffin Texts. "I do not forget this name of mine."[8]

Everything that exists operates through the energy that emanates from the seed of God. Atum was the etheric atom that existed in the nothingness. What drew the universe forth from the void? Heka, the word that God uttered with the force of his voice and the power of his will. The hieroglyphs of Heka's name (𓎯𓄿𓎡) supply us with images of that divine force, using two symbols as part of the name itself—the wick upon which the fire of God is placed and the upraised arms that indicate spirit (the ka). That wick of two intertwining threads pro-

Heka, the god of magic, wears upon his head the ka *image that is the animating principle of the words of power.*

vides us with a symbolic image that indicates the use of dual mental energies—the intuitive right brain and the philosophical left brain. The arms of the ka show spirit reaching upward toward the sun, praying, raising consciousness, drawing down inspiration. If one stands with arms up and out at right angles to the shoulders, one can feel how that position opens the heart. Two determinative hieroglyphs have no pronunciation. They are simply images to indicate a symbolic idea.

The scroll shows that the words have been written on the papyrus, which has then been rolled up tightly and tied with string. On one level, that hieroglyph indicates simply the idea of the written word. On a more symbolic level, that hieroglyph implies that the contents of the rolled up scroll are not for everyone's view. The magical language is a secret kept from profane eyes. Three seeds appear waiting to be planted, to grow roots in the physical world. They are the material potency of mental energy waiting to take shape.

The energies inherent in the words themselves, in the divine intonation, and in its intent sent forth a stirring, then a vibration that created the ripple effect inherent in the sequences of vibrations that followed. Through meditation on the words of power, we fan the spark within so that its flame shines more brightly. By that I mean, we become "enlightened," and as the ancients would have seen it, we become aligned with the light that is Re.

The Gnostic Christians, a remnant of the native Kemetic people in Egypt, preserved their teachings about Jesus on scrolls that dated from 340 CE—a time that would have been contemporary with an active priesthood of Isis in her temple at Philae. (The temple was not closed until 535 CE when it was used as a Coptic church.) These sacred scrolls only came to light in the town of Nag Hammadi, Egypt, in 1945 CE. Among those texts is the Gospel according to Thomas, which recorded the sayings of Jesus the Christ.

This text tells us that the energies that the master and his disciples used to heal and to work miracles were a form of energy akin to the higher vibrations of light. Thomas's gospel records a conversation that Jesus held with his disciples. He instructed them, "If people ask you where you originated, tell them that, 'We have come from the Light, where the Light originated through itself.'"[9] Jesus goes on to say that the quality of this light is "motion and rest"—in other words, vibration.

In this gospel Jesus gives his disciples information they need about an esoteric magical tradition that was contemporary with that of Simon Magus, a follower of Christ's who also worked miracles of healing and was trained in Alexandria. With this training in the use of words of power, the disciples are able to go out into the world, as so recorded in other gospel narratives, and work miracles in his holy name, i.e., using words of power. These words of power, called heka, like the god Heka, were said to be created from the light, from the essence of the god of light (Re) at his manifestation. Spiritual light is the transforming power of magic.

The text of Thomas places the human in powerful alignment with the Divine. Through the power of God to name and shape the world, the neteru appear inside all of nature and within us whether or not we realize it. Some Egyptologists, such as Eric Hornung, assert that there is no "main" god or goddess in Egyptian theology. There are only manifestations of the Divine on Earth, whose energies we invoke by name. While all energies stem from one source, the energy inside the fruit of an apple tree differs from the energy inside a yew berry (which is usually fatal). The energies of Khepera in the morning differ from the energies of Re at noon. The Litany of Re, for example, names the seventy-five varying aspects of Re, including some of those that also stress his dark aspects. All things that have names are made through the process of light vibration and are part of the Aufu Re, or the total body of God.

By naming and calling on a particular energy in the magical tradition, we affirm that we understand how it uses its life function. At the same time we know that we share with it the universal power to create, to manifest, to transform, to regenerate. In the ancient esoteric tradition the name itself, called *ren,* has its own vibrational, ethereal, and mental body, one of the nine spiritual bodies that we possess.

For now it is enough to know that working with the energy of the name and through meditation we have the capacity to supercharge our work. We may choose to accept the natural world, its bounty and gifts, without identifying it as a divine and living form, or we may choose to amplify its transformative energies by naming, identifying, and invoking, which are powerful actions deeply aligned to a higher purpose. We may want to invoke particular divine energies by name (say, the healing energy of Bast or the esoteric wisdom of Thoth) in order to assist us with our work. That makes our efforts more conscious and willingly aligned with divine purpose. That will hasten to bring the unconscious material into our consciousness, so that we may use that transformative power as it exists at a higher vibration.

HEKA: A CONSCIOUSNESS AND A REALITY

Heka is the essence of magic. Heka manifests potential. Heka, or the words of power, make the invisible visible. It may be experienced in ritual acts of writing, praying, meditating, dreaming, working, or thinking, as well as through reading and incantation. To make conscious the collective unconscious mind means to move that god force energy through a receptive human vessel. This dynamic use of creative energy has a greater effect than simply riding the wave of a natural cycle of fruitfulness and decay. It is commanding the cycle of generation with conscious thought and desire—as Ptah and Atum did—to effect spiritual, mental, emotional, and physical changes. That is working as a cocreator with the gods.

Group meditations and work with heka can have a transformative effect on not only individual but also world consciousness. The unified minds of spiritually motivated individuals working together can affect changes in the outer world. Even individual consciousness raising has the ability to raise the vibration of those around us. Holding a good thought, it turns out, is part of leading a charmed life. We may plant ideas like seeds in the minds of others. We can plant seeds of possibility in our own minds through the powers of affirmation. These seed thoughts may be our own, or perhaps they are the seed thoughts that originate in the mental energy of the Divine. All three use creative thought processes, working on multiple energetic levels.

In his preface to *The Temple of Man* by R. A. Schwaller de Lubicz, translator Robert Lawlor described the mind-set of the French art historian as he explored the ancient Egyptian creative impulse. Schwaller de Lubicz and the Egyptians themselves, Lawlor says, conceived a symbolist view of the ancient land "[in which two or more] concurrent, simultaneous levels are at work in any given instance. One is the study of Egypt as a civilization that existed in a factual geographic place and time, its people, mythology, social forms, its chronological unfolding, its monuments and artifacts, but this is only a backdrop, or support, for another Egypt, which might be called a quality of intelligence. This Egypt is outside of chronological considerations; it is rather, both an ever present and recurring possibility of consciousness."[10]

HIEROGLYPHS AS THOUGHT MAGIC

Far from the primitive worldview that Egyptologists in the past have ascribed to the early Egyptians, the ancient mind from the start exhibited the characteristics of thinking and observing along a high order. Rational minds will not crack open the mystery of hieroglyphic thought. We must acquire an Egyptian frame of mind that has the capacity to see a world in which several elements are at work simultaneously.

The first enigma is that hieroglyphs can be read from right to left, or left to right, depending on the wall on which they appear. The directions the images face and their proximity to a door, gateway, or portal provide a clue as to the direction of the reading. The words themselves may work phonetically as well as metaphorically. The images and sounds carry embedded cultural myths with them. Hieroglyphs provide an initiation into multidimensional thought. To understand the text, one must peel back each symbol layer by layer. To read hieroglyphs, one must be willing to enter the words themselves and unfold their intersecting realities.

First, everything that exists includes its opposite. The ideas are linked by association. Mut the mother goddess is depicted as a vulture. She lays her eggs to give birth to her children and she feasts upon the dead, feeding those children life energy derived from dead matter. The hieroglyph for *mut* means both "death" and "mother."

Second, all understanding is interwoven. Meaning is derived not only from the image of an object but also from its sound, from the oral tradition that accompanies it, from the science that surrounds it, from its colors, and so on. We must learn truth through all of our available senses, including our intuition.

Third, there are cycles of time and there is eternal time, and these all occur simultaneously. In the hieroglyphic writing of the Old Kingdom, especially, things seem always to be happening now rather than in the past. The star Sirius rises with the sun to announce the flooding of the Nile that renews the land and that makes a new Earth out of the Nun. It's not just reenacting the event of Zep Tepi. It *is* Zep Tepi, the first day of the world, and the ancient Egyptian calendar always begins on this day. The pharaoh, who embodies the god on Earth, is always reborn when the world first comes into existence; therefore he always celebrates his birth as Horus, the solar hawk god, during the helical rising of the star Sirius. Sirius is called Sothis and is the celestial image of his terrestrial mother Isis.

THE POWER OF IMAGINATION

One of the best ways to understand the hieroglyphic images—such as those that appear on the walls of the Pyramid of Unas—is to think of them as dream images. While you sleep, images are projected onto your mental screen. Each image has a meaning, and the more frequently these images occur, the more meaning the image will hold. Dream images link to other images, creating puns at times. In this way, the images offer us a second tier of meaning. The images form constellations of meanings that can continue to be unfurled and revisited even years later to reveal deeper levels that we did not glean the first time. It is the stuff of poetry. It is how the ancient Egyptians lived. Say metaphysical writers Alan Richardson and Billie Walker-John in their revelatory book, *The Inner Guide to Egypt:* "Creative imagination . . . can open up possibilities and considerations that would not otherwise be possible. It is, in fact, one of the fundamentals of magic. The imagination creates doors into a greater consciousness, rather like those false doors on Egyptian tombs where the spirit of the deceased was believed to appear—and really did."[11]

A scribe spent many years learning the hieroglyphs (its images, sounds, art, and grammar) and the stories of the gods and goddesses. Writers were priests and priestesses who served as Egypt's first healers and magicians. The high priest and scribe grasped the connections between magic, image, and naming. Hieroglyphic writing was God's language. When writing became more common during the Middle and New Kingdoms, scribes used hieratic or demotic scripts to record lists of offerings, judgments, and legal transactions. The true hieroglyphs, however, stayed in the realm of religious tradition. Thoth, the creator god of number, magic, and language—known to Greek mystics as Hermes Trismegistus—is the legendary architect of the hieroglyphs. In Hermopolis, he is an aspect of Heka, older even than Re, for he assisted Atum in Re's evocation from the bubbling cauldron of the Nun.

The ancients used symbols, including color, number, image, and word, to elucidate the universe and our place in it. The hieroglyphs created a precise constellation of meanings to the ancient Egyptians who had cultivated an acute perception of the many natural phenomena— from the rising of stars to the natural laws that govern our universe. Every hieroglyph—even the phonetic ones—carried a rich tapestry of meaning that could be gleaned about nature and about the cosmos.

We know when an image does not ring true. More than likely Jesus was not the blond-haired, blue-eyed man pictured on a kitchen magnet on my friend Caroline's refrigerator. We similarly distrust the Zeus-like iconography of the Jewish Yahweh or Christian God who resembles Santa Claus with a full beard and long, flowing, white hair. In hieroglyphs, the god Atum, the complete one, is impossible to depict. There is no literal way to depict the Divine. It has no face, and so the symbol is needed.

The Egyptians used hieroglyphs to suggest the many possible faces of God. The understanding could only be gained through a study of the language, symbols, and myths. Egyptian priests were reluctant to teach outsiders, especially Greeks, to read the hieroglyphs or to discuss their sacred teachings. Even the Leiden Papyrus, a demotic Greek magical text found in Thebes and said to provide the Greco-Roman initiate with the magic he needed to manipulate the cosmos, did not divulge the secret name of God. "His image can never be drawn, nothing can be taught of him, for he is too mysterious for his secret to be unveiled, too great and too powerful to be approached."[12] The ren, the secret "true name" of God, cannot be spoken and is unknowable.

The power of symbol relies on a true understanding of the magic of heka, and heka harkens back to a nearly ineffable supernatural consciousness that began first to perceive itself and its particularities. To name those particularities became the first creative act—an act that projected what we know as gods and goddesses into the forms found in the natural world. It is the power known by the Hebrews as the Great I Am.

In fact, John Anthony West says, "It is possible to say that Egypt regarded the entire universe as a gigantic act of magic, the transformation of consciousness into the material world."[13] There was not religion, per se; there was a spirit-infused state of mind that used heka to worship the Divine, to secure future regenesis for the dead, and to provide health and stability to the living. "Magic was sacrosanct and unchangeable, the oldest and most characteristic element of the so-called religion," says Walter Addison Jayne. "It was applied religion, and all rites and ceremonies were full of it."[14]

DEFINING HEKA

E. A. Wallis Budge, former curator of the British Museum's Egyptian wing, defined heka as "words of power" or "effective utterance." Ancient Egyptians described the dynamic power of heka as the proper words in the proper sequence spoken with the proper intonation and the proper intent. That prescription contained the power of the gods that expresses itself in the laws of the natural world. The inalterable truths that come to us from the gods are our legacy. The essential message of the Hellenistic treatise of Thoth (Hermes Trismegistus) is that Egypt was built in the image of heaven; in other words: as above, so below. The hieroglyphs were the word of God.

When the hieroglyphs first appeared inside the Pyramid of Unas, they were perfectly executed, ritually infused, and considered holy. The artistic images contained not only meaning but also a grammatical order and lyricism that makes them the first known religious poetry. The appearance of the glyphs is precise, showing the delicate stroke of the scribe's hand. Chant lines and images repeat in a kind of hypnotic trance. Even the stones that hold the hieroglyphs were chosen for their resonant properties, so that the vibration of a high priest's voice would create the proper tones. The texts were physically aligned to the doorways or worked as mirrors to the text on the opposite wall. A whole philosophy appears inside each hieroglyphic image and sound. All of this produced not only a work of art but also an invocation of the Divine that opens a doorway between worlds. Every aspect behind these holy glyphs is part of the sacred language of the gods, a gift to humanity from the beginning of time.

ALIGNING WITH DIVINE WILL

Our human bodies partake of the divine body. We, too, have the power to invoke our lives into being, to create form from the desire of our hearts aligned with the will of God. That is a key ingredient to the power of heka—the proper intent. Aligning oneself with divine will is a prerequisite to creation through heka. The earthly ritual action mirrors the act that occurs in the divine realm. The two are drawn together in mutual attraction. Intention is as much a part of magical sequence as the spoken words. Having a command of the language and the vocal presence to invoke the holy sounds during rituals gave the high priest the ability to open the portals of heaven.

Correctly chanting a divine name brought its spiritual energies into our consciousness and into our presence. The spiritual essence that we speak and acknowledge by name we ourselves already possess. In speaking, a resonance is made. As my friend Gloria says, "From your lips to God's ears."

In *Sacred Science,* Schwaller de Lubicz suggests that abstract meaning is secondary to reading the hieroglyphs. "Actually the pronouncement of each sound of the language," he says, "puts very precise nerves and breathings into action." The sound excites certain nerve centers, and the breath works its magic upon the chakras. "Physiological effects are evoked by the utterance of certain letters or words which make no sense in themselves."[15]

The ancient Egyptian Book of the Dead identifies every part of the individual as part of the body of the Divine. Nothing exists that is not a part of the original Creator. Says Chapter 42 in that text, "My hair is the hair of Nu [like the watery waves]. My face is the face of the sun disk. My eyes are the eyes of Hathor. My ears are the ears of [the jackal] Apuat."[16] This is not a petition to become like this or that. The text does not say, "Make my eyes like Hathor's." Rather, it affirms that the spirit-filled physical world exists right now, right here, all the time. Who has not looked at the face of a newborn child and thought in amazement, "You are a child of God."

RITUAL ACTS

A ritual action is a sacred action. Whether blessing a body, making a child, or writing a text, what makes the act sacred is the attention one brings to it. Through ritual, one recalls the power of God in the original act of creating the universe and uses that energy to create and bless other actions. Ritual creates a mirror action on Earth of a divine act that already exists and continues to exist in the eternal time of the neteru.

The Shabaka Stone suggests that after Ptah uttered the first visible and vocal vibration, the divine impulses floating upon the name vibration moved outward into manifestation. The priests of Memphis said that "[t]he gods entered into their bodies (that were made) of every kind of wood, of every kind of stone, of every kind of clay, of every kind of thing that grows upon them, in which they have taken form."[17] The power of heka draws the divine energy into its earthly form. (This idea that the gods and goddesses make themselves visible in nature and in objects of the natural world is an idea that should point us to a more deeply spiritual understanding of environmentalism.)

The Egyptians knew this meant working in a sacred manner with the divine energies of the natural world. The more one knows about the neteru, the more one can use the varied forms of energy that they exhibit. Because every part of the natural world is divine, or can be infused with divine energy, the spirit finds many ways to manifest in the material world. For example, the black granite sarcophagus inside the king's chamber of the Great Pyramid comes from an igneous stone—a rock formed in Earth's fiery processes and which the Egyptians used to symbolize the death and rebirth of the *bennu* (phoenix). Ritual objects reflect the gods inherent in the magical field.

More important than seeing the gods within a ritual object, we come to see how the neteru manifest within us. Not only do we see the image of Isis in the mother who breast-feeds her child, or in the cow licking her newborn calf, we actually see the real Isis that is within. And we see the feminine face of the Divine, the deeper part of the Creator that is one aspect of the Great He/She.

During burial and temple rites, Egyptian priests used words of power to draw in and maintain the order and truth set down at the beginning of time. As a healer, he brought our bodies into alignment so that we functioned as intended. As one who read horoscopes, he divined the perfect hours for activities. As a high priest, the pharaoh recited the words of power that awakened the indwelling spirit in all things—in the temple and its statues and in himself.

WORKING WITH NUMBER AND VIBRATION

The proper words, the proper sequence, the proper intonation, and the proper intent—that was what the ancient Greek philosopher Pythagoras learned in Egypt. He understood heka to mean that everything worked according to vibration. All is number. Language, architecture, music, astrology, healing—everything came alive through the law of vibration, and vibration is not static. Vibration changes things. Thought is a vibration that changes things. Waves of light flow in the pattern of the mind that observes that light, yet when the mind turns its attention aside, light reverts to particle (or seed form) rather than focusing and forming a light wave vibration, or an intentional motion. Light appears in both wave and particle forms, but applied mental energy, such as observation, changes the vibration. Attention equals intention and that attention works both up and down the scaffold between heaven and Earth.

Remembering and honoring the gods keeps them close to us and calls in their vibrations and emergent energies. Because all that is originated in the light vibration that created the universe, everything shares in the light and everything that exists has a consciousness. In Utterance 262 of the Pyramid Texts, Unas solicits Re, Osiris, and Thoth, saying, "Be not unaware of me. . . . You know me, and I know you."[18]

Language used properly in this way literally puts a "spell" on us. I tend not to respond to people as well when my name is mangled. We all like to hear our names pronounced correctly. That is also the idea behind what our fourth grade teachers were trying to put across: use good grammar and learn to spell. Being able to articulate that which we know—or even that which we wish to know—provides us with insights we may not ordinarily have had. In the process of writing, especially in the process of writing this book, I have tried to articulate things that were glimmers in my consciousness until I was able to ferret them out. In chapter 1 in *Awakening Osiris* (chapter 15 in the Book of the Dead), the freed spirit of the priest Ani asserts: "That which is named can be known. That which is unnamed is unknowable."[19]

Spoken language has a kind of encoded vibration. The consonants that became the Kemetic language were based upon the sounds one heard in a daily setting. The sound of two lips spitting (*p-tooh*) became the name of the god who spat forth light, Ptah. The energetic roar of the lion (*rere*) became the name of the lion, which was the name of the sun god Re. The shushing sound of the wind became the air god Shu, and the secretive name of the invisible was *sheshet,* which kept that soft, low, shushing vibration that referred to a deep mystery that one needed to lean toward in order to hear. Like their counterparts in the Hebrew language, Kemetic vowels operated on the sacred flame of breath. Vowels were considered to be sacred sounds that could not be duplicated in written ancient Egyptian language because of the breath, which carried the soul essence, as when Atum breathed upon the waters and drew forth life.

Consider that after the mummification ceremony, there follows a burial ritual in which the mouth of the dead is symbolically opened in the underworld. Here an ankh, the symbol of life, is held to the lips and nose. This provides the soul with spirit, or the breath of life, needed to speak in the next world. Now the newly dead may invoke the names of God, as they did on Earth.

The ancient priests probably sang their incantations. Incantation literally means "singing in" and is connected with the idea of enchantment. Enchantment involves a vocal pattern that fixes the vibratory energy and, in a literary sense, binds the listener to a story. In a magical sense, it binds the energy of the Divine to a cult object or within the individual. When a religious person speaks of "heeding the call," she means that the voice of the Divine has called down and drawn her toward it. In the same way, the priestess draws down the energies from above.

BOTH *WHAT* YOU SAY AND *HOW* YOU SAY IT

Imagine how the "Hallelujah Chorus" by Handel, or the song "Hallelujah" by Leonard Cohen for that matter, might sound if we did not know how to intone the word without seeing its sacred vowels. Imagine that the phrase we know as *praise God* derives from the trilling sound of ululation—a sound that accompanies the weddings and funerals of both ancient and modern Egyptians. Does it change our understanding of the song if we know the etymology? Ululation was part of the most ancient Pyramid Text—a part of the chanted shamanic rites that allowed Pharaoh Pepi to leave his mortal remains behind and ascend into Akhet, the shining Field of Reeds equivalent to the Greek Elysian Fields. Knowing the connection intellectually is fascinating. In reality, though, the meaning of that joyful and bittersweet intonation already exists in the breathy vowels themselves.

One more example of the delightful power of heka comes from Jonathan Cott's book *In Search of Omm Sety,* which tells the story of Englishwoman Dorothy Eady who found herself in Egypt devoted to the Temple of Abydos built by Pharaoh Seti I. She took on the Egyptian name Omm Sety. The new name aligned her energy more closely to that of the native women living in Abydos.

Cott tells the story of a modern-day policeman in Abydos who riled a cobra that had crawled out from a chink in the temple wall. Omm Sety decided to repel the snake by repeating a spell of protection from the Pyramid Texts. The last word to be said was *seben* (depart). Omm Sety kept saying "seben, seben, seben," but nothing happened. At last, she changed the tone of the word, emphasizing its last syllable—seb-EN. The cobra put down its hood and slunk back into its crevice.

To the miracle, Omm Sety responded, "I think a lot of ancient Egyptian magic must have been based on vibrations that we don't understand, because it's important that you use the correct tone of voice when uttering the spell."[20]

Could it be that all things have a soul vibration and that we pull on that vibration when we call a particular thing by its true name? Amun's name has a particular vibration that even Roman Catholic priests intone at the end of every Lord's Prayer. "Our Father, who art in heaven. . . . Amen."

For each sacred name, the goddess Seshet writes an akashic (soul) record. The pharaohs had multiple names, some for their public lives, some for their spiritual lives, and some for their personal or familial lives. Seshet wrote our names with light upon the leaves of the *ished* tree, or the Tree of Eternal Life. We live, die, and live again. It is more than a change of skins, or even a change of consciousness; it is a change of record and vibration. Like the recording secretary at the courthouse, Seshet details all our incarnations, marriages, birth and death dates, places of origin, children's names, gains, losses, accounts due, accounts paid, and so on. Wouldn't seeing each of our vibrations written in light constitute enlightenment—rather like seeing a DVD of the soul? That is one function of the Pyramid Texts and the Book of Coming into Light.

"Constant and ceaseless becoming" is one meaning of the dung beetle Khepera. Things end and things begin again. There is no single beginning and no end. The psychospiritual language of the hieroglyphs points to a grammatical certainty that there is but one reality, yet the story at the end of Pharaoh Unas's life is one filled with verbs of potentiality. Utterance 264 of the Pyramid of Unas Text says: "The reed floats of the sky are set down for me that I may cross on them to the horizon. The canal is opened. The Winding Waterway (both Milky Way and Nile) is flooded. . . . I am ferried over to yonder eastern side of the sky, to the place where the gods fashioned me, wherein I was born, new and young, when there comes this time of tomorrow."[21]

That grammatical construction reflects a spiritual truth that this life that has been lived is being lived now and is lived into eternity. The cosmos is eternally present and yet in constant motion.

Everything moves. All motion is vibration that came into being at the time of creation. At an unconscious level, it carries the knowledge of its origin and function within it. Throughout the universe, vibrations in each thing pulse and overlap. This creates unlimited possible connections and interactions between all of the intelligences in the universe. Imagine that. The differing rates of vibration create the shapes, sounds, colors, tastes, and odors that we perceive. Some frequencies create forms and move in cyclical patterns that we cannot perceive because these operate on a different wavelength than we do. Through mental means, like meditation, we have the ability to change our frequency. We can learn to match our vibration to the vibration of the other. Perhaps we can slow our vibration down to the rate that a granite boulder vibrates and in that way perceive the wisdom that rock has accumulated during its aeons of existence. If we vibrate at a higher rate, we can increase our contact with the spirit world, with the shades of the departed, with supernatural beings, with life-forms from other universes.

Energy also moves in cycles, creating a pattern that sometimes intercepts other cycles and patterns through accident or design. Radio signals that interfere with the flight patterns of birds might be an example of this, as would the changes seen in astrological contact between planetary energies.

THE LAW OF ATTRACTION

We can attract people, events, and energies to us. The mind and emotion form mental and astral vibrations that create a unified energy that travels over long distances through the cosmos in the same way that light or sound vibrates. Our actions reverberate out toward others. Our feelings and thoughts move outward across the universe, at times attracting that which we do not consciously know. Thoughts and emotions may draw to us positive or negative events and people. Throw a pebble into a pond and it creates a ripple. That ripple moves out toward the edges of the pond, and then when it bumps into something, the shore for example, the waves vibrate and move back toward the site of origin.

Now you can see how the law of vibration relates to the law of attraction. Remember that worry is a very strong thought vibration because it combines both mental and emotional energies. You may bring negative events toward you simply by worrying over them. Worry, I learned, was a prayer for something I did not want. I now invoke what I really want, and then consider it a done deal. Assured of a positive outcome, I tend not to worry or "overpray" the issue.

Knowing the power of a thought and how to form clear, strong thought energy allowed ancient Egyptian priests to heal, protect, and elevate the lives of those around them. To learn magic and the words of power took years of priestly training. For the *sem* priest, or a high priest, that knowledge was as essential as breath. In *Conception of God in Ancient Egypt,* Eric Hornung describes magic as "the nuclear energy of early civilizations because of its dangerousness and its power to transform the world."[22] Used correctly, as we have said, magic heals, protects, empowers, and invokes. Used wrongly (willfully, or with intent to harm or manipulate), magic has disastrous consequences.

DEVELOPING AWARENESS

We have looked at mental energy, the will, and the emotions as they relate to creative energy. It is through the applied use of these vibrations that things can be made manifest in the physical realm. The most important prerequisite to using heka properly, however, is developing the proper state of consciousness. This requires the wisdom of the heart—the pure alignment of love with divine laws. Just because we can do something does not mean that we should do it. We are responsible for the results of whatever action we take and whatever magic we make. The energy of the neteru is not evil. It is just energy. Our misuse of will and our thoughtless actions make error, sin, and evil.

Ancient Egyptian temple priests and priestesses performed all their magic in accordance with *ma'at*. Ma'at can be understood as truth, balance, and the foundation of the universe—in other words, *natural law*. One works in concert with Ma'at, the goddess of truth, as well as with the ma'at principle. One does not attempt to sway the balance or change universal law. Although we know that life is filled with recurrent cycles and patterns, Ma'at's truth is inalterable. Every being that exists in the universe has consciousness, and that innate knowing of its essential nature flows through all life-forms throughout eternity. Corn seeds naturally know their essential function and grow in the same manner as corn grows throughout the span of the aeons. The original begets an inherent essential self-knowledge within its progeny. Adaptation to the environment does not take away from the essential nature of the seed. The corn stalk in my garden is not the maple tree in my yard.

We expect the consciousness of every thing to do what it knows how to do. Every unit of the universe inherently knows what its function is. Humankind sometimes mucks up the cogs of the universe, either through human error or misused intention, and that can change the natural order of things. Egyptian pharaohs did not attempt to dam the Nile because to do so ran counter to the laws of Ma'at established at the beginning of time. The kingdom relied instead on the blessing of Hapi, Khnum, Satis, and other river deities to send the waters at the right time and at the right levels.

In the modern world's haste to control a natural, that is neter-ed, process, a hydroelectric dam was built on the Nile near Aswan to generate more energy. That dam backed up the river, flooded Nubian farms and homes, and created a mass exodus of peoples from their native land. The massive social and environment stresses caused by the dam have been felt throughout Sudan and Egypt and as far as the Mediterranean Sea.

Over time, farms that were once fertilized by the river were overgrazed and overproduced to feed a growing population. Thus the land grew poorer because it was no longer fertilized by the floodwaters. The exhausted land now needs chemical fertilizer to replace the minerals that the flood had naturally provided. Egypt created a number of industrial plants to generate the chemicals necessary to replenish the land, and most of the electricity generated by the Aswan High Dam was required to run the factories. One wonders whether the willful change in the river's natural cycle created a better or worse situation.

One can see that there is a problem here. As the old Chiffon

Margarine commercial used to say, "It's not nice to fool Mother Nature." Environmentalists try to draw attention to what happens when we blow up mountaintops and throw coal slag into rivers or mess around by altering the genetic codes of the food we eat. That is not good magic. That is not technological advancement, and it is certainly not working in accordance with Ma'at. In all likelihood, eating genetically altered foods will kill us. It will have the same effect as intentional and willful black magic. In essence, it's not magic; it's arrogance.

Conversely, the potential exists in every atom to return to its perfect state. The energy field exerted by our thoughts and desires—and a deeper understanding of how we grow—can affect our bodies, our environment, and our lives for the better. By our choices, actions, and states of mind, we alter the rate at which the atoms of our bodies vibrate. This is the underlying principle of personal growth and spiritual unfolding. Nothing is inanimate in the universe. Nothing is static. No energy is ever destroyed. It only transmutes, and this mobility makes things better over time. Our lives are influenced by our own mental and environmental vibrations and by the active innate intelligence of God.

HU, SIA, AND HEKA: INVOCATION, WISDOM, AND MAGIC

The Pyramid Texts show us a journey that Re makes through the neterworld every night. He made this same journey on the first day of the world when he sprang from the lips of Atum. After death, the soul makes this same journey on its quest for regeneration and greater enlightenment. Three divine beings accompany Re during his nightly travels in the *meskhet* boat. They are Hu, Sia, and Heka. In brief, we might define them as invocation, wisdom, and magic.

We have already examined Heka at some length, but certainly Re derives his power from his creative partners Sia and Hu. The two gods were said to be born from the fluid of the phallus of Atum as the Great He/She united with the hand of God. With Sia (wisdom or perception) and Hu (divine utterance or invocation), Atum uses Heka (magic) to create the cosmos at the beginning of time. Every day Re renews himself using this same magic.

Hu is magical breath, inhaling and exhaling; he is the vitality that sets the waves of being in motion. Sia is wisdom and understanding; he is the power of conscious thought and focused attention. In the realm of the gods, Sia is omniscience and divine knowledge, foreknowledge and understanding; Hu is the voice of authority; and Heka is spiritual intention, the force behind magic. All three divine beings exist in the realm of God as the light and life force that extends into the universe. All three must be kept in the mind of the high priest shaman and within the heart of the pharaoh from the opening of day to its close—and especially on the soul's journey through death, the dreamtime, or through the night.

The three companions of Re appear on the left-hand side in Re's solar boat. They are Hu, Heka, and Sia. Altogether they represent the breathy voice vibration, the magic, and the creative intelligence that accompany creation from light.

One creation myth says that when Hu drew in his first breath, there came a sucking sound that is the essence of his name. Hu is also the sound of an expelled breath. His two hieroglyphs, ⌂ ◦, are a house with an open door and the circle that represents the spiraling winds of a dust devil.

The hieroglyphic images of this name impress me with the idea that the breath of God exists within the form of all. A deep intake of breath that fills the lungs entirely followed by a complete exhalation that expels air from the bottom of the lungs is a called bellows breath. This breathing pattern automatically raises our receptivity to divine inspiration. With each breath that Hu expelled, creation took place. His first inhalation created the soul of Osiris and the exhalation that followed created Re.

At death the soul leaves the body upon its last breath. It ascends into the night sky and becomes a star in the body of Nut, and Hu is with him. This is a beautiful image of the cosmic swirl of galactic stardust circling to form new stars and solar systems.

Certain mystical traditions believe that the Sphinx is an image of the god Hu. When the river had reached its flood height, Hu's fiery breath stirred the water and caused the sun to rise. To reenact this sacred calling, people gathered on the river banks before sunrise to chant "Hu-Hu-Hu-Hu-Hu" until the sun rose. As a god in the company of Thoth, Hu also may have been present as a baboon, which is known to raise its palms in the morning and huff at the rising sun. Sri Harold Klemp, spiritual leader of Eckankar, notes, "Hu is the ancient name of God, a love song to God. When Soul has heard this sound, Soul yearns to go home."[23]

Sia holds an inner vision, while Hu expresses that vision. One might imagine them as the third eye and throat chakras. Spell 1006 of the Coffin Texts says that Sia exists in the Eye of Re and Hu exists on the tongue.[24] In some texts, Sia and Hu lose their more human traits and take on the symbols that represent their qualities. Sia takes the form of a white plume upon the pharaoh's forehead and touches in with the light of Re—the spiritualizing consciousness that enters the third eye then moves down to the throat to become an embodiment of the god Hu. Sia is part of the Eye of Re and represents "seeing true," an accurate perception that is inseparable from divine understanding. Sia is at work when that special light goes on in our head and we perceive truth in a lightning flash. This power of awareness offers insight and intuition to protect us from unknown or disavowed ego errors that might well up from the unconscious or elsewhere. Sia is a god whose wisdom diverts an adverse event by overpowering the shadow, or "any hidden god."

SIA AND THE AKASHIC RECORDS

In the solar boat of Re, Sia carried the sacred papyrus that contained the wisdom of Re. For the soul in transition, Sia carried one's personal book of life, or akashic record. Says Utterance 250 of the Pyramid Texts: "I have come to my throne, which is over the spirits (*akhu*). I unite hearts, O you who are in charge of wisdom, being great. I become Sia who bears the book of god, who is at the right hand of Re. . . . I, even I, am Sia who is at the right hand of Re, the proud heart, who presides over the Cavern of Nun."[25]

In the constellation of the neterworld, the Cavern of Nun becomes both the void from which Re must be reborn each morning and the dark grave from which the soul of the dead must arise. In the Book of Coming into Light, Sia accompanies Thoth, lord of wisdom, when the heart is weighed in the Halls of Osiris. Sia's scroll can be seen as the complete sacred text written by Thoth himself, a wisdom text that the scribe has studied throughout his lifetime. More likely it also represents the central karmic document of the neterworld—a record of the soul's knowledge of good and evil.

The texts that accompany the chapter "The Weighing of the Heart" in the Book of Coming Forth by Day (called Pert em Heru by the Egyptians) suggest that we write the akashic records with every breath

(Hu) and every action. Coffin Text Spell 321 says that the king's soul has taken the shape of Atum and is coming again into consciousness. "His utterance is what goes forth from his own heart; he has gone round in the company of Shu upon the circuit of Hu and Sia."[26] In our book of life, Sia records our actions, our changes, our entrances and exits. The text is shown to us and to the neteru in the neterworld as we traverse the winding way toward the stars.

Sia often takes a serpent shape similar to the serpent on the king's crown. Sia not only keeps personal records; he also keeps the scrolls that contain the wisdom and supraconsciousness of the gods. In another culture's Genesis story, Sia might have been the serpent that tempted Eve to take a bite of fruit from the Tree of Knowledge. As a serpent, he is one of those magical beings that understand the polarity of the universe and can thus transverse the upper and lower worlds. Omm Sety suggests a reason that the spirit of the pharaoh rides with Heka (magic) and Sia (wisdom) in the boat of Re. "What kind of magic would it be," she asked, "without wisdom to guide it?"[27]

In Utterance 255 of the Pyramid Text the soul of the dead conquers an enemy of Re named Khebdje. The name refers to a place of shadow, of occult darkness—a hidden place. To conquer the darkness, death, or the realm of the unconscious, Unas draws upon the powers of Hu and Sia. Unas sheds light into the darkness, saying, "I have assumed authority [Hu] and have power through understanding [Sia]."[28] We quell unconsciousness with consciousness; we expel darkness with light, the magic of Hu and Sia.

THE MAGICAL POWERS OF THE NETERU

Every neter possessed the magical, incantatory power of Hu, Sia, and Heka in varying degrees. Thoth and Isis were mighty in their words of power. His words became the essential shamanic texts (Book of the Dead, Coffin Texts, Pyramid Texts, and so on) of creation and regenesis. He taught those particular words of power to Isis who was mistress of the great magic. She, in turn, awakened her dead husband Osiris, conceived her child Horus by magic, and protected him from the henchmen of Seth. The magic of Atum and Ptah was so great that they merely breathed and life began. Sekhmet, Ptah's consort, knew the magic of healing and of life and death.

The Shabaka Stone of the Memphite trilogy clearly shows that all three divine qualities were necessary. "When the eyes see, the ears hear and the nose inspires breath, they convey that to the heart; that (the *ab*) causes every decision to go forth. It is the tongue which pronounces what the heart has thought. It (the tongue) fashioned all the gods, and the Ennead, and every divine word, also came into being through what the heart conceived and the tongue commanded."[29]

To me, this idea implies that we understand through image, sound, and rhythm. Those three are the principal elements of all Egyptian magical literature. Working as symbol and vibration, these bypass an intellectual understanding. Meaning is more easily apprehended by the heart first. When the tongue forms the speech of a feeling, it is translated into thought, but the heart knows the true meaning of language, and desire for the heart is the seat of consciousness. By speaking the Great Word, the bolts of heaven were unlocked, and the boat of Re, which is enlightenment, was able to flow forth as fresh and powerful as the first ray of sunlight.

The shamanic texts of the ancient Egyptians show us how these energies work on behalf of the gods, on behalf of the dead, and on behalf of the priest-magician. Swiss Egyptologist Eric Hornung saw these texts as the first examples of spiritual narrative, as did Carl Jung who traveled in Egypt in 1926. "The Egyptians were the first to practice a Jungian psychology of archetypes and to recognize the fundamental restorative power of the unconscious. They realized that in sleep and dreams, one experiences these depths as a psychic reality in which one may encounter gods and the deceased alike."[30]

CONNECTING TO THE LIFE FORCE

The same principles that connect pharaoh, shaman, and priest to the universal god force keep the living in contact with the ancestral spirits of the dead. One might think of it as an ongoing supernatural conversation. Since energy is never exhausted and nothing that is born ever dies, the spirits of our loved ones simply change vibration when they move into the other realm. It is still possible to connect with them through such rituals as holding feast days for the dead, dreams, and through mediumistic contact. What works in the boat of Re works also in the realm of the living. While this physical world is temporal, it is a means through which the soul can gain awareness. The true task of the living is to raise consciousness and learn about the soul's immortality through knowledge of the Divine. Thus spirit and matter are interconnected.

We might equate Hu with the medium's clairaudient abilities since Hu is connected with the voice, effective utterance, and the tongue. Hu provides a channel for the words that the spirit wants to convey. A medium may connect strongly with a spirit by allowing it to use her voice, while she lifts her own consciousness out of the way. A priestess of Nephthys who served as a ritual trance channel for the goddess was called "true of voice."

Sia is perception, clairsentience, and that inner knowing that we call gut feeling. The medium uses the serpent channel of kundalini energy to move up and down the chakra centers feeling the presence of spirit. There is a range of knowing that includes mental imagery and gut feeling. It might be more properly called receiving impressions from the energetic vibrations that hover around us.

Coffin Text 816 suggests that sensing and speaking true were a part of the Opening of the Mouth Ceremony. "I have seen Sia, and he opens my mouth and tells a true matter to the Lord of All [Atum]."[31] Coffin Text 1143 refers to Sia as existing within the Eye of Ptah,[32] indicating a similar relationship between the power of perception and an understanding of the workings of the Divine. Seeing may refer to feeling perception, or it may point toward a third type of vision, likely *ma'a-ir* (⟼ ◁▷), meaning true vision. The word *ma'a-ir* uses the hieroglyph of ma'at (the word for truth) and *ir* (the eye). The hieroglyph suggests the eye within the watchtower, which conjures up the image seen on the tarot card of the same name. To the ancient Egyptian mind, it may have been linked to the phoenix, or bennu bird, who built its pyre upon a pillar in the city of Anu.

The Leiden Papyrus contains several magical spells written in demotic script around the beginning of the Christian era. The Greco-Roman instruction book offered the novice sorcerer information on creating magical spells. While the book seems a little cookie cutter by ancient Egyptian standards, it does suggest clairvoyant mediums were being used at the time. For Greco-Roman Egyptians, scrying (or gazing into a crystal or bowl filled with water) was a way of visioning to acquire foreknowledge of events. For Kemetic Egyptians, it offered an understanding of life karma and an ability to witness the transformations the soul has made during its time on Earth. Ma'a-ir could imply true clairvoyance or possibly remote viewing, but it is less about seeing upcoming events than it is about seeing the truth of the spirit world, backward and forward.

In *Egyptian Divination and Magic,* Eleanor Harris suggests that scrying focuses one's concentration on an object. By creating a shift in brainwaves during trance, it then unlocks the secret (open sesame) to a universal understanding. In a theta brain wave state, we hear without physical ears and see without physical eyes. We move beyond the space-time continuum and travel into the core of the transcendent mind, until by accident a rational thought causes us to pop back out.

The Opening of the Mouth Ceremony (Spell 816 of the Coffin Texts), which is performed as a funerary rite, helps us to access the ageless wisdom. Sia is made able to speak through the vehicle, the etheric form of the deceased. "I have seen Sia, and he opens my mouth and tells a true matter to the Lord of All [Atum]."[33]

Now the glorified dead (*khu*) will have the capacity to speak through a medium using the faculty of Sia. The impressions received from the other side, thus, can be named. Using the symbols, the sound puns, the double meanings—in effect, the hieroglyphic record of a name, the tool of the spirit to speak the language of the living—establishes that the speech of Sia is in accord with true precognitive perception.

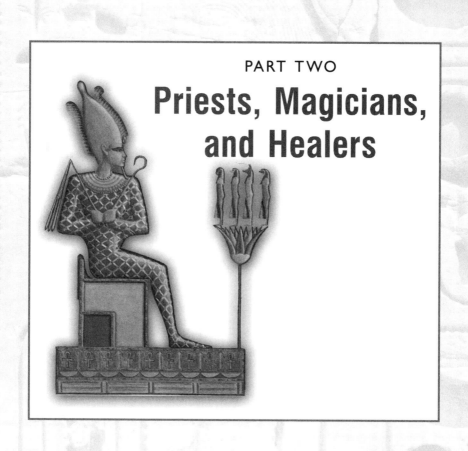

PART TWO

Priests, Magicians, and Healers

Isis and
Her Words of Power

Throughout this book, you will find the ancient legends and myths retold. Some of these stories are of divine beings, like Isis and Osiris; others tell the story of historical characters, like Khaemwast, son of Ramses II. Retelling these stories underscores the ways in which the human world and the divine world intersected within the ancient Egyptian mind. Mythologist Joseph Campbell has said that "[m]yth is the secret opening through which the inexhaustible energies of the cosmos pour into human cultural manifestation."[1]

Great stories are like dreams. To understand our lives, these must be told and told again, analyzed and reanalyzed, drawing into them new interpretations and deeper layers of meaning. The images that appear on the tomb walls and in the context of the Egyptians' sacred books are dreams. At this juncture in time, some five, six, or ten thousand years past, even history can become like a dream. If we view the entire study of ancient consciousness and its impact on our lives as if it were a dream language, it becomes easier to peel back its layers and open to its possibilities.

Isis and Osiris were a goddess and a god descended from heaven to live on Earth and to become the role models for all human life. As the first divine sparks on Earth, they were similar to the archetypes of Adam and Eve in their garden. They lived as a couple, tended their gardens, and built a community, and when Osiris died, he was mourned by his wife, Isis. She also magically conceived a child by him and resurrected him.

The magical myths of Isis and Osiris are important because they depict them as beings both human and divine. The myth of how Isis learned to use the words of power reveals how the ancient Egyptians saw the goddess Isis as a model magician. It depicts the ways in which magic could affect the divine realm as well as be put to practical use to serve humanity.

Isis was a conjure woman. She used words of power to control the forces of nature. The goddess could stop time, ease the pains of childbirth, and heal the lame and the blind. At her command, the waters of the Nile rushed forth to inundate and fertilize the land. She taught humanity the civilizing and healing arts. With the help of Thoth, as we will see later, she could even raise the dead, and it was she who taught the Egyptians the conduct of home and of temple.

Her magical arts grew even stronger when she learned the secret name of Re. Secret names were powerful tools, and so the secret name was protected and never spoken aloud. Its magic was so powerful that, if it fell into the wrong hands, great damage might befall the world. Even the other gods did not know a particular god's secret name and most of them were unpronounceable. And so how did Isis come to know the secret name of Re? The legend appears in the Turin Papyrus. Here is my own retelling.

One day the sun hung low in the sky casting its pink glow onto the distant hills, the fields of tall reeds, and the papyrus blooming beside the river. A cacophony of birds whirled through the air and settled in the leaves of the acacia trees. In the cool of the day, the sun god Re walked. Leaning heavily on his walking stick, he trudged beside the marshes. Already he was an ancient god, having exhausted himself with multiple risings and settings. Most of the time he lingered seated on this throne in one of his two horizons; his hair had turned silver and his bones were brittle. But still he was a vain god who adored the adoration of all the other gods and creatures.

"Say my name," he commanded his servants, "and strengthen me."

"You are the Most High Creator."

"You are the Sun in his morning and evening boats."

"You are King of Heaven and all of the Universes."

"You are the Mighty One."

"Lord of Time," said another.

"What another gorgeous day I've made," Re said. His servants agreed, helping him to stand and begin walking, moving his legs for him and his cane under him, propping him up. "Just look at the lions I made. See how they roar and call out my name? Look at the rams, the bulrushes, and the hoopoe wearing their yellow feathered crowns. Don't you think I am the most powerful creator god in all of Egypt?"

"Of course, you are," each servant answered. They ignored the fact that Re was by this time so old that whenever he spoke his spittle dribbled from the corner of his mouth to the ground. Every day he lost more precious fluid and some of his power leaked away.

Drooling all the way, Re continued to admire his beetles, his ibises, and his salamanders. "Why without me there would be nothing at all. The days come and go at my command. All the plants, the animals, and the people live because of me. Isn't that so?" Re demanded an answer.

"Yes, boss," they replied. "Just as you say it is."

In the garden, the sorceress Isis sat listening to Re's boasts. He did not see her there dressed in a green cloak that caused her to blend in with the papyrus and reeds. Already skilled in magic because, after all, she was a goddess, the veiled and hidden Isis scooped up some of the vital fluids that had leaked from Re's lips. She rolled them up in a ball of clay, molded it into a coiling serpent, and then breathed her magic on it.

Now she released it, and the dark-skinned cobra slunk through the overgrowth and shadows until it came into contact with Re's foot. When he stepped down on it, it released its poison. Re screamed at the serpent's fiery bite as its poison tore through him. He shivered and quaked, falling to the ground. "Help me," he cried with chattering teeth. "One of my creatures has risen up against me!"

Re's companions shook with fear themselves. "Oh, the world is coming to an end," they moaned. "Re has been bitten, and we all will surely die."

"Help me!" Re cried again. "Do something!"

The servants looked at each other in confusion, saying that they did not know what to do. "You are the Creator. You are the Mighty One. We are mere mortals. If you cannot heal yourself, we all are doomed!"

Now foam bubbled around Re's lips, sweat dripped from his forehead, and his eyes rolled back in his head. Colder than water and hotter than fire, Re writhed on the ground, moaning and quaking. He asked all who had magical powers to come to him and try to vacate the poison. His companions did as they were told and gathered in the garden all of the children of Re and the most powerful village sorcerers and magicians.

Among the weeping humans and children of Re stood a medicine woman named Isis. She calmly approached the god, asking him what was the matter. "Tell me, Father of All," she said. "Has one of your creatures risen up against you? Was it a serpent? If it was, I can banish its poison with my words of power."

Re nodded, and Isis replied, "Then you must tell me your true name so that I can heal you."

Re refused because to know the true name, the secret name, the name never to be spoken aloud, was to acquire all of the god's magic. That power could be used for evil purposes.

"Well, if you will not tell me, I can't help you," Isis said and turned away.

Reconsidering, the sun god blurted out, "I am Khepera in the morning. I am Re at noon. I am Atum at eventide."

"Of course, you are," Isis said. "Everyone knows that." She turned to leave the garden, but Re called her back.

"I'm the maker of heaven and Earth. I am the father of the gods. I am all that is."

"If you don't tell me your secret name, your soul essence name, then I can do nothing," she said. "Say your true name, and you will live."

Re, motioned her near him, saying that he would give her his name, *but that he could not do so in front of the other gods. Isis then gathered up Re, covered him with the cloth of her being, and in this way, his soul and his secret name left him and entered her. Having what she needed now to work her greatest act of magic, Isis chanted the words of power to save the god. "Flow, poison, out of Re," she said. "It is Isis who works her magic, and I have made the poison to fall on the ground. The secret name of the great god has been taken from him. Re shall live and the poison shall die."*

Perhaps it was in this way that Isis accumulated what became several more of her sacred ten thousand names. Apparently the magic worked its charm. The sun and his solar energy came back the next day as powerful and mighty as ever and without any sickness in his limbs. He no longer commanded all Earth, however, so he withdrew to a more distant place in heaven where he could watch over his creation. In this way, Isis became great of magic, a goddess equal to Re and Thoth in her powers, and a patron saint of all shamans in Egypt.

Before we feel sorry for Re and get upset about how Isis tricked him into letting her usurp his magic, consider that Re was the solar authority in the celestial realm, but that kind of solar dynamo power on a planetary level would have burnt out every living thing on Earth. It was necessary for him to withdraw and for the future king, Horus, the son of Isis, to become the embodiment of the solar energy manifest on Earth through the physical presence of the pharaoh. Osiris is the first ruler of Egypt, but when he dies and vacates the throne, it must be Horus who reigns and not the overpowering influence of Re, or the barren Seth.

In this way, the pharaoh embodied the magical power on Earth. He was the high priest of the Egyptian tradition, and the priests of the temple worked magic on his behalf for the benefit of the country. They did so through a number of means: temple rites, sacred text and practical magic, or the applied skill of healing and transforming the natural world through the words of power.

Because Re's name was something that could not be spoken aloud, it was believed that the magic of the god could be absorbed by writing the words of this legend on papyrus, dissolving the ink in a glass of water, and then drinking the water. The magician is not content to read; he swallows the texts, puts pieces of papyrus in a bowl, drinks the magic spell, and ingests the words that hold the meaning.[2] Upon drinking the water, the magician acquired the words of power needed for spells that healed venomous serpent bites.

This may sound ridiculous to us, and yet it was a rite that was passed down to the guilds of cathedral masons thousands of years after the drinking of magic was performed by Egyptian scribes. It may have been the laborious copying out of the text that imprinted it upon the scribe's psyche, but it certainly was the act of ingesting it that stated his spiritual intention to retain that knowledge within himself.

Practical Magic
for Egyptian Healers

For people living along a narrow strip of green land in the midst of a desert, every day was a gift. The Egyptian culture stayed in close contact with the divine world—the natural world, the world of sun, moon, sand, water, acacia trees, crocodiles, and lions. It was a world filled with the living forms of the Divine. Because the people worked with the natural world, it was not superstition to address the gods and goddesses and to petition them as if they were standing at one's side.

The Divine is always all around us. In the modern world, we have grown accustomed to only a weekly experience of God. During a church service, we call that intentional talking to the Divine praying. Still, in our private time, we may continue to call upon the Divine; for example, saying, "God bless you," when a child sneezes. We have Saint Christopher statues in our cars to protect us while we drive. We tuck lucky four-leaf clovers inside the pages of our books to remind us of the day we received a sign of God's blessing.

PRAYER AS MAGIC

In his letter to the Macedonians living in Thessalonica, the disciple Paul advised them to pray without ceasing. Specifically, he enjoined them to "Rejoice always. Pray without ceasing. In all circumstances give thanks, for this is the will of God for you in Christ Jesus. Do not quench the Spirit. Do not despise prophetic utterances. Test everything; retain what is good" (1 Thessalonians 5:16–21). Except for the reference to Jesus, an ancient Egyptian might give the same advice. Actually the Thessalonians, who were part of the Greco-Roman empire in 53 CE, had well-established fellowships of Isis and Osiris. The initiates of Isis in Egypt and elsewhere throughout the Mediterranean were already encouraging common meals among their fellow members, regardless of race, gender, or social class.

Isis offered a salve for physical, emotional, and spiritual wounds. Her adherents received healings and the assurance of immortality. As part of the sacred initiation rites, confession and humility were required. It seems clear that the Roman Catholic Church aligned itself with some of the teachings of the Isian and Osirian Mysteries. Icons of the Virgin Mary often are derived from temple images of Isis with the infant Horus seated on her lap. (Please see plate 15 of the color insert.) In other places, the goddess Isis trampled the serpent aspect of Seth underfoot, and in similar fashion, Mother Mary stamped upon the serpent Satan. Other books, including *Dreams of Isis* and *Feasts of Light,* address that subject. The Vatican even moved and reerected an obelisk originally erected by Tuthmosis IV in Egypt; it sits now in the middle of Vatican Square—a "magical" means of acquiring the potent energies of Egyptian religion.

WORKING WITH VIBRATION

In this modern era, we are more accustomed to relying on technology for our power. We understand things with our rational minds. Radio waves and magnetic energies surge forth every time we change channels on the television with a remote control. We rely on invisible energies whenever we remotely call a person on a cell phone. Our armies can even look with infrared goggles at creatures walking through the dark forest, or look at the bones—even the cells—inside our bodies. One cannot see the vibrations that cook our dinners, keep our radios tuned, or power our Wi-Fi; nevertheless, we accept the possibility of doing such things as ordinary and common. A remote control is an ordinary magic wand, and a cell tower is this century's answer to the obelisk.

All these things—seeing and talking remotely, altering perspectives, peering within to gain information, healing diseases, listening to voices from long ago—ancient Egyptians attempted to do through altered states of consciousness. In both these modern and ancient scenarios, the magic has been similarly produced—through vibration.

We do a disservice to the concept of Egyptian *heka* when we think of it only as magic, by which most people mean primitive superstition. We are the poorer for having no word in our vocabulary to define the powerful relationship between the minds of gods and humans. Heka is a visible manifestation of inward devotion and mental vibration that has an effect in the outer world. To put it in simple religious terms, prayer changes things.

All peoples have the capacity to pray. While all ancient Egyptians and their deities possessed the power of heka in some degree, priests, healers, and magicians were particularly good at it. They understood certain rules about why and how magic could be used.

RULES FOR EVERYDAY MAGICAL PRACTICE

Magic had practical uses. Inside the vestibules of sacred tombs and temples, the sick were healed, the soul journeyed safely through the underworld into the light, and the gods were praised. On a daily basis, heka combined with images (talismans and charms) could be used to heal, to balance, or to enliven the body by either warding off or drawing toward the individual certain kinds of energies. The magical images of heka were used to determine the divine plan for our lives (divination and dreams); to heal physical ailments (medicine and potions); to communicate with the Divine (prayer and supplication); and to make contact with departed ancestors (spirit communication). Temple music, offerings of food and drink, perfumed oils and incense, and meals shared with the gods (communion) were the ways ancient Egyptians kept up a strong connection between themselves and the creative mind, or logos, of their god.

The energy of heka involves using the human vessel as a generator or as an alchemical vehicle through which spirit-infused change may occur. We know that energy is never destroyed and that the magician's forte is the transmutation of energy. He knows what energy is available, how and when to use it, and how to amplify it. Just because energy *can* be manipulated does not mean that it should be. We saw that destructive energy unleashed when we transmuted hydrogen molecules to create the atomic bomb. We saw also what horror Adolf Hitler created in his attempt to destroy the Jews with not only hate speech but also the use of occult power.

Black magic, or the unfettered use of magic and words of power for personal gain, is a human attempt to control divine will. We understand that we are given free will; but as it is below in human families, so it is above. We warn our children of the dangerous effects of some of their actions, and if they willfully insist to do something anyway, they must suffer the consequences. A good priest or priestess does not attempt to manipulate divine will, although many a sorcerer has been known to try. The law of *ma'at,* however—the application of what is right and true—must always remain one's first thought.

There are many ways to approach the Divine, to pray, or to infuse spirit in our lives. Robert Masters, author of *The Goddess Sekhmet,* a treatise on Egyptian magic and psychology, suggested that ancient Egyptians made effective ceremonial magic because they relied upon several centers of cognition. These included "elaborate and potent symbol systems; words of power; consciousness-altering sounds, gestures, postures and sacred movements."[1] These activated the energy systems of the subtle bodies, or chakras, which allowed a healer to diagnose illness and to heal the body by changing the energies. Egyptian healers knew that people needed defenses against physical and mental attack; they understood that this type of healing offered psychological and spiritual well-being. To battle the forces of chaos and dissolution, the priest-healer-shaman had at his disposal a well-developed theology of the cosmos and multiple ways of interacting with the neteru.

PRIESTS AND SCRIBES OF THOTH

A well-developed higher mind was a prerequisite for the job of priest and scribe.

Practicing magic in ancient Egypt required knowing the written word. All priests were literate and devoted to Thoth, the god of the papyrus and ink pot. Among the oldest deities in the Nile Valley, Thoth created magic for the benefit of humankind. He kept the lunar and solar calendars and oversaw the work of architects, scribes, priests, judges, doctors, and viziers, and he worked his magic on behalf of the dead. As the ancient stories say, he even worked magic on behalf of the other gods and goddesses. From the beginning of recorded history, the scribes of Thoth governed Egypt by the rules that the god laid down. In Hierokonopolis in Upper Egypt, an image of his shrine appears on a stone artifact as early as the First Dynasty of King Narmer.

Thoth's temples became the training ground for future priests and scribes. It was said that the god was great in magic. "With his own fingers" the god composed forty-two sacred texts to assist souls in transition.[2] All magic derives from his mythical book the Book of Thoth, which was like the Holy Grail of Egyptian mystery traditions. Alchemists and adepts still seek the primary text. Like the Ark of the Covenant, which the Jews believe contains the commandments inscribed by God and given to Moses, the Book of Thoth was so powerful that it had to be kept from profane eyes. The sacred texts of Thoth were hidden inside multiple sealed chests, which were finally buried somewhere at the depths of the Nile or in the darkest, most remote recesses of a cave. In this way, the power of its sacred words could not be abused by those with evil intent. Securing the text this way kept others safe from harm.

The most revered priest-scribe in all of Egypt was the chief vizier of King Djoser during the Third Dynasty. Imhotep was not of royal blood, but to him were attributed all kinds of medical miracles, architectural wonders, literary compositions, and administrative coups. The ancient Egyptians saw him as a genius on the caliber of Leonardo da Vinci. He built the first known pyramid of the Old Kingdom, the Step Pyramid, and was a priest of the sun god Re. His fame lasted more than two thousand years. During the final New Kingdom dynasties, Imhotep became part of the trinity of Ptah and Sekhmet, replacing the god Nefertum as their son.

Considered the father of medicine, Imhotep founded a school of medicine in Memphis. It is possible that the Edwin Smith Papyrus, which may be as old as 2400 BCE, contains his medical wisdom.[3] So laudable were his healing powers that the Greeks equated him and his healing temples with the god Asclepius. Later, Imhotep became a kind of patron saint to scribes through the ages. Egyptologist James Henry Breasted wrote about Imhotep's potent legacy: "In priestly wisdom, in magic, in the formulation of wise proverbs, in medicine and architecture, this remarkable figure of Zoser's reign left so notable a reputation that his name was never forgotten. . . . [Scribes] regularly poured out a libation from the water-jug of their writing outfit before beginning their work."[4]

MAGIC: THE WORK OF SCRIBES

Magic and writing were woven together through the fabric of Egyptian culture. If there was a strictly oral tradition, it has disappeared. Most scribes were men, although some priestess scribes served in the goddess temples. Certainly Queen Hatshepsut learned the art of letters from her father, Pharaoh Tuthmosis I. The oral tradition was also alive and well. In the artisan and workers' village of Deir el Medina, located near the many tombs and temples in the Valley of the Kings, several texts mention a wise woman living there who may have been clairvoyant.

Most magicians, sages, and healers, however, learned their art by studying ancient scripts. They would have been priests and priestesses who bore titles such as prophet of heka or chief of secrets. The most sought-after magicians were the lector priests whose jobs were to keep the sacred books, record new rituals, and recopy or update older text as needed. These books of rituals contained a variety of formulae and instructions. Each temple kept a scriptorium called the house of life.

Some magic could be recited from memory, but written magic was the most prestigious. Written spells of protection and healing were family heirlooms, kept in storage to be copied onto papyrus and dissolved to make a magical drink or worn as an amulet on the body. Words offer powerful magic. Words speak to us in visible and invisible ways. The texts of the temple libraries were zealously guarded, and many an ancient Egyptian teacher refused to let his words be copied down. The Nag Hammadi Gnostic text known as the Apocalypse of Peter summed it up succinctly when it said, "Words are a mystery." These sacred words, the text warned, must be guarded and kept secret. In profane hands and in profane mouths, their true meanings would vanish.[5]

An efficacious spell had to use the exact words spoken aloud and accompanied by the proper actions. The deities' secret names needed to be pronounced correctly, and each priest guarded the names of the gods, the king, and the spirits so that not anyone could work the magic. This protected magician, pharaoh, and temple, keeping their secrets safe from potential sorcery.

Priests never let profane eyes see their texts. Greek sorcerers were especially notorious for trying to misappropriate the secret language of the Egyptians. Amun, the primary god of Thebes and the New Kingdom pharaohs, kept his sacred names intact. If his true name was not revealed, his energy could not be stolen; thus he was always called the hidden one to preserve the power of his priests, the power of Karnak and Thebes, the might of the pharaoh, and the god force of the universe. Even the Greeks were in awe of how long he managed to hang on to his secrets. Says the Leiden Papyrus:

Your first form by which you have begun was Amun—namely, he who hides his name from the gods. . . . Amun is one! (He) who hides himself from the gods . . . whose nature is unknown. . . . His nature is not recorded (or displayed) in sacred scriptures; he cannot be described and taught. He is too mysterious for his power to be laid bare; he is too great even to be asked about, too immense to be perceived. One would fall dead suddenly, in fear, if one were to pronounce the god's mysterious name, unknown to everyone. Not even a god can call him by his name, the vital one, because his name is secret.[6]

PHYSICIANS, PRIESTS, AND MAGICIANS

Temple magic for the most part remained in the temples. If one needed spiritual assistance or magic, one called a priest. The general population saw magic conducted outside the temple walls as a practical alternative either to mucking around in spiritual matters, of which they knew little, or to doing nothing at all. Everything in the universe had a reason. Ordinary folks may not be able to see it, but in that case, they relied on a knowledgeable local priest or magician. Magic allowed people to see the relationships between causes and effects. Symbols were easily understood, and analogies underscored the principle of like affecting like. Garlic oil, for example, was seen as similar in kind to the fatty oils that induced gout in a man's foot, and was therefore used to treat the kind of lameness caused by gout. The Egyptian healer worked on the premise of like affecting like. Meaning accrued through the association of one object and another, or one event and another. Thus, through observation of apparently coincidental occurrences—say, the rise of certain stars and the coming sandstorm or flood—meaning arose and future events could be predicted.

While the lector priests of the Old Kingdom era could perform all manner of heka, including casting out demons, healing the sick, shape-shifting, and commanding waters to part and winds to whirl, the Middle and New Kingdom priests acquired a specialist mentality. Originally, lector priests in the temple only performed rituals to protect their king and to assure rebirth for the dead. By the first millennium BCE, they became more associated with magic. Priests of Sekhmet, the goddess of pestilence, became healers—for who knew better how to heal than she who brought disease. Local women, most of them priestesses of Isis or Hathor, were prized as midwives skilled in magic.

There were snake and scorpion charmers who repelled noxious creatures and seers who counseled those whose ghostly relatives or neighbors were causing trouble. Somewhat related, but not necessarily considered magicians, both male and female artisans made amulets. Certainly an amulet needed to be crafted in a ritually correct manner—with the proper intent and constructed with the appropriate materials—but it was the lector priest who wielded the words of power to activate the magic inherent in them. The lector priests were known as the *kher ab,* meaning the true of voice. Their incantations had to be recited precisely as written and delivered with authority and intention. A priest was highly valued for his oratory skill as well as for his magical ability.

Physicians, priests, and magicians—there seemed to be no separation between the three roles. All three called upon providence to attain the desired results. Priestly services were paid for primarily through bartering goods or services in kind. It was not considered debased to request payment; Egyptian physicians were paid in barter and goods rather than by monetary means. During the Roman era, financial reward and coinage gained a toehold and at that time, payment in coin became the defining edge between practical magic and sorcery.

PRIEST-SCRIBES WITHIN THE TEMPLE

I love walking through the Cairo Museum looking at images of scribes, priests, and priestesses. One evening I went to the museum and found myself gazing raptly into the face of Ramses-Nakht (1150 BCE), one of my favorite statues. The first prophet of Amun sat cross-legged with a scroll partially unrolled in his lap. I gazed at the features of his perfectly chiseled face. His eyes were downcast, half closed in meditation. The baboon of Thoth was perched upon his shoulder, hanging on tightly to his head. While Ramses-Nakht seemed to dream, the baboon's eyes blazed, staring straight into me, deeply alive.

Here is what draws me back to that statue over and over. What does that scribe know that I don't know? And how can I get one of those baboons to help me write my books?

To become an ancient Egyptian priest-scribe one usually had to be born into a family of priest-scribes. Through those family associations with the temple, one came into the community of the priesthood, but it was the pharaoh who eventually appointed the higher level priestess and temple servants. Of course, the other prerequisite was to study a great deal. In fact, study might be considered a lifelong endeavor for scribes. The scribe's education meant more than being able to copy the sacred texts. Scribes attended a scribal school attached to the temple and went through several initiation rites. Among those rites for young boys was circumcision; another was baptism for all in the sacred lake. The individual initiation rites for the various deities varied, as did initiation into higher grades. After many years of serving in lesser roles, a scribe might become initiated into the proper ways to conduct temple services, approach the god, and so on.

A priest usually served a single temple as long as he lived. The Old Kingdom priests served a single divinity, but there were often many gods or goddesses in each community. The New Kingdom saw the predominance of the cult of Amun, which became more or less the state religion, especially after the aberrant and nearly disastrous Atenists of Akhenaten in the Eighteenth Dynasty. In time, Amun assumed the qualities of the Old Kingdom creation god Atum and the local god of fecundity, Min. The qualities of Re's radiance were now attributed to the hidden god. In time he was known simply as Amun-Re.

While separate priesthoods served other gods and goddesses in their temples, the Temple of Amun at Karnak was the largest, government-funded temple, acquiring a hierarchy of priests and priest-esses to serve it. The pharaoh put most of his energy into the temples of Karnak and Luxor, although he made sojourns to other sites for their festivals. One might say that around the time of Ramses the Great, the cult of Amun was the wealthiest and most powerful national religion—more so than any single deity had been in previous centuries.

Except for the pharaoh and his wife, a priest usually served a single temple his entire life. The temple was always open because the god is almost always home in it, which meant there was never any time in which a crew of priests was not employed there. There was no lack of work to do, and specialized priesthoods were not uncommon. Some priests were fine musicians; others accomplished astrologers. There were foods to be prepared, linens to be kept clean, liturgy to prepare for three daily services and feast days. These men and women lived in and served the temple for three months a year, usually one month at a time. The rest of the year, they lived in their communities going about their lives as civil servants, farmers, bread and beer makers, mothers, fathers, sons, and daughters. High priests and others who maintained the daily rites of the cult and who kept the festival rites as oracles lived in and kept the temple running at all times. Whenever the pharaoh visited, the king performed the rites of the high priest.

A few rules applied. Only peasants ate fish and pork; priest were semivegetarian, eating a bit of poultry and beef. Clean linens and clean bodies were a must for the priesthood. Bathing in the sacred lake three or four times a day while serving the temple was practically mandatory as was shaving all body hair, except for the eyebrows. Only papyrus sandals and linen dress were worn. One exception was the *sem* priest, or high priest, who wore the ceremonial leopard skin draped across his back. The priesthood abstained from sex while they served in the tem-ple. (Outside the temple walls, they were fathers and mothers, husbands and wives.)

Sometimes the priests and priestesses who were employed as stolists, lector priests, or oracles would fast up to ten days to become "a pure one." These servants of the god or goddess frequently lived in an almost ecstatic trance state. In this way, the divine being could more easily inhabit and speak through the human vessel while he or she was in trance. Just as the sacralized, enlivened statue could contain the spirit of the god, so could the pure human vessel be inhabited by the god's essence. Outside the temple, lector priests who were practicing magicians made use of this talent for channeling. They aligned their energies with the god and let the divine life force work through them. For example, one spell found on ostracon at Deir el Medina provided the script a magician might say to control an enemy. It should be noted that ancient Egyptians were not proponents of free form channeling, such as is common to modern metaphysicians. A god in ancient Egypt chose to present himself through a medium who was well prepared, one who had studied and knew the authentic words that had been composed by the god himself (as were the words of Thoth), and written by his own fingers. "I will say: 'Come to me, Montu, lord of the day. Come, that you may put (name) born of (name) into my hand like an insect into the mouth of a bird. I am Montu whom the gods adore.'"[7]

Priests were channels for or servants to the Divine. It was not the task of a temple priest to preach to the community, deliver sermons, or minister to the needs of anyone other than the pharaoh. His duties were not pastoral. They were to ensure the well-being of the country by tending after the needs of the pharaoh and the goddesses and gods. If all was well with them, all would be well with Egypt. At times, the high priest, who had a broader contact with the public through the lower castes of the priesthood, would counsel the pharaoh on matters of concern to the nation. In this way, he acted more like a chief of staff. This particular individual—the older, wiser, and more experienced high priest of the temple—was given the title First Prophet of the God.

Among the temple staff were horologists who kept track of the hours and the length of the days. This was an extremely important task that determined the precise time that the sun would crest the horizon. The gates of the temple and the doors of the shrine had to be opened at precisely the moment that the sun's first rays would strike the golden face of the deity. Due to the different latitudes of Egypt's temples and the sun's variation during its equatorial dance of the seasons, this priest had to be a good astronomer and mathematician. The astrologer priest needed similar skills. He or she observed the calendar of the seasons, marking the feast days and assisting in the foundation and laying out of the temple so that it met certain astronomical configurations. By watching the sun, the stars, and the constellations, the priest-astronomers determined precisely when the annual floods might arrive, when the seasons would change, when to plant, when to sow, and when to reap. In other words, they were the keepers of the Egyptian farmer's almanac, advising when to plant the first seed and when to roll out the Osirian mystery plays.

THE ROLE OF TEMPLE PRIESTESSES

Women were not often high priestesses except during the Old Kingdom, a time in which there seemed to be more equity among the sexes. Nefertiabet, a high priestess of Neith and the daughter of Fourth Dynasty pharaoh Khufu, is beautifully depicted on a slab stela seated before her offering table. Queen Meresankh, wife of King Khafre who succeeded Khufu, held the office of high priestess of Thoth. Obviously a woman of letters, Meresankh taught her twelve children the scribal and priestly arts. Her eldest son, Prince Nebemakhet, was the chief lector priest, high priest, and vizier married to Nubhotep, who was a prophetess of the goddess Hathor.

The influence of women disappears during the Middle Kingdom but reappears in strength during the years between the Eighteenth and Twenty-third Dynasties when the high priestess of Amun held the title Hand of the God. The high priestess, the highest-ranking woman of the temple with the exception of the queen, was expected to remain celibate. Unable to have children of her own, she was required to adopt and train a daughter to succeed her. She had administrative control of the area of Thebes, rather like a mother superior. Most of the New Kingdom priestesses, if they did not sing, dance, or make music in the temple, acted in the passion plays of the season. They also stayed busy as full-time mourners employed to keen, sing, and follow the coffin to its final resting place in the Beautiful Valley.

OF ORACLES AND FEASTS

Unless they were attending a passion play, a public feast, or a funeral, the public did not have access to the permanent staff of the temple. Many made their offerings to the gods at the courtyard altar inside the first pylon. Each hoped that his or her rare or luxurious gift might catch the eye of the priest who would draw the individual forward. Otherwise, the public never had an opportunity to witness the inner workings of the temple, its rites and rituals performed by the priests. On rare occasions, particular individuals were called out to come beyond the hypostyle hall into the inner chambers. There, perhaps, they might receive a special message from the high priest or from the neter itself.

Certain temples became famous for their oracular powers, for healing, and for dream incubation and interpretion. Among the more famous oracular temples was the Temple of Amun at Siwa Oasis, which legend says was founded by one of two African sibyls who were banished to the desert from the Temple of Amun in Luxor. One priestess founded the oracle at Siwa and the other founded the Temple of Zeus (Amun) in Dodona, Greece. Oracular temples are usually located in naturally occurring geologic anomalies, such as Delphi's geological fissure, which was said to release mystical vapors. (Some have suggested the vapor may have been ethylene gas fumes.)

The appearance of the lush Siwa Oasis in the midst of the vast Libyan Desert may be one reason why the oracular temple was founded here. Its simple presence in the midst of emptiness seems miraculous, so it would seem other such vibrant miracles might follow. Possibly the arduous trek to the temple through drifting sand and blindingly intense sun and heat might cause enough heat prostration to alter the consciousness of the supplicant. When that exhausted individual is taken away from her everyday life and falls into a dream state inside an oracular temple, all manner of unusual visions, spirits visitations, and dreams might occur.

Olympia, a widow and the future mother of Alexander the Great, was thought to have visited the Temple of Zeus (Amun) at Dodona in northwestern Greece. While in a dream state, the god impregnated her with her divine and royal son. That would make Alexander the son of the Egyptian god Amun and therefore a future ruler of Egypt. The oracle of Siwa confirmed the story to Alexander when he visited it during his Egyptian campaign. Having been led through a desert sandstorm first by two black crows and then by two snakes who kept him on his path when the desert threatened to overtake him, the future king of Egypt spent the night inside Amun's temple with Siamun, the high priest.

The oracle seemed to confirm that Alexander was on a divine mission and would soon become the next king of Egypt. In other dream oracles, the coronation of a king was presaged by a dream of two serpents, one on the right and one on the left, and two birds indicating the two forms of the goddesses Mut and Wadjet who represent northern and southern Egypt.

As a part of the morning service, the oracle priest opened the doors of the shrine just at the moment that the sun's rays crested the horizon to strike the gleaming face of the god or goddess. Usually the shrine remained closed except for opening, midday, and closing ceremonies. The god resided like the radicle of a seed within the husk of his shrine within the seedpod of the temple, awaiting the moment that first light called the god to life. Some ceremonies involved offering the god food, clothing, and drink. At night, the high priest closed and sealed the doors of the shrine, bowed low, and retreated, walking backward and sweeping away his footsteps. Alone in the dark, the god seed remained silent but still alive inside the temple. The next morning, the divine one was again awakened, bathed, praised, fed, and lauded as a living member of the community. As always, the gods were appreciated for their divine protection, benevolence, and renewal.

Outside the temple compound, oracular statues became the centerpiece of festival processions. At the appropriate time agreed upon by the astrologers and priests and in accordance with the calendars, the gods' festival days were celebrated. In Dendera and Edfu, mutual festivals called the Beautiful Reunion were held. The dual feast day celebrated the sacred marriage of Hathor of Dendera and Horus of Edfu. During the weeklong feast, the goddess was taken from her Dendera shrine and sailed up the Nile in her sacred boat, until at a time approved by the horary and oracular priests, the boat landed in Edfu. Then the shrine of the goddess was paraded on the shoulders of priests through the streets, adored by crowds of devotees, and finally carried into the sanctuary of Horus at Edfu. There the god and goddess had their conjugal visit until the goddess departed three days later. Again, amid great celebration, she returned home.

The Opet Festival honoring Mut, Amun, and Khonsu was a similar common oracular festival that took place in the vicinity of the temples of Karnak and Luxor. Temple priests carried on their shoulders the divine images seated in their open shrines inside the divine boats. Individuals might place a bit of ostraca at the feet of the god Amun and ask yes or no questions. For example, "Shall Seti be appointed as a priest?" or "Will I become foreman of the crew?" An affirmative answer was indicated by a forward movement of the statue; a negative answer by a backward movement. Often those who were ill claimed miraculous healings after a glimpse of the golden deity in his or her shrine.

OF DREAMS AND INTERPRETATIONS

In the dream state, one contacts the unconscious mind as well as the higher mind and the presence of God. The ancient Egyptians would have made little distinction between the upper and lower realms of the dream state, seeing all dreams as an opportunity to have direct contact with the Divine. In fact, the realm of Osiris could be accessed through the dream state both during night sleep and during daytime meditation.

The operative part of the word *rs* (⬯⎮) and the hieroglyph of the opened eye occur in all three of the words: Osiris, ⬯⎮⬭; dream, ⬯⎮⬭⬯; and to awaken, ∼∼⎕⬭⬯. The dream state was another kind of seeing—perhaps a truer form of sight because the ego stood apart from it. It is possible that the underworld Res-tau, ⬯⎮⬭∿, which has been identified as residing in Amentet (the hidden land), is an astral dreamworld to which both the living and the dead had access. Even the Egyptian words for *to dream* and the *underworld* have similar sounds.

In Deir el Medina in the workers' village, the New Kingdom scribe Kenhirkhopeshef (1235–1191 BCE) maintained a library with what appears to be his very own and very ancient dream book. It contains unusual dream associations to the modern mind, but when one considers that much of dream life, whether ancient or modern, engages in word puns, the meanings of the hieroglyphic dream book may be lost in translation. Note that the hieroglyphic words for *donkey* and for *greatness* are homophones, both *ur*. Thus, to dream of eating donkey meat meant that something very good was about to happen in one's life.

Some of the 108 dream symbols found in Kenhirkhopeshef's book are images that may appear in an individual's dream life. Certainly they also appeared in the various chapters of the Book of the Dead, which the workers of Deir el Medina were employed to carve upon tomb walls in the Valley of the Kings and Queens. The dream book, for example, mentions a man eating his own excrement, while in the Book of the Dead there appears an underworld guardian of the gates whose name is Eater of His Own Excrement. In the dream and in the afterlife as well, knowing the name of the formidable being was a good thing.[8]

Many dreams are only partially understood or recalled. Thus, dream incubation and interpretation became important temple functions. Dream interpretation was a skill that was god given; not just anyone could do it. Dream symbols in Egyptian hieroglyphs work in a similar fashion to the way dreams work in any language. (Sometimes falling off a cliff means "Watch where you're going," and sometimes falling off a cliff means being angry with your husband named Cliff.)

Most temples offered dream consultations to the supplicant who entered as "a pure one, washed and fasted." Revelatory dreams were common in the temples of Isis, Anubis, Amun, and Re—even in the temples of Imhotep and Seti I. Often the particular dream neter was chosen because he or she was known to provide help of a specific nature. Women hoping to conceive or to glimpse their future children came to the dream temples of Isis. Some oracular dreams prophesied future destinies, like the dream of a boy, Tuthmosis IV, who was hunting one day and fell asleep beneath the chin of the Sphinx. The Sphinx told him that if he removed the sand that clogged its neck and body, he would receive the throne of Egypt. Some dreams offered transactions with the Divine, such as the forgiveness of mortal errors committed or similar judgments that meant that the gods understood the dreamer's secret needs.

The gods could peer into one's soul, and by interpreting the dream images, one could divine the future and make amends before things happened. Through dreams one could stay in contact with those family and friends in the other world. These dream incubations also had a healing aspect. Myrrh, a plant the ancients called guide of Isis, was associated with the rituals of burial and mourning, having been the plant that Isis was said to use when contacting Osiris in the dreamworld and raising him from the dead.[9]

Dream time during the Old Kingdom differed from dream time in the Greco-Roman period when dreaming was a kind of national pastime, similar to attending a spa for a treatment. Skilled priest-dreamers who acted as shamans for their country, including the pharaoh himself, may have engaged in dream practices that were more along the lines of remote viewing, astral travel, and vision questing. The high priest who performed the secret rites of the pharaoh's Heb-Sed, or renewal, Festival probably created a scenario in which the pharaoh experienced his death.

Perhaps with the aid of plant medicines, the pharaoh entered a trance and connected with the ancestral spirits, the animal spirits, and the gods of the neterworld. All that the public may have known about the initiation rite at Saqqara was that every pharaoh in Egypt experienced one in his thirtieth year. To survive the grueling ordeal was a testament to the king's vitality and integrity.

This long history of vision questing here may have led to the Saqqara Serapeum (built by Khaemwast during the Eighteenth Dynasty) becoming known as a dream temple during the Greco-Roman era. Most certainly there was a connection between the famed priest-scribe Khaemwast, son of Ramses, who toured the underworld during his vision quests, and his father, Ramses II, the most long-lived pharaoh who boasted having completed thirteen jubilee festivals. He completed the first vision quest Heb-Sed Festival during his thirtieth year of reign and the subsequent festivals every three years thereafter.

The big dreams came only seldom. More often, dreams were of a more mundane, personal nature, such as dreams of overeating, losing status, losing one's teeth, being naked, being elevated in stature. Many scribes kept copies of dream books, which they consulted and in which they recorded their interpretations. Still, dream interpretation was up to the individual consultant to determine the true nature and meaning of the dream.

Dreamers came to the temple to meet with the priest-scribe in the house of life and receive dream charms, healings, dream interpretations, or counteractions against psychic attacks. The priestly dream interpreter saw symbols, whether in hieroglyphic scripts or in dreams, as direct communications from the Divine. The library contained many sacred texts, including the texts of all the temple rites and secrets, and so the library was well protected and kept shrouded in great mystery. The sacredness of its contents automatically elevated the lector priests who attended it and who kept the *medjat,* or the papyrus scrolls. From this word for the holy words, we derive the Greek word *magikos* and the Old Persian word *madju,* or magi.

The dream charms often included words directed to the African protector god Bes and the lion goddess Sekhmet. One such spell suggested drawing an image of Bes on the left hand in black ink mixed with myrrh, frankincense, cinnabar, and rainwater (hard to get in the desert!), along with the juice of wormwood and the blood of a black cow and a dove. Then black cloth dedicated to Isis was wrapped around the hand. Incidentally, the rest of the cloth was wound about the neck. After an invocation was made at sunset, the dreamer went straight to bed without saying a word. If one spent that much time in the pursuit of an important dream, the subconscious mind would receive a very powerful suggestion. Having made oneself receptive to its possible appearance, more than likely the big dream would come.

Dreams were important to the Egyptians because dreaming was Isis's preferred method for contacting Osiris in the underworld. Likewise, dreams were the manner that Osiris used to train his orphaned son Horus to become powerful enough to defeat Seth who was trying to kill Horus and take the throne. Anyone who has traveled in Egypt for some time knows that when one returns home, the dreams of the ancient world are imprinted so strongly in the brain that we continue to dream about and to receive nightly visitations from the terrain we had explored psychically and physically by day.

The ancient Egyptians held an absolute belief that life existed on other planes and that this alternate life was similar to the world already known to them. After they became familiar with the gods and goddesses who might one day people the Elysian Fields in the underworld, it became easier for them to see the gods in their dreams or walking through the town streets. The ancient Egyptians used their affirmations to remind themselves that when we sleep our consciousness astrally travels. The body rests, but the mind is at work, learning and exploring in other dimensions.

Another divination method mentioned in the Greek magical papyri and used in a similar fashion by the Golden Dawn involved the invocation of both Isis and Re, using the same technique that Isis used to locate the severed body parts of Osiris. On twenty-nine leaves of the male date palm the names of twenty-nine deities were written. These names were linked to the twenty-nine letters of the Coptic alphabet. After praying above the leaves, one picked them up two by two. Only the last two leaves provided the omens and their interpretation answered the question clearly.[10] This technique is similar to the divination method that I witnessed by a Peruvian shaman who read coca leaves.

HEALERS BEYOND THE TEMPLE WALLS

Like most of us, the ancient Egyptian wanted to enjoy life on Earth and to feel comfort in his passage into the next realm. Health consciousness was life consciousness, and that included seeking medical advice when needed. The local off-duty priest or priestess living in the community was accessible. All manner of people, from farmers to housewives, sought Egyptian priests for spiritual advice, for the production of funerary books, for talismans, for special prayers, or, when necessary, for magical incantations. Some asked the priests to prepare feasts for family members who had gone to the western lands and into the Fields of Peace. Others worked in courts of law. One of the best things to be said of a priest was that "[h]e was discreet concerning what he saw and learned, capable in his work, and well-loved by his people."[11]

For nearly three thousand years, Egyptian physician-scribes treated all manner of injuries, illnesses, and diseases and even performed surgical procedures. They fully documented their medical arts, the Old Kingdom having especially revered its doctors and medical professionals. Of all the healers working in the ancient world, the Egyptian physician was most likely to have based his understanding of medicine on scientific inquiry and the successes of physicians before him. Paintings in an Old Kingdom tomb show Ankhmahor (2300 BCE) cradling and massaging the foot of a patient and applying reflexology. Hesyre was the first dentist in ancient history, employed by Pharaoh Djoser of the Third Dynasty (2400 BCE), and he was probably a contemporary of

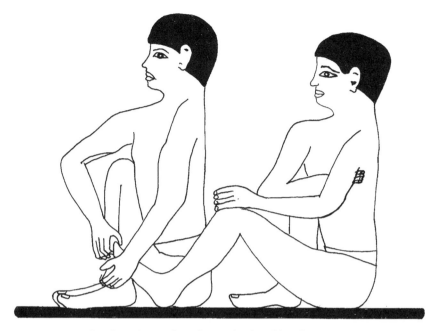

*Foot reflexology depicted in the tomb of Ankhmahor (2300 BCE),
a healer during the Old Kingdom era.*

the famed physician Imhotep. Lady Peseshet is the first known female
physician. She served as director of female doctors during the Fifth
Dynasty (2350 BCE), which indicates that she was not an anomaly.
Many more women than she were practicing medicine. An intriguing
statue of the Fifth Dynasty physician Niankhre (2300 BCE) provides
us with a portrait of the wounded healer. The high priest of Heka was
a cripple whose magical medical arts were used to combat the poison of
scorpions.

Throughout the years, ancient physicians worked as surgeons, gyne-
cologists, proctologists, ophthalmologists, dentists, gastroenterologists,
and pharmacists, as well as alternative healers, such as aromatherapists
and reflexologists. The Nineteenth Dynasty physician Iwty (1320 BCE)
kept a great many scrolls as references and was considered an expert in
the preparation of herbs, oils, poultices, and medicinal plant extracts, as
well as providing instructions on treating the diseases he encountered.

During Greco-Roman times, physicians treated their patients

inside rock-cut chambers on the upper terrace of Hatshepsut's temple at Deir el Bahari. The hospital was devoted to the Third Dynasty physician Imhotep, to local healers of the Eighteenth Dynasty, and to Amenhotep, son of Hapu. For Greco-Romans receiving treatment from physicians trained in the techniques of Imhotep and Amenhotep, a visit to Hatshepsut's temple hospital was equivalent to taking the healing waters in Lourdes, France. Sanctuaries previously dedicated to the god Amun by Hatshepsut now allowed priest-physicians to treat their clients. Over fifty graffiti attest to the miraculous cures performed in the name of Amenhotep and Imhotep. Such stories of healing increased the fame of Egyptian medical science in the ancient world.

Doctors in the ancient world made house calls: one Middle Kingdom statue shows a physician carrying his medical kit, which might have contained some of the accoutrements seen in later carvings on the walls of Kom Ombo. These included knives, drills, saws, pincers, beakers, jars of oil, pots of herbs, powders, and salves, as well as measuring scales and amulets. (Please see plate 24 of the color insert, which illustrates medical instruments inscribed on the walls of Kom Ombo.) Both the Roman anatomist Galen (129–199 CE) and the Greek physician Hippocrates (460–370 BCE) attribute their medical knowledge to the texts they studied in Memphis at the Temple of Imhotep.

In all probability, the healthiest people were the priests, scribes, and physicians. The prescription for a healthy life outside the temple was similar to the life that was maintained inside the temple. One should keep to the regular purification rituals that encouraged much bathing, shaving one's head and body hair to reduce lice, and keeping dietary restrictions against raw fish and other unclean animals.

Working-class life was hard. Builders, sailors, soldiers, and manual laborers had many injuries, and few people were immune to disease. Even Egyptian royalty, who had the best chance for a long happy life, suffered from polio, infertility, and physical weaknesses—perhaps caused by intermarriage. Because of the climate, all castes of people could be plagued by illnesses. The ubiquitous flies and the sandstorms that howled across the desert created many problems, including skin diseases, respiratory infections, and eye ailments such as cataracts, conjunctivitis, trachoma, and night blindness, the latter of which could be treated successfully by eating animal liver. Dental problems were endemic. The gritty texture of bread baked in the sandy climate wore down teeth over time; tooth decay and gum disease were common. Broken bones, headaches, urinary tract infections, stomach ailments, and all matter of sexual difficulties from problems conceiving to impotency were treated by physicians.

All physicians (and magicians) were known as priests of Heka. The Heka priests devoted to Anubis practiced as embalmers; therefore they possessed an intimate knowledge of the workings of the human body from its bone structure to its internal organs. The priests of the lion goddess Sekhmet, lady of pestilence and the plague, possessed knowledge of what caused disease as well as what healed. Sekhmet was also the lady of drunkenness, and her priests and priestesses, as well as those of Isis and Hathor, probably knew of anesthetics and pain relievers. The priests of Selket took command of working with serpent bites and scorpion stings. Priestesses of Isis and Hathor were adept at gynecology, and those dedicated to Ptah, Amun, and Thoth possessed the words of power and were mighty in a number of fields, including incantations.

What moderns have come to associate with the doctor's prescription signature, the R_x, actually dates to the use of the *wadjet,* or healing Eye of Horus (👁), by physicians of ancient Egypt. The Eye of Horus alluded to the mythic battle between Horus and Seth for the vacated throne of Osiris. During their fierce eighty-year war, the god Seth was said to have plucked out the left eye of Horus. Hathor, the cow goddess, healed his eye with her sacred milk—milk being one of the physician's more frequently used medicaments. (Please see plate 27 of the color insert, which features the Eye of Horus on the ceiling of Dendara.)

In addition to writing the sign of the wadjet as a healing notation, the various hieroglyphs depicting parts of the eye were used to indicate

In the myth of the Contendings of Horus and Seth, the Eye of Horus was blinded by Seth and later healed by Thoth using the milk of the cow goddess Hathor. Thereafter, the Eye of Horus was known as the healing eye and used by physicians dedicated to the healing arts and scribes of the god Thoth.

a fraction of the whole eye; for example, the eyebrow ⌒ is one-eighth, the pupil ○ is one-quarter, and the left cornea ⊲ is one-half. In other words, the parts of the eye indicated what was needed to heal the whole being, as in how much or what fractions of ingredients were to be mixed in a poultice or herbal remedy. The Eye of Horus also indicated a homeopathic understanding of healing, with like being used to treat like, much as antidotes for poison are made from snake venom.

Again we have an ancient healing image of serpents intertwined about the caduceus of the physician. Note that the serpent goddess found in Lower Egypt was called Wadjet, just as the healing Eye of Horus also was called wadjet. Both signs are linked to Thoth, the god of scribes and healers.

PRESCRIPTIONS FOUND IN MEDICAL PAPYRI

Those who buried the dead often looked for the causes of the person's death. Most likely the work of priests in mortuary temples led to standardized medical practice in ancient Egypt. Embalmers had a working knowledge of anatomy and used careful observation skills to determine what disease might have taken the victim. In determining the cause of death, they began to study its possible cures.

Medical papyri were a part of every temple. Two of the most important medical documents to have surfaced from the ancient world were the so-called Edwin Smith Surgical Papyrus, whose glosses date to the seventeenth century BCE, but which originated during the early dynasties of the Old Kingdom, and the Ebers Papyrus (1500 BCE), a medical compendium that ran up to sixty feet in length.

Probably the most pragmatic manuscript of the ancient medical arts, the Edwin Smith Papyrus groups together similar illnesses and injuries, starting at the top of the head and moving down the body. Unfortunately the fragile papyrus manuscript has broken and is missing the rest of its contents. Of the forty-eight injuries noted, most are related to the head, including lacerations, fractured skulls, dislocated jaws, and the like. The text ends abruptly at discussions of spinal injuries.

The Edwin Smith Papyrus describes presenting problems and details treatments or surgeries that are needed. The physician announces how favorable or unfavorable the situation is and whether or not he is able to treat it. The text includes advice on examination procedures, symptom relief, the application of salves, or the isolation of the break or wound. This prescription is followed by either advice to rest for a few days or to return to daily life.

In one case of throat injury, the text describes the presenting symptoms: "a gaping wound piercing through to his gullet. If he drinks water he chokes [and] it come out of the mouth of his wound. It is greatly inflamed and he develops fever from it."[12]

Following the announcement that the wound is treatable, the physician stitches the wound together and then will "bind it with fresh meat the first day." Each day thereafter, he treats the wound with grease, honey, and lint (bandage) until the patient recovers. If the wound becomes inflamed, dry lint is applied to the "mouth of the wound," and the doctor will "moor [him] at his mooring stakes" until he recovers; that is, send him to bed.[13]

Advice regarding blows to the head are given in great detail, suggesting that the physician check for feeble pulse and fever, blood, or bone fragments in the ear, as well as blood-shot eyes, deafness, and aphasia. These injuries were considered among the few untreatable cases in which the manuscript advises the physician do nothing, approaching the whole case with a wait-and-see attitude.

The priest-physician mentioned in the Ebers Papyrus provides his full credentials and assures us that he has the support of the gods. He learned his trade, the papyrus says, in the temples of Sais and Heliopolis. Furthermore, he is a priest of Re, and his healing powers are given to him by the god Thoth. The Ebers Papyrus contains medical advice that was a combination of medicine, magic, and affirmation. One might think of the medical papyrus as an ancient record of trial and error with some remedies that are later proven as scientifically based, like the use of urine as an antiseptic or the application of honey to burns and wounds.

Some advice appears in both the Ebers and Edwin Smith papyri. The following text refers to medical practices that moderns might recognize, such as having a Sekhmet priest take a pulse by laying fingers on the back of the head, the hand, both arms, or both legs. "Then he will feel the heart," advises the text, "as there are vessels in every limb of the body and the heart 'speaks' at the beginning of the vessels of all body parts."[14]

Among the more common cures that we might recognize today are honey and milk for sore throats and coughs, belladonna to relieve pain, willow to cure headaches, and poppies to cure insomnia. Physicians of the day created suppositories and herbal dressings and advised having enemas or taking castor oil. Frankincense cured throat infections and stopped bleeding, cardamom treated flatulence and indigestion, myrrh stopped diarrhea, and tamarind was used as a laxative. Egyptian healing gardens probably included many plants common in gardens of today— dill (mixed with wine and raisins as a pain killer), cumin (for stomach upsets), parsley and celery (diuretics), and chicory (for liver upsets). Gum and mouth diseases were treated with cinnamon and dentists used gold to bind loose teeth to healthy teeth.

In some cases, beauty and health went hand in hand. To reduce the glare of harsh sunlight and glaring reflections from the sand—both of which led to cataracts of the eyes—ancient Egyptians painted the upper and lower eyelids with crushed malachite. The green copper mineral extracted from the mines in Sinai was dedicated to Hathor, the goddess of beauty and joy. Applications of galena powder also protected the eyes from sand, wind, and insect plagues. (Using galena, the lead-based powder, is not advised.)

Ancient Egyptian doctors even created prosthetic devices made of wood and leather. These were fashioned as functional limbs rather than simply for cosmetic purposes. In the Cairo Museum one can see a prosthetic toe that dates from between 1000 and 600 BCE. Still attached to the foot of an elder female mummy, the toe shows signs of wear and the amputation site is well healed. Furthermore, the toe actually bends and functions as it should. An artificial leg from 300 BCE is housed in the British Museum.

THE MIDWIFE PHYSICIAN

Many temple inscriptions and medical papyri concern themselves with conception, childbirth, nursing, rearing children to adulthood, and, in some cases, with contraception. Giving birth was both miraculous and dangerous. The Temple of Horus and Sobek at Kom Ombo may have operated as a healing temple and perhaps as a school of medical arts.

Several chapels there contain illustrations of medical practices, including images of pregnant women seated on birthing bricks and giving birth. Noblewomen may have come to the temple to give birth and to be helped by the midwives and priestesses who served the temple. A *mammisi*, or birth house, was attached to each temple to celebrate the birth of a child of the divine couple, usually dedicated to the divine birth of the pharaoh who built the temple. At the mammisi in Dendera, Queen Cleopatra appears in honor as the goddess Hathor having given birth to her son Caesarion, depicted as the god Ihy, whose name means "joy."

A birthing story from the Westcar Papyrus reports the prophesied birth of triplets by Ruddjedet, the wife of Rawoser, a high priest. In this story, several divine beings appear at Rawoser's house, disguised as traveling musicians. They are the goddesses Isis and Nephthys who bore the children of Osiris, the creator god Khnum who fashioned the children's bodies and their souls on his potter's wheel, the birth goddess Meskhent, and the frog goddess Heqet. (Please see plate 29 of the color insert.) The musicians told Rawoser that they were skilled midwives. After gaining entrance, the entourage quickly sealed themselves inside the room with Ruddjedet. Isis stood before her, and Nephthys supported the woman from behind, while Heqet's frog magic of turning tadpole to child hurried each child's birth. Isis called forth each child by name. The goddesses washed them and cut the cords. The goddess of the birthing brick Meskhenet decreed their fates as royal kings, and Khnum gave each child health in body and spirit.

The story provides the narrative thread running alongside common birth practices. Women gave birth in a crouching position or seated in a birthing chair, yet another association with the goddess Isis whose hieroglyph is the throne, ⌋◠◦⌐. The child dropped through an opening in the birthing chair and into the hands of the midwife. During labor, the mother's body was supported and tended by the midwife and her assistants, while chants were sung to Isis and Hathor. The woman's belly was massaged with herbs. The birthing bricks on which the woman in labor crouched were painted with images of Hathor and the seven Hathors. These seven birth goddesses were linked to the Pleiades and functioned a bit like fairy godmothers to ensure the destiny of the future child and to protect both the mother and child from harm. One might think of them as guardian angels that surround one's bed during life and death transitions.

The Kahun, Carlsberg, and Berlin papyri, as well as the Ebers Papyrus, offer fragmentary but overlapping prescriptions for conception, birth, and protection for mothers and children. Amulets were a strong source of birth magic, and fertility charms were popular. Women hoping to conceive were known to wear, or even tattoo, girdles made of cowrie shells, similar to those worn by African women. The magic drew upon the visual similarity between the vagina and shell. Fish pendants, a form of Isis that refers to her as the *abtu* fish that swallowed the phallus of Osiris, were popular hair ornaments.

After conception, amulets were needed to keep the growing fetus safe from miscarriage. Knotted cords may have been inserted into the womb during menstruation, an ancient version of the tampon. During pregnancy, these knots of Isis called *thet* (𓋹) were worn as amulets to contain the blood that was creating the body of the child within the body of the mother. "Listen, O Isis," says one amulet invocation. "I am offered unto Isis for I am the Uniter of Worlds. I am the Living Blood of the Goddess poured out into the universe."[15]

The connection between the fertility of the fields and the fertility of human beings was strong. The ithyphallic god Min watched over the fields, and the seeds from his sacred lettuce plants were gathered and pressed into an oil. To this day, Egyptian men still use the oil as an aphrodisiac.

The mother goddesses Hathor, Isis, and others watched over the well-being of women. Ancient medical texts from 1350 BCE suggest that pregnancy was verified by using barley grain and wheat seeds. When a woman believed she may be pregnant, she urinated on both the wheat and barley. If the barley sprouted first, a male child would be born. If the wheat sprouted first, the child would be female. If neither sprouted, no child would be born. Archaeologists and medical researchers have determined that the ancient test is 70 percent accurate, even in the earliest stages of pregnancy. The test works because the urine of pregnant women contains a high level of estrogen and progesterone, which helps the grains to sprout.

BIRTH MAGIC

As the birth time approached, great caution was needed for both mother and child. Childbed fever and stillbirth were common. It is no accident that the hieroglyph of the vulture Mut is used for two opposing concepts: mother (🦅 ⌒ ○ 𓀭) and death (🦅 ⌒ 𓀐). The borderland between the world of the living and the dead was quite apparent to those giving birth. Often when a mother and her infant died during childbirth, they were mummified together, placed side by side, with the child near the hips of its mother.

Birth amulets offered some protection from these dire events. The goddess Tauret often appeared as a hippopotamus with full belly, her tongue pressed between her teeth—reminiscent, perhaps, of birthing techniques for laboring women. The plumed African dwarf god Bes rose in national popularity as a birth god who often accompanies Hathor and Ihy. Images of Bes were placed on the birth mother's forehead, a protection for her while she was in that altered state of giving birth, and as a way for the midwives to call forth the child from the womb using their words of power. (Please see plate 22 of the color insert.) "Come down, placenta, come down! I am Horus who conjures in order that she who is giving birth becomes better than she was, as if she was already delivered. . . . Look, Hathor will lay her hand on her with an amulet of health! I am Horus who saves her!"[16]

Repeating this incantation four times assured its efficacy.

Dates mixed with wheat and herbs bandaged across a mother's belly loosened the child in the womb. Topically applied saffron and beer relieved childbirth pains. Fenugreek not only eased childbirth but also increased the flow of milk. Childbed fever and stillbirth were common; surviving infancy was difficult. When a child cried *ihy* at birth, the midwife knew that she would live; if she cried *mbi,* made a creaking sound, or turned her head downward, she would not.

Naturally, Isis and Horus amulets protected birthing mothers and their children from harm. When Horus's wicked uncle Seth was hunting him and his mother Isis, she hid Horus in the papyrus swamps. Because the goddess Renenutet protected them with her fiery cobra energies, amulets that depict the serpent nursing Horus abound in Egypt. The pharaoh received his serpent wisdom through this nurse mother's milk. Making sure that the mother had enough milk for the child was of the utmost importance. Poultices of cucumber were often used to aid lactating women.

In ancient times, many children died of malnutrition. It was best not to have too many children close together. Rather than having many children, the Egyptians preferred to have healthy ones. Because lactating women appear not to conceive as readily as the mothers of children who have been weaned, the Egyptian mother allowed her child to nurse into his third year. Charms existed to prevent the birth of twins, which would have created a burden for the mother as well as for the children, especially during the drought season. In addition, the ancient Egyptians practiced contraception and used herbs (tampons of plant fiber coated with honey, crushed dates, and gum acacia) to encourage spontaneous abortion when the health of the mother and child were at risk.

THE USE OF HEALING TALISMANS AND AMULETS

Outside the temple, the healer used many of the same healing techniques that a priest of Heka used inside the temple. This included the use of amulets and incantations—what modern people might think of these days as affirmations. Says the Ebers Papyrus, "Magic is effective together with medicine. Medicine is effective together with magic."[17] This strongly suggests that true healing is a state of mind.

As Mary Baker Eddy, the mother of the Christian Science religion, suggests, "All is infinite mind and its infinite manifestation, for God is All-in-all. Spirit is immortal Truth."[18] Egyptologist Geraldine Pinch rightly surmised that magic gave the mind something concrete to attend to as one struggled with an illness. "Modern medicine is coming to realize that the mental and emotional state of the patient has much more effect on their physical condition than was originally allowed for the scientific model of disease. Egyptian medicine never neglected these aspects."[19]

One reason that amulets work is that they are culturally agreed-upon symbols. They offer an aggregate of group thought that intensifies the power of the icon. While ancient Egyptians may have had more than three thousand years of common understanding of their particular symbolic images, most First World citizens in the modern era have two thousand years or more of understanding of Christian iconography. Historically symbols are built upon symbols, taking on some of the cultural patina that preceded them.

Thus it would not be surprising to find that the protective Christian symbol of the cross hanging above one's bed is related to the protective and similarly shaped ankh, the life-giving symbol linked with Isis. One may be anointed in the healing waters of Lourdes, France, or the healing waters of the Nile; both are said to flow from the throne of heaven. Far from feeling perplexed by the similarity of pagan and Christian references, we ought to feel invigorated that the language in which the Divine spoke with the ancients is just as alive and vibrant in our age as it was in theirs. A Catholic supplicant might request a healing through the auspices of the Blessed Virgin Mary, or the Lady of the Miraculous Medal, or Our Lady of Guadalupe. Egyptian healers sought the help of Isis, who was great of magic, and often began their incantations by saying, "May I be granted the words of power of Isis."[20]

Some charms literally get under our skin. Sacred drama is one way of empowering us through a deeper understanding of spiritual principles. A Catholic or Protestant walking the Stations of the Cross during Lent takes on either the role of Christ who suffered or the crowd who betrayed him in the court of Pontius Pilate. On festival days, ancient Egyptians reenacted the sacred dramas of the death of Osiris, the mortal battle between Horus and Seth, and the birth of the Holy Child.

In the confined space of a temple or in the home of the client, the magician often called on the powers of gods and goddesses, going so far as to embody the divine healer. In sacred healing rituals, the priest or priestess became an empty vessel through which the voice spoke and the hands of the god or goddess worked. Through the power of the "true voice" of the god, the healer commanded evil to leave and the patient to thrive. These practices resemble Christian ideas about exorcism through amulet, prayer, and faith. Psychodrama is a cultural shamanic technique used throughout the world from prehistory to the modern era. African traditions allow a healer to contact and work with ancestral spirits.

While modern "family constellation therapy" developed by German psychotherapist Bert Hellinger has a less religious agenda, its effects are as deeply and powerfully felt as a shamanic journey. In this case, an individual "stands in" for the client's living or dead family members and allows the healing drama of those family members during a particular life event. Becoming empty vessels, the participants in the constellation allow a family story to be told through them for the benefit of another's healing and understanding.

THE LANGUAGE OF HEALING

Hu, a third powerful component of words of power, appeared alongside the gods Heka and Sia. Hu became the impassioned power of speech in combination with human will aligned with divine will. Hu drew forth the healing powers of the heart, the seat of consciousness. The healer commanded the gods' energetic words of power. "Without 'words of power' there would be no Egyptian magic, rituals or ceremonialism," says Wim van den Dungen, Belgian educator and philosopher. "The magical actions were important, but absolutely impotent without the words necessary to empower them."[21] The magic works because the thought and word vibrations create mutal responses in each other.

Having studied both the oral traditions and the ancient texts at length, the scribes knew all of the stories about the powers of the gods they called upon. Often healing incantations were the script of a myth that pertained to the illness or to the act of healing itself. The doctor or the patient recited the words, identifying themselves with particular divine energies. Physicians often claimed to be Thoth who healed the wounded Eye of Horus. Thus the physician's pronouncements, magical actions, and use of implements, herbs, poultices, and the like would all suggest to the patient that he, too, would receive the same cure as Thoth gave Horus.

This refers to the mythic words of power that Thoth prescribed for Isis. She must first learn the secret name of Re to stop time. Stopping time is a prerequisite to healing as it calls back the energies that have been sent forth. These same words of power were used by Thoth and Isis to heal the child Horus who had been bitten by Seth disguised as a poisonous snake in the papyrus swamps. Momentarily forgetting her words of power, she calls on Re and Thoth to come to her aid. Thoth reminds her of her skill as a magician and says that he has commanded the barge of the sun to move backward so that Isis now will have time enough to save the child. She recites the charm that all healers of serpent bites knew by heart. "Back, O poison! You are exorcised by the spell of Re himself. It is the speech of the Greatest God which turns you away!"[22]

When snakebite threatened the life of a patient, a Sekhmet priest might reenact Thoth's command to the solar barge. The priest used the voice of the god to "threaten" the illness, saying that if the disease did not return to yesterday's location (nonexistence), then streams would dry up and the plants would wither until this patient, as Horus, recovers and his health returns.

To increase the potency of healing images and incantations, the hieroglyphic symbols or words were written on a papyrus. After being read aloud, the papyrus and its healing words were soaked in liquid and imbibed by the patient. Magical *stelae,* or *cippi,* were often erected outside a temple for public healing. These cippi depicted the child Horus overcoming dangerous animals and reptiles through the healing power of his mother, Isis, and the god Thoth. The magic inside these words and images was acquired by pouring water over a cippus. The water was then drunk by the patient or used to wash a wound. The notion was that by drinking the water the patient would be healed, as Horus was healed.

In this way, the healing words were not spoken into the air over the patient's head but were circulating throughout the entire system. Similarly, the words might be inscribed on a patient's skin in ink mixed with the juice of healing herbs. The patient then licked the spell from his body. The idea of eating and drinking the healing properties of the neteru may have begun as early as the Old Kingdom. In the Fifth Dynasty Pyramid of Unas Text, Utterance 274 declares that Unas "lives on the being of every god." He "eats their magic" when they appear to him.[23]

The amulets used in ritual were given to the client as a visible reminder of the invisible powers of the universe that controlled life and destiny. In some sacred places, archaeologists have found ostraca inscribed with prayers for healing, as well as amulets depicting whole and healthy body parts. Those in search of healing placed faience amulets near the Serapeum at Saqqara inside the tomb that was thought to belong to the physician Imhotep. Eyes and ears accompanied requests for the divinized healer's help in seeing and hearing. Egyptians of all classes wore protective amulets that took the form of powerful deities or animals; for example, the lion goddess was worn for protection. (See plate 21 of the color insert.) As early as the predynastic era, men wore bracelets fashioned in the image of the hawk, and women wore tadpoles, hippopotami, and cowrie shells.

Often hieroglyphic signs were used as amulets by both the living and the dead. The ubiquitous ankh magically endowed the wearer with long life and prosperity, the *djed* (spine) of Osiris returned stability and strength, the *waz* scepter bestowed power, and the Eye of Horus generally bequeathed good health. Scarabs were worn by both the living and the dead, although only the dead wore the winged scarabs inscribed with the chapter of "The Heart of Coming into Being." Presumably the living already possessed their beating hearts.

The material used to make the amulet also carried an inherent energetic field. Obviously the pharaoh and nobility prized gold as the symbol of perfect radiance, which made their amuletic jewelry the target of obvious looting when tombs were disturbed. Because stones of malachite, green jasper, lapis lazuli, carnelian, or turquoise were not always available to those in need of an amulet, faience items appeared in the sacred healing colors.

AFFIRMATIONS AND BANISHING SPELLS

It was understood that sometimes a negative thought or fear created a dreaded disease. An affirmation, along with an applied amulet or healing potion, was used to combat physical problems caused by spirits of the dead. One bit of Late Kingdom ostraca found at a Theban gravesite was a banishing spell that, perhaps, helped a widower quell the spirit of his departed spouse or the departed spouse of his new wife. It reads: "Get thee back, thou enemy, thou dead man or woman. . . . Thou dost not enter into his phallus, so that it grows limp." The text goes on to fret over other possible complications like seed in his anus, limp feet, deaf ears, and pressure on the chest, among other things.

At any rate, the most important line to me seems to be: "Thy head has no power over his head."[24] Perhaps this means that the thoughts of the departed spirit may not control the speaker's thoughts. The text does suggest two possibilities: first, that there is some unacceptable mediumistic type spirit communication occurring and, second, that the living have the ability to use the power of the mind and will to overcome the negative thoughts of others. Possibly the text offered the new priest-scribe-in-training a compendium of possible complaints that could be adapted for any circumstance that might require a banishing spell. This particular ostraca contains the kinds of errors that a practiced magician probably would not have made.

Many banishing spells targeted supernatural beings, based on the belief that someone who wields a greater magical authority than you has likely bewitched you. Thus a sorcerer great in magic was required, one who possessed the words of power of Thoth or Isis. Knowing the names of these evil beings gave the healer the power to act against them and overcome them.

A statue of King Ramses III (1184–1153 BCE) was placed in the desert and provided with spells that would protect his emissaries by banishing snakes and curing snakebites. Other statues had less intentional healing aspects. Statues of the goddess of pestilence Sekhmet were established on the borders of the Egyptian empire as a warning to invaders. Statues of Sekhmet may have been dusted with plague-inducing spores like anthrax and infused with magical incantations for good measure. In individual consultations, a physician using the law of like attracts like might go so far as to use animal dung to entice some repellent disease to exit the body—since foul things attracted foul things. The likelihood is that the odor alone might make the patient vomit, thus expelling whatever poisons might have been in the stomach.

If the magic hadn't worked, physicians of the ancient world would have been out of business a long time ago. Instead, their work was lauded throughout the ancient world—in Greece and Rome, Syria and Babylon. In the second century CE, an anonymous Greek sailor was in Egypt when he was overcome by blindness. Fearing death, his companions led him to the healers in the Temple of Ptah in Memphis. There he called upon the goddess Isis to heal him, and she did. Because of her magical cure, he copied the aretalogy to Isis that he found written on the temple wall, and he erected it on a stone stela in the seaside city of Cyme in Asia Minor. The Temple of Ptah in Memphis and the original Hymn to Isis are now rubble, but we have this hymn, beautifully translated by Frederick C. Grant, that reminds us of a sailor's devotion and the love and might of Egypt's mother goddess. In part, it reads:

> I am Isis, mistress of every land and I was taught by Thoth and with Thoth I devised the letters both sacred and common. . . . I am she who rises as Sothis. I am the goddess of women. For me Bubastis was built. I divided Earth from heaven. I revealed the map of stars. I commanded the ways of the sun and moon. I created creatures in the sea. I fortified the gods' truth. . . . I release those in bondage. I am Queen of sailing ships. I dam the rivers if I please. . . . I rise beyond destiny. Fate listens to me. Blessed art thou, Egypt, who has nourished me.[25]

HEALING THOUGHTS

The healing prayers of the Egyptians were less supplication and more invocation. They assumed that the world was in perfect order because it was made by a perfect being. The natural world was the living expression of God's presence in the world. The healing invocations, actions, amulets—even the hieroglyphs themselves—were, in part, the means to reassure the individual that all was in right order (ma'at) in the world through right connection with the Divine.

The use of the most efficacious cures and herbal treatments was further proof that the Creator existed in all things. It was up to humans to observe and correctly use those divine powers bequeathed to them. Above and beyond all of this, it was understood that vibration was the substance of all substances and that all forms were an extension of thought. The mind of man was but a reflection of the mind of God, and both God and man possessed the ability to use that greater mental power. In other words, we have at our ready a great untapped capacity for creative energies.

Isis and
Her Scorpions

Fear, anger, jealousy, insecurity, grief, exhaustion—these are the troubling emotions. We all feel them. Sometimes we act on them, but not without consequences. Your life is a creative act—your every thought and feeling appears mirrored in the world around you. Misery or happiness often is a matter of choice. Everyone has disappointments and trials. It is how we respond to them that may differ, and that response may determine not only our happiness but also our health.

Clear and loving mental energy can change the effect of a negative event. To respond to a negative emotion with a negative thought is to create a string of negative outcomes. Becoming aware of our feelings and making a conscious choice to respond lovingly and calmly will create a more positive outcome. Feelings are simply energy forms, and energy of one kind attracts similar energy from another.

Priest-philosophers and teachers used the myths of ancient Egyptian gods and goddesses to illustrate the differences in human and divine interventions. In the story of Isis and her scorpions, we see the goddess Isis as worried, frazzled, and angry. This story offers us a view of how the thoughtless act of a human evokes the wrath of the goddess. Similarly, an act of kindness by another woman appeases the goddess and offers a change of heart. It might also be viewed as an ancient example of how similar energies attract each other.

The story "Isis and Her Seven Scorpions" comes to us from the

Metternich Stela found in ancient Alexandria and is probably of the era of Pharaoh Nectanebo, last pharaoh of the last dynasty of Egypt. More than likely the stela was erected outside a temple dedicated to Isis as healer and was used as a part of a magical cure for scorpion stings. The text is told in the first person and begins and ends with the statement: "I am Isis, mistress of magic, speaker of spells . . ." This was a common way in which to invoke the healing powers of the goddess.

Now, after Seth, her brother, had murdered Osiris, her husband, in a fit of jealous rage, the pregnant Isis became imprisoned in the house of Seth. He locked her up to keep an eye on her pregnancy so that when she delivered her child, he could take Horus from her, kill the infant, and then secure all of Egypt for his own. The imprisonment of Isis bears a similarity to the German tale of the miller's daughter locked in a prison and forced to spin straw into gold.

Locked in Seth's prison and numbed by the sorrow over the loss of her husband Osiris, Isis resigns herself to this dreadful outcome. Thoth, the god of wisdom, "who understands the truth that is in heaven and on earth," called her to come forth. The day was waning as the sun was going down, but Isis heard Thoth calling her forth, and so she disguised herself and left the prison.

Alongside Isis scuttled her seven scorpions: Tefen and Befen walked behind her, Mestet and Mestetef walked beside her, and Petet, Thetet, and Matet walked ahead. (The scorpions were named for the seven major stars in the constellation Scorpio—Antares, Graffias, Dscubbe in the head of the scorpion, Shuala and Lesath at either side, and Acumen and Aculeus in the scorpion's stinger.) They stayed close to Isis in order to protect her. As she walked, she whispered to them, "Beware the Black One. Call not the Red One." She did not want to even mention the contention of Osiris (the Black One) and Seth (the Red One) because she did not want to draw toward her any trouble. It was the enmity between these two brothers that had caused her misery in the first place. Isis warned her scorpions not to look at the children or at any innocent creatures for fear that even their glances might call forth some misfortune. (Scorpions are so hard to control.)

The goddess and her entourage hurried along the hot desert roads, a place without shade or any place to stop. With Seth and his militia following close behind, Isis and her scorpions headed toward the green delta as fast as they could go. As Isis and her entourage traveled along, they came to Per-Suit, the City of the Crocodile, the first township that opened up into the papyrus marshes and swamps. Isis kept walking north toward the great green waters of the delta.

She searched for a place in the papyrus swamps to hide herself, a place where she might give birth, for by this time, Isis was heavy with child. She had been on the road so long: she was bedraggled, her hair shorn and her clothes ragged. She had covered herself all over in dust in the way that women in those days mourned. The beautiful goddess was nearly unrecognizable. With the seven scorpions skittering at her feet, tails reared and claws clacking, Isis was a fearsome sight to behold—a filthy, dangerous, bedraggled woman.

At last, she and her seven scorpions walked through the streets of the City of Two Sandals, the city that celebrated the twin goddesses. As they approached the houses, Isis hoped to find a place where she could stop to lie down for a while, for she was bone-weary. At the first house stood a woman named Gloria; some called her Strength. Gloria stood in her doorway, and from a long way off, she saw Isis coming down the road—a woman surrounded by scorpions and covered in filth. As Isis approached, Gloria shut the door in her face. A little ways farther, Isis came to the home of another marsh-woman. This woman opened the door to Isis and invited her to come in to rest.

The seven scorpions were not ready to rest. Feeling the sting of the door shut in their faces and angered at the sorrow this insult had caused their mistress, they decided to get together and put all of their scorpion's poison into the stinger of Tefen, the leader of the group. Having done that, the poison in Tefen's sting now contained seven times the power of a normal scorpion. Now Tefen returned to Gloria's house. The door was still shut, but there was a narrow crack between the door and threshold, so he crawled under the door, entered the house, and stung Gloria's son to death.

The poison was so strong that the child died with the first sting, and fire broke out in the house. Gloria cried out, running into the streets and carrying her dead child in her arms, her house engulfed in flames behind her. Her screams were loud, and yet no one came to help her. She realized that this unkind fate had occurred because of the unkindness she had shown the beggar woman. The mournful sounds of Gloria's lamentations fell upon the ears of Isis, who was at rest in the house of the other woman. The sound of Gloria's grief stirred the heart of Isis, and the two women now felt each other's sorrow.

In that moment, a great miracle occurred. The sky opened, and water fell from heaven onto the house of the woman. It was not the time of the inundation, and so water from heaven was seen as a gift from the Divine. The raging fire was extinguished. In the falling rain, Isis got up and returned to the place where the dead child lay. Because she is Isis, the mistress of magic, her voice can awaken the dead. In her throat lie the words of power—the life-giving words that even the dead can hear. Gloria gave her the child, and Isis wrapped her arms around him in order to bring life to his lifeless body. The child lay cold and still, the scorpion's poison in him.

Then, with her magic words of power, Isis called forth all of the poison, saying, "O poison of Tefen come out of him and fall upon the ground. O poison of Befen, advance not, penetrate no further, come out of him, and fall upon the ground. For I am Isis, the great enchantress, the speaker of spells. Fall down, poison of Mestet. Hasten not, poison of Mestetef. Rise not, poison of Petet and Thetet. Approach not, poison of Matet. I am Isis, the great enchantress, the speaker of spells. The child shall live, the poison shall die."

The child recovered, the house fire was quenched, and the rain ceased.

In thanksgiving, Gloria brought all of her wealth—bracelets and necklaces, gold and silver pieces—to the house of the marsh-woman who had opened the door to Isis. She laid them at the feet of the goddess, which was her way of repenting for shutting the door on a weary woman.[1]

The story was accompanied by a recipe for using wheat flour and salt on a scorpion wound to draw forth the poison. The words that Isis recited to heal the poisoned child were the same words spoken by ancient Egyptian medicine men or women to heal a scorpion sting.[2]

We can glean a few things about magic and healing from this story. Clearly we draw some circumstances toward us by our thoughts and actions. The woman who shuts her door and her heart against Isis draws the energies of the stinging scorpions. The names of the fixed stars of Scorpio, in fact, could be seen as the names of negative attributes. For example, Acumen was the star known for gossip and all that occurs in shadow. Aculeus, while depicting strength and leadership ability, was a star known to generate anger and outrage. Antares, the lead star of the constellation and probably linked to Tefen in the myth, is the brightest star, which depicts how the mighty fall from grace through their own ruthlessness. Gloria, the translation of the ancient Egyptian woman's name, perhaps thought too highly of herself to have a bedraggled woman in her home. The mighty were brought low in this case.

In this story, Isis expresses her wrath, but unconsciously. The city of Per-Suit, the crocodile, symbolized the unconscious and that which lurks beneath the surface. Isis does not send out her scorpions, but rather the subconscious energies on their own return to Gloria's house. They are the embodiment of another's ill temper drawn toward the woman who expressed fear and loathing in the first place.

When Isis heard the wails of Gloria, she could have hardened her heart to her, but she did not. The scorpion energy was unconscious in its sting. The kind and generous spirit of the unnamed second woman toward Isis allows kindness and sympathy to flow in turn. Hearing Gloria's sorrow caused hidden feelings to be made known. In a conscious response to Gloria's sorrow, Isis decided to act in goodness and love to heal the child. It was a conscious act to take the negative event and emotion and turn these toward a positive outcome. With love, with attention, and with the help of the Divine, total disaster is averted.

The city into which Isis came was called the City of Two Goddesses, and we see the faces of two women there (perhaps goddesses in hiding). One is known by name, and the other has no name but works anonymously. The first is visible to her community, and the second works behind the scenes. These are the aspects of every woman—and every human being. The lesson here is that there is indeed a difference between what we do for show and what we do for love.

Healings and miracles do occur through love, through contrition, and through understanding. We may never know completely the effect of our actions and words, but through this myth, we see that turning the other cheek in difficult circumstances benefits more people than we realize. Kindness begets kindness.

Help may come from unexpected and unexplained sources. The Divine, like Thoth whispering in Isis's ear to guide her, does intervene in human affairs. When we listen to the voice of the Divine and not to our own egoistic desires, then we are able to accomplish great things. And it is right when great bounty is given to us that we offer that blessing back to the source.

The magicians and sorcerers of ancient Egypt did perform many miracles—not the least of which was keeping a culture alive and vibrant for over three thousand years. Most of the time, the high priests and scribes worked behind the scenes to keep the country going. At other times, they used a little magic on the side to turn the tide of fortune their way or the way of the pharaoh. The danger occurred whenever ego, rather than alignment with divine will, was allowed to enter into the equation. Even in ancient Egypt, a difference was seen in the magician who served as a healer and in one who acted as a sorcerer.

We might even see this story set in the City of Two Goddesses as two sides of the same face—the goddess who giveth and the goddess who taketh away.

Shock and Awe
Magical Spells for Protection

A chink appeared in the doorway that had been sealed for three thousand years. The breech was wide enough for a man to put through his face and his hand holding a candle. Imagine how the flickering yellow light glinted off the golden and bejeweled mummy case, how the candlelight revealed the staring eyes of the shadowy black guardian, the jackal Anubis. Imagine everywhere the glint of gold—the chariots, the beds, the grave goods piled in a corner, and, too, the brightly colored images of gods and goddesses that danced in reds, blues, greens, and yellows upon the white-washed plaster walls.

"Can you see anything?" Lord Carnarvon demanded of the dusty and exhausted archaeologist in his employ.

"Yes," replied Howard Carter. "Wonderful things!"[1]

THE MUMMY'S CURSE

As wondrous as it was for Carter and Carnarvon to find the boy king Tutankhamun's tomb, it was equally terrible. The ancient Egyptians had protected the graves of their pharaohs with magical spells and incantations. Was it a mummy's curse that caused Lord George Carnarvon, who had funded Carter's expedition, to die of blood poisoning from a mosquito bite five months later? Was it an ancient curse that sickened and killed so many of the excavation workers, or was it because a bacteria dormant inside the tomb had stayed alive, feasting on all the food intended for the afterlife? Could the curse be scientifically explained? Perhaps the deadly spores of an ancient fungus became activated by the fresh air when the tomb was opened.

The tale of the mummy's curse abounded in the press in 1923 because the general public had heard that ancient Egyptians believed in protecting the bodies of their pharaohs (and equipping them in the afterlife) with magical spells. Howard Carter denied that he ever found such a curse inscribed in Tutankhamun's tomb, but magical spells and curse bricks have appeared in other tombs.

A similar protection spell comes from the Sixth Dynasty tomb of Vizier Ankhmahor at Saqqara. Ankhmahor provided a beautiful blessing for his ancestors and for those who tended his tomb, but for tomb violators, he had harsh words. "As for anything that you might do against this tomb of mine of the West, the like shall be done against your property. I am an excellent lector priest, exceedingly knowledgeable in secret spells and all magic. As for any person who will enter into this tomb of mine in their impurity . . . I shall seize him like a goose (wring his neck), placing fear in him at seeing ghosts upon the earth."[2]

The dead and their resting places needed protection, but history has proven that ancient curses, strategically placed pits in dark corridors, and noxious spores have not been enough to keep out the tomb violators, most of whom beat the archaeologists to the draw thousands of years earlier. In that case, the curse that extends beyond the grave provides the final recourse. Says a Sixth Dynasty inscription found at the mausoleum provided for the house of Meni, "A crocodile against him in the water; a snake against him on land. He will do something against that same one. At no time did I do anything against him. It is God who will judge."[3]

In a later chapter on the Osirian Mysteries, we discuss spiritual matters of the underworld at length. Here we will concern ourselves primarily with the magical protection and outfitting of the tomb.

SPIRIT HELPERS

There were as many chores to do in the underworld as there were on this side of the sod. Domestic duties or agricultural labor that needed assistance on Earth also needed doing in the land of the dead. In the next world, the *ushabti* spirit helpers functioned as stand-ins for the tomb owner. The Chinese emperor had his terra-cotta soldiers; the Kabbalist had his Golem; and the Egyptians employed ushabti, meaning "the answerer." On an earthly, human level, imagine a slave on a plantation or a soldier in the army who is told not to speak until spoken to. Because the ushabti is a miniature human created by humans to do human work, there is some resonance to the Old Testament allusions in which God made humans in his image for a similar purpose.

Sturdy ushabti with the features of the tomb owner were carved of tamarisk or thorn wood. Some of King Tutankamun's 413 ushabti were simple faience figurines, while others bore gilded crowns and carried spears. The craftsman inscribed true words of power upon the figure. One word written on the forehead enlivened the statue. Coffin Text 472 describes this concept in language similar to the biblical stories of humans who were created by God's hand. "Look upon this man, ye gods, transfigured souls and spirits of the dead, for he has acquired force, seized his moment, and taken on royal authority. He is a pharaoh, ruling mankind, controlling them like cattle. They were created to serve him. The gods themselves ordained it."[4]

Ordinary folks commanded ushabti. Everyone wanted at least one. The more one had, the better. Coffin Text Spell 472 was written in advance and attached to or inscribed on an ushabti. The text appears to have intentionally kept the tomb owner's name blank until it was purchased. "Ushabti, if, in the world of the dead, anyone calls (name) to move bricks, or resurvey the flooded ground, or till new fields, you will say; 'Here I am!' . . . If (name) is called to oversee workers in the newly planted fields, or tend to irrigation, or to move the sands from east to west, or vice versa you will say 'Here I am!' and take his place."[5]

Plate 1. Looking toward the city, the Fourth Dynasty pyramids of the Giza plateau are comprised of (left to right) the Great Pyramid of Cheops, his son Chephren's pyramid with limestone cap, and the smaller pyramid of Chephren's son, Menkaure. Scholars believe that the three pyramids were positioned to align to the stars of Orion's belt. (Photo by Jane Brantley)

Plate 2. A damaged bas-relief scene in Philae. Note how the heads in particular seem to have been obliterated. (Photo by Jane Brantley)

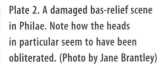

Plate 3. A date palm prepares to flower, then fruit. Festivals celebrating the fecundity of the earth were woven into the cosmology of the ancient Egyptians. (Photo by Jane Brantley)

Plate 4. Sunrise over Cairo
(Photo by Jane Brantley)

Plate 5. The columns at the Temple of Isis in Philae bear
the face of Hathor, goddess of beauty, one of the most
esteemed in ancient Egypt. (Photo by Jane Brantley)

Plate 6. A beautiful grain field along the banks of the Nile near Kom Ombo (Photo by Jane Brantley)

Plate 7. Khepera, the dung beetle, represents the aspects of light, particularly the god Re coming into manifestation. (Photo by Jane Brantley)

Plate 8. The mallet and rolling pin are two tools used in the ancient art of making papyrus. (Photo by Jane Brantley)

Plate 9. Seshet, goddess of Scribes, Karnak is here depicted in the act of writing the story of the pharaoh's life. Some scholars speculate that the petals of her horned headdress represent stars of the Pleiades, establishing Seshet as goddess of both astronomy and writing. (Photo by Jane Brantley)

Plate 10. The Nubian Museum contains one of the predynastic burial pits found in Egypt. Buried with its clay offering bowls, the fetal position of the corpse indicates a return of the dead to the womb of the Great Mother. (Photo by Jane Brantley)

Plate 11. These magical *ushabti* represent the army of Nubian warriors in service to the king. (Photo by Jane Brantley)

Plate 12. A row of ram-headed sphinxes, Karnak. The avenue of ram-headed sphinxes leading to the first pylon was built in approximately 656 BCE. Originally there were three avenues of sphinxes, one of which, two miles long, linked up with the avenue of human-headed sphinxes of the Temple of Luxor. (Photo by Jane Brantley)

Plate 13. A typical rural scene on the Nile, comprised of fishermen and sheep (Photo by Jane Brantley)

Plate 14. Activities of everyday life were depicted on papyri such as this one, housed in a museum in Cairo. Many papyri were used to illustrate the specifics of medical cases and the treatments needed. (Photo by Jane Brantley)

Plate 15. The Virgin Mary and the Christ child appear in the Coptic Church in Aswan. They bear a striking similarity to the ancient statues of Isis and Horus. (Photo by Jane Brantley)

Plate 16. Hapi, the Nile god, is source of all abundance. He controls the flood from his cavern below the Island of Elephantine. (Photo by Jane Brantley)

Plate 17. In this relief from Abydos, Seti I is on the left and Thoth, as healer, with his magic wand (or caduceus), is on the right. The caduceus features two entwined snakes and two wings at the top; symbols of healing and regeneration. (Photo by Jane Brantley)

Plate 18. Hathor, the goddess of beauty and joy, and also the mother goddess of the regenerative power of life, is depicted here at the Temple of Hatshepsut. Note the cow ears of the goddess, which identifies her as the Great Mother goddess of Egypt. (Photo by Cathleen Shattuck)

Plate 19. The Eye of Horus represents wholeness in that it reminds us that, even in the minutest fraction of the human being, God exists and we are all part of the divine plan. As such the Eye of Horus is a bridge between worlds. (Photo by Jane Brantley)

Plate 20. Amun, the hidden god is seated on his throne, receiving an offering. The fact that he is also a god of the air is indicated by the feathery plumes on his head and the blue color of his skin. (Photo by Jane Brantley)

Plate 21. The three emblems—ankh, djed, waz—empowered the pharaoh with the energies of life, stability, and power. (Photo by Jane Brantley)

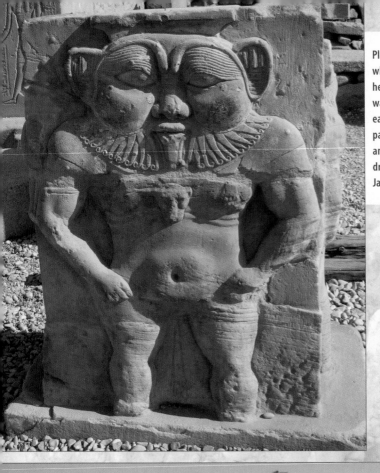

Plate 22. Bes, the dwarf god who accompanies Hathor (seen here at her temple in Dendera), was the protector of children, easing a mother's childbirth pains, providing merriment, and chasing away the bad dreams of children. (Photo by Jane Brantley)

Plate 23. The pyramid of Chephren, son of Cheops who built the Great Pyramid, sits on the highest point of the plateau, which gives the illusion that it is the larger pyramid. It is the only pyramid to retain a portion of its limestone casing. (Photo by Jane Brantley)

Plate 24. The healing chapel at Kom Ombo depicts a number of medical instruments, including the Eye of Horus amulets and scales for measuring medicine. (Photo by Jane Brantley)

Plate 25. The author (at left), with noted alchemical healer Nicki Scully, at an altar of their own arranging in Karnak (Photo by Jane Brantley)

Plate 26. Recycle bins at Movenpick Hotel, Aswan (Photo by Jane Brantley)

Paper ورق

Plastic بلاستيك

Glass زجاج

Plate 27. Hathor, the healing cow goddess (among her other attributes), is credited with healing the stricken Horus with her milk, after Seth put his eye out in a fight over the throne. The Eye of Horus on the ceiling at Dendara is a tribute to her healing act of kindness. (Photo by Jane Brantley)

Plate 29. The frog goddess of Hathor's temple carries the knives used to cut the umbilical cord. The magical frog goddess Heget was the goddess of transformation and birth because of the embryonic tadpole figure of developing fetuses. (Photo by Jane Brantley)

Plate 28. An egret on the Nile, Luxor (Photo by Jane Brantley)

Plate 30. A lady bakes wheat bread in a clay oven for a restaurant in Saqqara. (Photo by Jane Brantley)

Plate 31. These hieroglyphs spell the name of the Egyptian city Aput, located near Qena. Here, the glyphs appear on the wall of the Temple of Hatshepsut, on the west bank of the Nile near the Valley of the Kings. (Photo by Jane Brantley)

Plate 32. The lion goddess Sekhmet, daughter of Re, was an important part of the Heb-Sed Festival in that she symbolically devoured the pharaoh so that he could be born again. This underscores the theme of cyclical renewal so important to the ancient Egyptians. (Photo by Jane Brantley)

Plate 33. The lotus petal columns form the hypostyle at Kom Ombo on the right bank of the Nile between Edfu and Aswan. They are still glorious millennia after it was built in approximately 180 BCE on the right bank of the Nile between Edfu and Aswan. (Photo by Jane Brantley)

Plate 34. The enigmatic Sphinx gazes toward the rising sun. The exact age of the original Sphinx may predate the First Dynasty. (Photo by Patricia Haynes)

Plate 35. Seti I, second pharaoh of the 19th Dynasty (1314–1304 BCE), is depicted here, on the walls of the temple he built at Abydos. In the building projects that he undertook, the quality of architectural design, relief sculpture, and painting were rarely surpassed by later rulers. (Photo by Jane Brantley)

Plate 36. Pigeon roosts overlook the Nile River in Aswan. Many families raise pigeons to sell, which are a restaurant delicacy. (Photo by Jane Brantley)

Plate 37. The Hall at Karnak is the largest known example of a typical hypostyle hall (a building in which columns support the roof). This hall was called many things at different times, including the designation "the Hall of the two crowns." The name probably reflects a coronation ceremony performed there; a coronation ritual is depicted on its walls. (Photo by Jane Brantley)

Plate 38. A sphinx highlighted along the Avenue of Sphinxes in Luxor at night. The Avenue of Sphinxes dates back to the reign of Amenhotep III in the Eighteenth Dynasty and runs from Karnak to Luxor. (Photo by Jane Brantley)

The dead needed the same protection from chaotic forces that faced the living. Not only did the ancient magical Opening of the Mouth Ceremony allow the dead to ingest the spiritual essence of food and drink, but it also allowed them to use the words of power. Open mouthed, the spirit of the dead could say the secret names that provided safe passage through Duat, and it opened a channel for communication between the worlds. With the power of *heka,* the dead commanded threatening animals to devour tomb robbers. Noxious serpents that might devour the dead departed at a magic command to leave the tomb and slunk back into the desert.

FUNERARY AMULETS AND TEXTS

Healing amulets worked equally well on either side of the tomb. Tucked between the winding sheets of mummy cloth one found, for example, the *djed,* or backbone of Osiris, placed along the lower spine; the *thet,* or buckle of Isis, at the throat; the two fingers to uplift the deceased to the sky; and the healing Eyes of Horus located throughout the body but especially placed over the embalmer's incisions. The all-important scarab of the heart carried with it inscriptions that assured the veracity of one's memories and wisdom garnered during life. It assured that the heart, when weighed in the balance after death, spoke favorably of the deceased to Osiris and to the forty-two judges in Duat.

The funerary texts provided the dead with esoteric magical knowledge. Magic allowed Egyptian shamans, priests, and sorcerers to manipulate the energetic vibrations of various situations so that one could perform exorcisms and healing, as well as receive the good graces of the Divine. Magic also had important pragmatic aspects, which were exploited to achieve the aims of humans (living or dead), spirits, and gods. Intuitive archaeologist Omm Sety believed all magic should take the form of prayer and be used only for healing people or warding off evil. The practice of magic for personal gain, she felt, was often against the will of the gods.[6] But in ancient Egypt not all magicians worked with life and death energies. Magicians of the mundane dealt with such matters as creating good luck charms, controlling pests, and making love potions.

THE USE OF MAGICAL FORCE

The use of ushabtis in Duat was intended as spiritual assistance for the "disembodied." Reciting magical spells over wax or wooden figurines in order to control living and breathing human bodies turned the use of ushabti into sorcery. The most effective magical figurines incorporated a physical part from the intended victim, such as hair or bodily fluids. The ancient Egyptians used spittle to target the right person for the intended spell. (In this same way, a forensic scientist uses DNA from spittle to pinpoint the perpetrator of a crime.) Names inscribed on clay pots, tablets, or figurines were cursed with magical spells and then splintered, pierced, burned, broken, or buried in cemeteries in the belief that the spirits of the glorified Egyptian dead would help to bind, weaken, or destroy the enemy.

Sometimes magical force was needed for the stability of the country. (See plate 11 of the color insert.) Magic became part of the first line of defense. The Teachings of Merikare, which was part of every scribe's lessons, assured the priests in training that the use of magic was a gift from God—"to repel the thunderbolt of what is to come."[7] One might find this idea quaint until one considers that the use of formidable divine energies is precisely what scientists have harnessed in their atomic arsenals in this modern age. Eric Hornung put the idea in perspective when he said, "Magic is the nuclear energy of early civilizations because of its dangerousness and its power to transform the world."[8] When used wrongly by man, with evil intent and perhaps even as a weapon in the name of one's blind religious conviction, both modern and ancient kinds of magic have disastrous consequences.

The myth of Queen Dalukah reveals an Egyptian-African sorceress greatly feared by the Syrians. According to her legend, after the pharaoh's army drowned in the sea, Queen Dalukah built a wall on the borders of Egypt. Around the walls, she erected stone crocodiles, lions, and other threatening creatures. If an army crossed the Arabian Peninsula to attack Egypt, she recited her words of power and buried the offending figurines head first in the sand, causing the sand to swallow her enemies. Her reign, it was said, lasted thirty years.

The Arabesque legend of Queen Dalukah combines several elements of Egyptian magical lore, including the appearance of legendary queens, such as Nitocris (2152–2150 BCE), Hatshepsut (1479–1458 BCE), and Cleopatra (69–30 BCE), among others. The sands that swallowed Dalukah's enemies may refer to a similar story in which the Red Sea swallowed pharaoh's army in Exodus 15:12. Or it may refer to the sands that swallowed the Persian army of Cambyses, the remains of which only recently were found in the Sahara Desert outside Siwa Oasis. It appears that all fifty thousand soldiers, lost in a storm, drowned in the sand.[9]

A VOICE OF MAGICAL AUTHORITY

The most powerful heka that a sorcerer could wield was that belonging to Isis or Thoth, both great of magic. Thoth created the world from nothingness, composed the sacred books, and taught all he knew to the goddess Isis. Her magic became powerful enough to stop time and the sun god Re in his tracks, to raise Osiris from the dead, and to immaculately conceive the god Horus.

Spell 123 from the Metternich Stela allows the eloquent magician to command magical language. As Egyptologist Robert K. Ritner points out, the spell itself shows off the linguistic acumen of the magician through its punning play on the language of sacred language. Says Spell 123: "I have spoken (*djed*) by your spell (*ri*). I have recited (*shed*) with your magic (*hekau*). I have spoken (*djed*) by means of your sayings (*djed*). I have conjured (*akh*) with your conjurations (*akhu*). I enchant (*shen*) using your words (*medju*) which you created through the magic (*hekau*) that comes from your mouth (*ri*)."[10]

All of the words (*medju*) spoken (*djed*) in the spell (*ri*) employ the varieties of enchantment (*shen*) or "encircling by magic," conjuration (*akhu*), and magic-making (*hekau*) from the mouth (*ri*) of the magician (one who knew *medju*).

THE TIME FOR MAGIC

Often in order for magic spells to succeed, elaborate preparations were needed. Naturally these preparations included knowing the right words to say, the right gestures to perform, the right symbols to invoke the right neteru, and the right state of consciousness in which to communicate on spiritual matters. The right time was equally as important.

Generally one avoided working on an unlucky day. For example, the third epagomenal day, the day that Seth was born, was considered especially malefic because Seth murdered his brother. The drought days of mid-May before the annual flood were also unfavorable. On August 12, the Cairo Calendar advised, "Do not go out today. Wait until Re sets in his horizon." On August 20, it advised: "The followers of Set and Horus are in conflict. Do not do any work." Favorable days bore a kind of fortune-cookie description, such as for August 28: "If you see anything this day, it will be good."[11] The Cairo Calendar horoscopes were not individualized but may have represented an understanding of fixed star astrology, since the Egyptian priesthood was closely attuned to the sky. The Cairo Calendar was one of three astronomical scrolls found, but it was the only one without major insect damage.

For the Egyptian priest-astronomer, keeping the calendars in their true order was a major undertaking and a complicated task, considering that the priests kept at least three calendars based on three different heavenly bodies—the moon, the sun, and Sirius. All three heavenly bodies moved at different rates. The electromagnetic moon cycles controlled the energies of the seas and the emotions of Earth's creatures; the solar cycles controlled the tilt of the planet and the energies of the seasons; and the Sirian cycles determined the precession of the equinoxes.

The magician regulated his life by cosmic laws; thus the twentieth day of the first month of the inundation was the day to receive and to send letters. Life and death go out that day. On that day one makes the book* entitled the End of the Work. It is a secret book that makes charms go awry, halts plots, and intimidates the whole universe. It contains both life and death.[12]

Meditations and magic performed at dawn and dusk were most auspicious. Ritually cleaned, fumigated, and darkened rooms, caves, or temple chapels gathered and held the energies. The space was charged with holy water carried from the Nile and kept in a bronze bowl, with aromatic herbs and oils, and with ritually scattered pure Nile sand.[13]

The instruments had to be purified as well. Some were easy to find—a new brick, the milk of a black cow, the blood of a black dog, one's own semen, or the milk of a woman who had birthed a male child. Other items, like shavings from the head of a dead man (possession of it was sorcery and against the law) or the gall of an Alexandrian weasel (an endangered species even in ancient times) were harder to find.

DIVINATION

The magician had to be ritually pure—to have spent time in meditation and abstained from sex, blood, or other matters of the flesh for three days before the rite. The demotic magical papyri also specified that the medium's assistant, or consort, had to be pure. The ideal medium was a woman assisted by a virginal boy. She stood behind him and vocalized her incantations into his crown chakra as he gazed into a scrying bowl.[14]

Seers needed to move in and out of trance quickly; thus a magical incense was prepared in advance. In a brazier a combination of crocodile bile, frankincense, stalks of anise, and eggshells burned together brought in "the voices of the gods at once." Another, much easier

---

*The phrase "makes the book" was used by ancient authors of the Cairo Calendar. Most likely it refers to a scribe's writing of a secret text. Any scroll of whatever length was considered a book.

demotic magical prescription brought the same results; it read: "Burn a frog's head on the brazier and then they speak."[15]

Once the magician had used these powerful energies, she quickly thanked and dismissed them. Energies that hung around could be unpredictable. A common dismissal included the noble attributes of the god, such as the ones found in the Leiden Papyrus. "Farewell Anubis, the good oxherd, son of a jackal, child of Isis . . ." The dismissal concluded with words to prevent harm from befalling those innocents that the energies might contact upon leaving. "Good dispatch, joyful dispatch!"[16]

RITUAL OBJECTS

Chief among ritual implements was the magic wand. Wadjet the snake goddess was the female form of Heka, god of magic, and the serpent or wadjet wand was highly favored among sorcerers. Wadjet also appeared on the uraeus of the pharaoh's crown, indicating the serpent energy that ran up the spine and across the crown chakra and emerged at the third eye. Made of bronze or iron, serpent wands contained powerful magic.

These same magic wands belonging to the priests of Egypt appear in Exodus 7. When the priests threw their wands to the ground, they turned into serpents. Moses quickly threw his hazel wand to the ground, and it, too, turned into a serpent, devouring the wands of the priests. Of course, Moses was raised by the pharaoh's daughter as a royal prince. More than likely he trained as a lector priest and was equally as skilled in the use of words of power.[17]

Fearsome deities decorated the semicircular, apotropaic wands. Often wielded during childbirth, they were carved from the curved ivory of a hippo's tusks, the full-bellied hippopotamus being linked to pregnant women. The heka warded off snakes, scorpions, and other dangerous creatures that might harm the mother or her child. It read: "Cut off the head of the enemy when he enters the chamber of the children . . ."[18]

An apotropaic wand carved with images of protections included the god Bes and the noxious creatures one intended to dispatch. The sorcerer's healing wand was carved from an elephant tusk, and its boomerang shape was a part of its magical ability to turn away misfortune.

Egyptologists disagree about which animal was depicted on the *waz* scepter of the pharaoh. I believe it to be the head of the Seth animal. Because the image was the hieroglyph for dominion, the wand may have symbolized the ability of the king to wrap his fingers around the neck of chaos and master it. The forked end of the *waz* could have been used to corral the erratic and destructive energies of vipers. In any circumstance, wands symbolized the ability of the pharaoh to summon powerful beings and to make them obey him.

THE CORONATION

Magic always accompanied the coronation of kings, which were often depicted as taking place in heaven first, then on Earth. In that way, images of the immaculate conception of Hatshepsut depicted the queen mother Ahmose and the god Amun greeting each other in heaven, their feet uplifted by angelic goddesses.

Coronations usually took place soon after the death of the previous king. Part of the ceremony included an elaborate and often-depicted Opening of the Mouth ritual performed for the mummy by the first prince. Through the ritual dialogue ascribed to the king and his predecessor, the sacred act was written in stone, so to speak. Magical knowledge and power emanated from the gods and was bestowed upon the pharaoh. At Queen Hatshepsut's coronation, we read the script of the gods that proclaimed her rule by divine right. "Utterance of all the gods: 'Amun-Re, this is thy living daughter and we are satisfied with her in life and peace. She is now thy daughter of thy form, whom thou hast begotten and prepared. Thou hast given to her thy soul, . . . [thy bounty, and] the magic powers of the diadem.'"[19]

The spirit of her father, Pharaoh Tuthmosis I, summoned Hatshepsut to stand before him as she receives the crown. "Come glorious one; I have placed you before me; that you may see your administration in the palace and the excellent deeds of your *kas*. All this is done that you may assume your royal dignity, glorious in your magic and mighty in your strength."[20]

PROTECTION OF THE PHARAOH

Protecting the king of Egypt involved necessary sorcery. A temple priest's job included cursing the king's enemies. Whenever the serpent Seth appeared in inscriptions, the hieroglyph was neutralized with knives stabbed in the snake's back. Because Apopis, the serpent of chaos, eternally threatened the creator sun god, fierce magic was needed to combat him, his soul, and his magic. Papyri depicted the god Re as the fighting cat Mau who shredded the serpent with knives. In temple rituals, Apopis was drawn onto a papyrus in green ink or shaped of wax. The image was spat on, stamped upon, stabbed, and burned. The exorcism against him read: "I have overthrown all the enemies of pharaoh from all their seats in every place where they are. See, their names written on their breasts, having been made of wax, and also bound with bonds of black rope. Spit upon them! Trample them with the left foot. Cut them with spear blades. Throw them on the fire of the melting-furnace of a coppersmith. Burn it in a fire with mandrake. Dissolve what remains in urine."[21]

Sometimes it took the magic of one god or goddess to combat the magic of another. Such a powerful spell was necessary to master the demon serpent Samana—a serpent form of Sama-el, sometimes called Samuel, or the angel of death. The magician here claims to have suckled from the breast of the warrior goddess Anat and to have the ability to use the serpent power of Seth against the foreign demon. The magician announces: "See, I have lots of words against you! From the big pitcher of Seth I have drunk them, from his jug I have drained them. Listen, Samana-demon, listen. The voice of Seth is roaring."[22]

Here the Egyptian serpent energy of Seth is mightier than the serpent energy of the foreign god Samana. The magician declares that he will throw the Samana snake on the ground. The deserts will consume him and cause him to wither until "the heat of your mouth does not exist."[23]

Priests also cursed the mortal enemies of the king in temple ceremonies. The looming portraits of the king riding in his chariot inscribed on the outer temple pylons attested to the might of the pharaoh and his magicians. Beside the king's chariot rides Sekhmet, the devouring lioness, also known as the powerful one, great of magic. Foreign enemies to the throne were shown kneeling and bound or sometimes slaughtered in temple scenes.

STRICKEN FROM MEMORY

Pharaohs were not immune to attack by negative magic. Despite having been the legitimate heir to Egypt, the monotheistic pharaoh Akhenaten was stricken from the list of kings. Nearly all traces of his thirteen-year reign were erased by his military general Horemheb. When Horemheb, who had married Akhenaten's daughter, finally acquired the throne, he began systematically to erase the works and the memory of his father-in-law.

Destroying the name of an individual was equivalent to inflicting a kind of second death, because one of the spiritual bodies of the Egyptian was his or her name. The elaborate tombs and the preparations for memorials and feast days for the dead assured that those whose names were read aloud in ritual were eternally remembered.

Despite the eternal beauty of her temple at Deir el Bahari, Pharaoh Hatshepsut's name never appears on the King List of names, and the King List purports to include everyone from the remotest reach of predynastic memory. In his book *Queens of the Pharaohs,* Leonard Cottrell vividly describes the devastation of her temple, monuments, and royal statues when Hatshepsut's nephew Tuthmosis III ascended to the throne.

> His [Tuthmosis III] workmen descended on her funerary temple, and amid the crash of hammers and scraping of chisels her rows of great statues were overthrown and then pounded into fragments. Not one was spared, and those which we see in the Cairo Museum, and in the Metropolitan Museum of Art, New York, were reassembled from the thousand pieces which [Herbert Winlock of the New York Museum] found. . . . The destruction was thorough and deliberate. First, the statue was thrown from its base, then its eyes were hacked out, and the uraeus, the sacred serpent, was struck from its brow. After that, the hammers and nails got to work and the columns splintered into heaps of rubble.[24]

Tuthmosis replaced her cartouches with his own to demonstrate the true order of succession. He made every effort to show that the queen had never existed. Pharaohs were also known to curse their enemies by painting the soles of their sandals with the abhorrent name or figure. With every step thereafter, the pharaoh trampled on his enemies and eventually rubbed them out of existence.

DEFENDING EGYPT WITH MAGIC

The Pyramid Texts tell us that the shamans of the Old Kingdom could cast out demons, heal the sick, shape-shift at will, and command nature. They could part waters, stop the sun, rent Earth, and stir up the wind and rain. The pharaoh had to have at his command—if not be one himself—the most powerful sorcerers in Egypt. No doubt that is what kept Egypt viable for more than three thousand years.

Not every story has a happy ending, however, as the following one will attest.

Callisthenes, said to be a nephew of Aristole and a contemporary of the last king of the Thirtieth Dynasty, had written that Pharaoh Nectanebo II (360–343 BCE) used magic to defend his country from outsiders. If the boats of his enemies came against him, he retired to his meditation room where he kept a bowl filled with water. Rather than losing his real soldiers in battle, he fought his battles with wax ships floating on the water in the bowl and wax soldiers; he caused the Egyptian figurines in their boats to fight the soldiers of his enemies.

Then, it was said, he put on the cloak of an Egyptian prophet, took up his ebony rod, and returned to the chamber, where he uttered words of power to invoke the Egyptian gods to work magic with winds and subterranean demons against those who opposed him. The magical figures then sprang to life and fought each other. Each time, the ships of wax swirled about and the Egyptian figurines vanquished the enemy. Nectanebo II watched as the figures of the ships and the armies of his enemies sank to the bottom of the bowl. Thus did the real ships sink and the foreigners drown. In this way, Nectanebo II kept Egypt safe from harm for nearly twenty years.

One day in his cloistered room as Nectanebo II's army fought with the army of the Persian king, Artaxerxes III, he watched with horror as his magical army was defeated. His own ships sank and not the ships of his enemies. Here the story becomes a bit vague. It was said that

Nectanebo, rather than go down with his ships, cloaked himself and fled first to Memphis, then to Upper Egypt, and finally into Nubia, where he disappeared, vanishing from history.

The ancient Greek writer Callisthenes, in his capacity as documentarian of Alexander the Great, remarked that the disappearing act was a ruse. In a continued magical act of national preservation, Nectanebo II disguised himself as the god Amun. He then impregnated the bereft Greek widow Olympias with her child, Alexander. Thus, not only did the god Amun confer power to Alexander to rule as Egypt's king, but this ruse also assured that he, being the son of Nectanebo II, was of Egyptian blood.[25]

MAGIC MISUSED

No magic was inherently evil, or black. Anyone who could read and pronounce the words of power could wield magic. Some did so with ill intent and that constituted criminal behavior. Intrigues in families, conspiracies among courtiers, acquisitions of power and wealth—it happened among common people, but one particularly spectacular case happened to an Egyptian royal. The magical acts of the conspirators against Ramses III were called "great crimes of death" and "abominations of the land" because the victim had been the king himself.

The acts were so horrendous that even the real names of the evildoers were not recorded in the records because to preserve their true names was to give them a longer life than they deserved. After they were convicted of high treason, the names of the criminals were changed to some equivalent name that meant "He who is cursed by the gods." Here is that story.

During the reign of Ramses III (1186–1155 BCE), Penhuibin, overseer of the pharaoh's herds, went to Messui, the temple priest, asking for some magic words that would bring him strength and power. The priest-scribe handed him the scroll that belonged to the pharaoh. Soon after, the herdsman conspired with members of the king's harem to use the magic of the gods against the pharaoh. They used the words they found in the scroll to make potions, write spells, and sculpt wax figurines that would harm the king and his entourage. The women of the harem were told to acquire from the king some bit of hair or bodily fluid since they had greater access to him. The plot failed. The conspirators were tried for sorcery and condemned to die by their own hands; that is, to commit public suicide.[26]

With the possibility of intrigue going on behind his back, a pharaoh needed a lot of magical protection. Angry deities, jealous ghosts, foreign demons, and sorcerers might torment the pharaoh's daylight hours, causing illness, accidents, poverty, famines, uprisings, and infertility. Thus the household furniture might possess both functional and magical applications. The claw-foot bathtubs and chairs that we so commonly associate with Victorian furniture imitate Chinese dragons, Greek griffins, and Egyptian lions—all magical beings whose protection began with spells to safeguard ancient kings and queens. These creatures likewise protected the Egyptian home, especially at night, when, as the light faded, the forces of chaos became more overpowering.

LOVE SPELLS

Magic serves many purposes; some are not as noble as others. Love spells were used to manipulate the feelings of another. One rather tame love spell found on a potsherd was intended to make a woman follow a man the way a cow follows her calf. Many Greco-Roman love charms used clay or wax figures pierced by needles, which caused a living being to experience pangs of love as if from the arrows of Cupid. Many love poems in the Chester Beatty Papyrus accuse the beloved of bewitching the lover. "My brother torments my heart with his voice. He makes sickness take hold of me. He is neighbor to my mother's house and I cannot go to him! Mother is right in charging him thus: 'Give up seeing her!' It pains my heart to think of him. I am possessed by love of him."[27]

Ancient love spells, like modern ones, sometimes had a way of backfiring. One legend of the Fourth Dynasty recounts a story of a magician's unfaithful wife, which is told to Pharaoh Khufu by his son Khafre. Unbeknownst to the magician, his wife was seeing a handsome young man in her service. When the butler reported the affair to his master, the magician molded a tiny wax crocodile. He had his butler carry it to the lake where the young man bathed each evening and toss it in. As the wax crocodile hit the water, it immediately became a giant living reptile. It snatched the adulterous man in its jaws and sank to the bottom of the water.

Sometime later, the magician invited Pharaoh Nebka to his house and told him about the crocodile. When he commanded the crocodile to appear, it came up out of the water and dropped the young man, unharmed, before the two men. Once the adultery had been revealed, the magician commanded the crocodile to snatch up the young man again. It did and disappeared with him to the bottom of the lake, never to be seen again. The adulterous wife was burned alive and her ashes thrown into the Nile.[28]

Khaemwast and Naneferkaptah

Yearning for Secret Knowledge

If a little knowledge is a dangerous thing, the craving for vaster knowledge could be worse. Among several magical stories of Ramses II's son, the story of Prince Setne Khaemwast is one that shows the power of *heka* and the razor's edge that a true magician and priest must walk. This particular story is my adaptation from text translated by Miriam Lichtheim in the third volume of her *Ancient Egyptian Literature.*[1]

One day, the high priest Khaemwast found a scroll that told the story of a powerful magician, Naneferkaptah, who had been the son of Pharaoh Amenhotep. Naneferkaptah had acquired the magic in the sacred Book of Thoth, one of the books that had been written by Thoth's own fingers. Desiring this knowledge, Khaemwast and his brother, Anherru, went to the tomb of Naneferkaptah, finding there the mummy still wrapped in silence and linen. Naneferkaptah lay in the dark earth, buried there like a magic seed in the center of the tomb. On either side of Naneferkaptah's stone sarcophagus sat two ghostly figures, the kas *of a beautiful young woman and a boy. On the chest of Naneferkaptah lay the holy Book of Thoth.*

The high priest asked for the papyrus, but the ka *of Ahura, Naneferkaptah's wife, warned Khaemwast that the papyrus contained nothing but misery. She knew because her body and that of her child,*

Merab, still lay far away in Coptos near the eastern desert. Naneferkaptah, she said, cared more for knowledge than for his family. He craved the wisdom of ancient texts and magical spells.

How did he become so obsessed by these magic spells? It seems that one day, while he was studying an ancient shrine, another priest taunted him, saying, "I can tell you where to find the Book of Thoth. After reading the first page, you will be able to enchant heaven and Earth, the abyss, the mountains and the sea, and you shall know what the birds, the beasts, and the reptiles are saying. When you have read the second page, your eyes will behold all the secrets of the gods themselves, and you will be able to read all that is hidden in the stars."

All the priest asked in return was one hundred bars of silver and a burial fit for a pharaoh when he died.

Naneferkaptah agreed.

The book lay in the middle of the river at Coptos inside an iron box, inside a bronze box, inside a sycamore box, inside an ivory box, inside an ebony box, inside a silver box, inside a golden box. And in the golden box lay the Book of Thoth. "All around the iron box are twisted snakes and scorpions," the priest warned. "And it is guarded by a serpent who cannot be slain."

Excited at knowing the whereabouts of the book, Naneferkaptah ran home to tell Ahura the news, but Ahura had a bad feeling about the matter and begged him not to search for the scroll. Rather than listen to Ahura, Naneferkaptah acquired a royal boat in which he, his wife, and his son set sail to Coptos. There the priests and priestesses of Isis welcomed them, and Naneferkaptah made sacrifices to Isis and Horus.

After his fifth day in Coptos, Naneferkaptah went alone to the river to work his great magic spell. First, he created a magic cabin filled with men and tackle. After casting a spell that gave life and breath to the men inside, he cast the nautilus into the Nile. Then he anchored his boat in the middle of the river above the nautilus and spoke his words of power. For three days, the men worked ceaselessly day and night until they reached the place where the book lay. Naneferkaptah raised the book out of the rivers and anchored his boat at a shoal. As the priest had predicted, he found that living, poisonous snakes and scorpions encircled the boxes, but Naneferkaptah's magic quieted them.

Around the iron box, Naneferkaptah saw a guardian serpent that would not die and his magic was useless against it. When he hacked off the snake's head, it still brought its halves together again until, finally, Naneferkaptah devised a way to separate the two halves with sand. Then he opened the bronze box, and the box of sycamore, and the box of ebony, and the box of ivory, and the box of silver. Finally he came to the golden box, and when he opened it, Naneferkaptah found the Book of Thoth.

Reading the first page, he suddenly acquired power over heaven and Earth and over the abyss, the mountains, and the sea. He understood the language of beasts and fish. Reading the second spell, he discovered the secrets of the sun in the heavens, the moon, and the stars. He saw the gods who were hidden from mortal eyes.

Clutching his papyrus, he ordered the workmen to return him to Coptos, where Ahura awaited. After she read the first and second spells, she also learned the magic that her husband had learned. Then Naneferkaptah copied all of the spells onto a clean sheet of papyrus. He dissolved the papyrus in a cup of beer, washed off all of the words, and drank it so that the magic of the spells entered his body and mind.

As the family left Coptos to return home, their son Merab fell from the boat and drowned. Using magic from the book, Naneferkaptah tried to save him, but, alas, his boy was dead. Calling Merab's ka, he asked his son what had caused his death. And the spirit of Merab answered that when Thoth discovered that his book was missing, he went to Amun-Re and complained that Naneferkaptah had stolen the book's magic and slain its guardians. Re replied, "Deal with Naneferkaptah and all that is his as it seems fit to you. I send out my power to work sorrow and punish him, his wife, and his child." The child said the power of Re and the will of Thoth drew him into the river and drowned him.

Heartbroken, they left Merab's body for embalming at Coptos and decided to return home. When the boat came to the place where Merab

*had drowned, the power of Re overtook Ahura. Falling into the Nile, she
drowned. Naneferkaptah called her ka and heard its story; it was just like
Merab's. Once more he traveled to Coptos for her burial, then set sail for
home.*

*On the day that the boat arrived in Thebes, it seemed to sit empty,
drifting restlessly against the shore. Pharaoh came to see what had
happened to his boat, only to discover Naneferkaptah dead. He buried his
son with the Book of Thoth lying on his chest and the kas of Ahura and
Merab came to watch over the man they both loved.*

*After Ahura had told Khaemwast of the misery that befell her family
because of the Book of Thoth, she warned Khaemwast to relinquish his
quest for magic. "You have no claim to it," she said. "Indeed, for the sake
of it, we gave our lives."*

*Still wisdom hungry like the magican before him, Khaemwast again
asked for the book. He even threatened to take it by force. Now the two
spirits were afraid of him, but the ka of Naneferkaptah rose up out of its
body to confront the magician. He challenged Khaemwast to a game of
senet—a game at which Naneferkaptah's skill excelled. Each time they
played, the high priest Khaemwast lost. With each win, Naneferkaptah
used magic to make Khaemwast sink deeper and deeper into the ground.
Finally Khaemwast found that he was buried up to his neck. He called to
his brother, Anherru, and asked him to quickly bring to him the magical
amulet of Ptah and place it on his head before the game was lost.*

*At the Temple of Ptah, Anherru asked the other priests for the
amulet. Making his way back to the tomb—just barely in time—he
placed it on Khaemwast's head. Before Naneferkaptah could make the
ground swallow up the high priest forever, Khaemwast sprang free and
grabbed the book from the corpse.*

*He and Anherru ran. Over their shoulders they heard Ahura's ghost
sadly cry, "Alas, the power is drained from him who lies in his tomb." Then
they heard the ka of Naneferkaptah answer, "Don't be sad: I will make
him return the Book of Thoth. He will come as a supplicant to my tomb, a
forked stick in hand and a fire pan on his head."*

When the high priest returned the amulet to his father, the pharaoh, he told him all that had happened. Ramses suggested that Khaemwast immediately return the book that had caused so much trouble. Instead, Khaemwast took the book home and began to study its spells and use its contents to counsel those who came to him for magical consultations and advice.

One day he met a woman named Tabubua, the beautiful daughter of the high priest of Bast. Khaemwast soon forgot everything—he forgot the book, he forgot his wife—everything, except Tabubua. When she sent a message asking him to come secretly and meet her at her desert palace outside Bubastis, he could not go fast enough. There he saw a tower inside a great garden with a high wall surrounding it. Inside, Tabubua welcomed him with sweet words and looks, led him to her chamber and served wine in a golden cup. Khaemwast confessed his love for her; she agreed that they were destined for each other, but she could have no rival. Khaemwast needed to divorce his current wife, she said, and to keep his children from plotting against her, they should be sacrificed and their flesh fed to the cats at the temple.

In his ardor, the high priest agreed. When he had written out the order, Tabubua handed him the cup of wine again and stood before him— lovely and singing her bridal hymn. Beneath the window where he sat came the death cries of his children, but Khaemwast drained the golden cup. To Tabubua, he said, "My wife is a beggar and my children lie dead. I have nothing left in the world but you—and I would give all again for you. Come to me, my love!"

When he reached out for her, he saw her beautiful form become that of a corpse. She and the palace disappeared, leaving Khaemwast alone and naked in the desert. He ran home to find his wife and children still alive and well. The gods be praised. The priest had learned his lesson. Pharaoh Ramses made his son promise to return the Book of Thoth to the tomb of Naneferkaptah, but to save himself he had to return as a supplicant, carrying a forked stick and a fire pan on his head. In humility, the book was returned.

The ghost of Naneferkaptah, though, was still angry. He assured the high priest that what Tabubua had foretold in his dream would happen unless he brought the bodies of Ahura and Merab and buried them together in his tomb.

In Coptos, Khaemwast searched for the burial records of mother and child, but they were difficult to find. He offered a reward to whomever could lead him to the graves. At last, an old man came saying he remembered his great-great-grandfather showing him the tomb of the woman and her child, but that a house had been built upon the grave.

The high priest paid to have the house demolished by the king's soldiers. Khaemwast ordered the men to dig beneath it until they found a rock-cut tomb, deep in the earth. Inside it lay the bodies of Ahura and Merab. Now the old man shape-shifted into the ka of Naneferkaptah and disappeared from sight. Khaemwast returned to the tomb of Naneferkaptah. Amid great ceremony, he reburied the magician, his wife, and his child, along with the Book of Thoth. The pharaoh's men heaped sand over the stone shrine and hid the tomb. It was not long before a sandstorm turned it into a great mound, then the sands shifted and leveled the place so that it could never be found again.

There Naneferkaptah lay, silent and dreamless, with his wife Ahura, their son Merab, and the magical Book of Thoth, awaiting the day of awakening when Osiris would return to rule over Earth.

PART THREE

The Secret of Coming into Light

The Learned Egyptians

Walking over the hot tilted stones of Saqqara, I suddenly discovered a new level of understanding about how the hieroglyphs appeared on the walls. More than the carvings on the wall, I saw the shape of the wall itself.

No group but ours was there at the close of day. The sun sets quickly in the desert, and the complex was closing any minute. We had spent the day at Saqqara, walking, meditating, reading glyphs—mostly me reading glyphs, I guess—and performing ritual. As we were leaving, I felt dizzy with hieroglyphs that still begged to be read.

The roof of the causeway leading upward toward the Pyramid of Unas kept repeating the hieroglyph for *ma'at,* drawing a sharp line of light down the middle of the darkened corridor through which we walked. As we strode down the causeway toward the bus, I kept stopping to look over my shoulder. An almost laser beam of bright sunlight fell from above between two slabs of stone that resembled the double ma'at. The light began leading my eye back toward the Pyramid of Unas, practically begging me to follow it. I felt myself caught in a balancing act between the two truths, the *ma'aty*—the light and the dark, the upper and the lower, the seen and the unseen, yesterday and tomorrow, the symbolic and the simple. It was a clear white line between two worlds. I was reeling from the sheer astonishment of what I was seeing.

I stopped and leaned against a wall, gazing up, because just for a minute there I thought I understood the symbolism. Then I felt my friend Bobbi's tug on my arm, nudging me along with the rest of the group, then pulling me, as if I were no more than a rag doll. "Come back to us, Normandi," she said gently. "Come on. There's water on the bus, and there'll be more hieroglyphs for you to read tomorrow."

Later, I recognized something of myself when I read the ancient Egyptian tale of Prince Khaemwast and the spirit named Naneferkaptah. The high priest Khaemwast had devoted himself to the study of ancient books, magic, and mysticism, but he was not immune to the lust of both knowledge and the flesh. Neither did the great love for wife and family keep Naneferkaptah from his wisdom quest. Such is the way of most shamans and initiates. As a pharaoh's son, Naneferkaptah kept no real job, so he wandered around the desert trying to read the hieroglyphs on ancient tombs. The priests laughed at him and at his crazy lifestyle of wandering through the desert, looking for truth.

Apparently this desert wandering is an endemic ancient Middle Eastern curse. For forty years, Moses led an entire people on such a walkabout. Many Egyptologists have similarly searched the desert sand and rubble for the yet-to-be discovered tomb of a yet-to-be identified pharaoh. Many *National Geographic* specials on archaeological finds have fueled interest in ancient Egypt, and Zahi Hawass, Egypt's former high priest of the ancient texts, recently entertained the world with his reality television show, *Chasing Mummies*. (The series began on July 14, 2010, and aired Wednesdays at 10 p.m. on the History Channel until the program was canceled following the Arab Spring of 2011.)

The allure of such mysteries can be all-consuming. Thirty years ago, I heard the spirit of a departed friend whispering in my ear: "If you want to read hieroglyphs and know the spell of living well, come to find me in Egypt. There is a book there that Thoth, the god of wisdom, wrote with his own hand." I had to teach myself to read hieroglyphs, wandering through ancient texts and labyrinthine stacks of libraries. Eventually I learned to read the stones, or as I like to say, "I learned the language of birds." In one of these books, I first encountered the Fifth Dynasty Pyramid of Unas text, its perfect hieroglyphs seeming to have descended straight out of heaven and onto the walls of the pharaoh's tomb. When I saw them for the first time in Saqqara, I fell to my knees on the floor with mist in my eyes.

Whether or not I learned to enchant, I was enchanted. I have spent years contemplating ancient scripts, comparing them, relishing the finds of others, making my own tiny discoveries—all too often kept in the secret room of my skull. Every night when the moon rises, I see Thoth setting out a new sliver of light for me to go by. Every morning, Re rises in my eastern window where a stained-glass beetle hangs above my desk (thank you, John!). Dawn's first light glitters through its glass wings. At night, I wander out into my yard looking for Orion above the house, above the trees. I am in love with Egypt every day of my life. Sometimes ancestral spirits walk through the rooms of the house. And Isis is always at my back, her wings enfolding me.

THE BOOK OF THOTH

The mysteries written by Thoth were not meant for the reading pleasure of mere mortals. High wisdom is hard to come by. To gain access to Thoth's book, both Khaemwast and Naneferkaptah had to go to great lengths. The book that holds all the secrets of our becoming was said to lie in the depths of the river at Coptos inside its strong, nesting boxes of iron, copper, cedar, ivory, ebony, silver, and gold. It has been called the Book of Osiris Becoming Re[1] and the Emerald Tablet.[2]

It may be the akashic record of Earth—a memory cell that exists within us and within time and space that recalls our personal and planetary histories. Or it may be a book that lies at the depths of our being—the secret of our own hearts. It is the secret of our longing, our devolving or developing states of consciousness, our lives lived in ignorance or to the best of our ability. The secrets of the heart are guarded by the serpents, scorpions, and crocodiles that are the errors of our mind, our thinking. Time and forgetfulness are the ouroboros, the eternal serpent that winds about the book of life, feeding on memory and devouring itself. It is the beginning and the end of things. It is

Thoth, the god of scribes and of magic, was also known as Hermes Trismegistus by the Greeks. He was said to be the author of forty-two books of magic, which the Greeks attributed to a book called the Hermetica.

the pattern of being and passing away and coming to life again.

Arduous tasks are required to retrieve the book. Once attained, self-knowledge is fleeting—as Khaemwast learned perhaps. The god's wisdom does not save us from our mistakes. We have to do that, with our lessons of the heart learned, and forgotten, and learned all over again. Think of the sad demise of a man too hungry for knowledge and power. (How Thoth guards his mysteries!)

It should not seem surprising that even to the ancient Egyptians, knowledge of the magical words of power and the ways of the gods was a subject that generated endless fascination. The knowledge was shrouded in secrecy, and the mysteries required faithful concentration and attention to the tasks at hand. The priests were advised not to let profane eyes see their texts. In volume two of his metaphysical treatise *Thrice Greatest Hermes*, G. R. S. Mead tells us that a pharaoh had been warned to "[k]eep our sermon from translation in order that such mighty mysteries might not come to the Greeks, and to the disdainful speech of Greece, with its looseness and its surface beauty, taking all of the strength out of the solemn and the strong—the energetic speech of names."[3]

It was not easy for even an Egyptian to become a priest or priestess in the days of Egypt's glory. It was almost impossible for an outsider.

And yet it happened. Eventually the days of the pharaohs drew to a close. Certain supplicants, who were deemed pure of heart, great of mind, and strong of will, came to Egypt to learn its sciences, its language of symbols, its creation stories, its mathematics, and its morals as bestowed to us through the patterns laid down by the gods and goddesses at the beginning of time.

EGYPT'S INFLUENCE ON GREEK PHILOSOPHY

Most Westerners believe that the shape of philosophical thought and culture derived from ancient Greek wisdom keepers like Pythagoras (570–495 BCE), the mathematician and philosopher from the isle of Samos. According to Porphyry (234–305 CE), the knowledge-hungry Pythagoras traveled throughout the ancient world in search of answers. His travels took him to the land of the Egyptian magi where he learned mathematics, geometry, architecture, astrology, music, and the treatises of harmonic vibrations. Pythagoras later taught his students that number is all, and sacred harmonics and geometrics ruled the universe. He also studied the origin of life and the transmigration of souls.

Legend has it that the pharaoh Ahmoses II of the Twenty-sixth Dynasty provided Pythagoras with letters of introduction to the priests of Heliopolis. The priests there met with Pythagoras but suggested that, rather than study with them, he travel to Memphis to study with the priests of Ptah because they were the older and more venerable cult. Pythagoras traveled to Memphis. Once there, the priests again turned Pythagoras away and sent him on a trip from Memphis to Thebes (Diopolis) more than three hundred miles away. Unperturbed, Pythagoras set out on the long journey.

He arrived dusty and still thirsty for knowledge at the great temples in ancient Thebes. The priests of Amun read the letters from their pharaoh Ahmose II and realized that they dare not turn the stranger away, so they took him in. Still, they kept him from the sacred rituals performed before the *naos* inside the holy of holies sanctuary by creating rituals that were excruciating, ridiculous, and demeaning to the Greek. All of these challenges were calculated to drive Pythagoras into despair and send him on his way. Pythagoras persisted, zealously completing every single task. The priests were so impressed by the dedication of Pythagoras that they taught him all that he requested, even allowing him to make sacrifices in the temple, which no foreigner had ever been permitted to do.

During the span of his twenty-two years spent sojourning in Egypt, Pythagoras visited every holy place and was well received by the priests with whom he studied. He learned through oral instruction from the sages. He sat with the scribe priests and learned their languages—the symbolic, the hieroglyphic, and the epistolic wisdom texts. He studied sacred geometry, architecture, and the rites of each temple. If he heard of an exceptional man somewhere within the kingdom who was venerated for his wisdom, Pythagoras went and studied with him.[4]

The ancient Greeks—from whom we derive our understanding of all philosophies, sciences, and religion and all matters of justice and moral integrity—came to study in Egypt if they possibly could. Why? Because, they said, Egypt was built in the image of heaven.[5] Many other Ionians, Greeks, and later Roman sages attributed their wisdom to visits in Egypt. After the death of Socrates, Plato (350 BCE) spent thirteen years living in Egypt, studying the texts of Thoth and the rites of Amun with a priest at Heliopolis. Living near the Great Pyramids, he learned the ancient history of the Sphinx, and from this history of the earliest Egyptians, he developed the story of Atlantis, from which the Egyptians said the oldest inhabitants of their land had come. Solon (638–539 BCE), the Athenian lawmaker before Plato, was said to have learned the same Atlantean story from the priests who read the temple walls of Sais.[6]

Thales of Miletus (circa 585 BCE) came to Egypt to study with priest-astronomers—astronomy and geometry being the two great sciences of which Egyptian priests were considered adepts. Anaximander (611–546 BCE), likewise of Miletus, learned from the Egyptians "the boundless" origin of all that is. Although he worked also in the fields of geography and biology—including the idea that all life evolved from the sea—Anaximander was the first speculative astronomer. He proposed that Earth is suspended in space and that all the planets move upon wheels. These facts he likewise learned in Alexandria and in Sais. The female teacher Hypatia, a mathematical genius, studied in Alexandria, even though certain Alexandrian boys and Greek men thought she acted too high and mighty for a woman of her day.

Eudoxus of Cnidus (400–350 BCE) came to observe the heavens from the Temple of Heliopolis, where he learned the mathematics of astronomy. Eudoxus developed an understanding of the function of fixed stars and pole stars. He is said to have copied and translated into Greek the ancient Egyptian texts and discoursed on the movement of the five visible planets. He, like Pythagoras before him, had petitioned to the pharaoh to introduce him to the priests at Heliopolis and Memphis. Nectanebo, the last pharaoh of the Thirtieth Dynasty, provided Eudoxus access.[7]

Perhaps it was time for the Egyptians to share their sacred knowledge with others who proved themselves to be worthy recipients of this wisdom. If they were watching the heavens, perhaps they saw their time was drawing to a close. The Age of Aries (and the ram god Amun) was giving way to the Age of Pisces (the Christian fish). The cycles of supremacy of the ancient Egyptians had ended. The Persians overthrew Nectanebo, and after two hundred years, Alexander the Great of Macedonia conquered Egypt, aligning himself with the ancient Egyptians as one of their own sons, the progeny of Amun.

THE SACRED LIBRARIES

The Serapeum built in Saqqara by the Ptolemaic rulers honors the earlier Greek philosophers who learned their wisdom from the ancient Egyptians. Greek rulers were buried side by side with the likes of the Sixth Dynasty sage Ptah-hotep and Imhotep, the deified priest, scribe, physician, and architect of the Third Dynasty. In the Serapeum, the Ptolemaic regents erected eleven busts of such Greek writers and philosophers as Plato, Pythagoras, and Heraclites and Pindar, the Greek poet who spent much of his life in Thebes.

In the Mediterranean city of Alexandria, just across the sea from Athens, sat the Library of Alexandria, which was also known as the Soter, or the Mansion of Books. Another library called the Serapeum, or the Mansion of Life, was situated in Saqqara. Each contained about 400,000 volumes. In the era of the Ptolemies, the Soter was the largest world archive of known science, history, literature, religion, harmonics, philosophy, law, and business. Most people owned no books of their own. Imagine how precious a scroll's treasures must have been. For thousands of years, scribes, who never kept ancient texts in great quantities, laboriously preserved by copying in a neat hand the books that were the foundation of their culture—copies of books so ancient that they were written by the very fingers of the god Thoth. The libraries of Egypt amassed their knowledge for at least two thousand years. By comparison, the U.S. Library of Congress, which is less than two hundred years old, holds 20 million volumes.

The Serapeum attached to the library of Alexander was, like the Serapeum of Saqqara, built by Ptolemy III (246–222 BCE) and maintained thereafter with a reverence for the mysteries that Egypt had imparted to its philosophers. Five hundred years later, however, the wisdom disappeared. The sacred texts of the Egyptians literally went underground when the Christian bishop Theophilus forbade the worship of Osiris or Dionysus in Alexandria. Upon finding the archival storage rooms beneath the temple, radical Christian mobs overran the temple, destroyed the monuments, and burned the ancient Egyptian texts for being heretical. (*Her-ese* [a contraction of Heru, another name for Horus, and Isis] may be the root of the word *heresy*, meaning to the early Christians the sin of suggesting that Jesus and Mary were akin to the Egyptian dieties Horus and Isis.)

Every temple in Egypt—and some Mycenaean temples—were built on the remains of the preceding temple it replaced. In Abydos, for example, the temple built by Seti I reportedly rests on ten previous temples dating back into prehistory. The zodiacal ceiling in the Ptolemaic temple to Hathor at Dendera depicts the pole star as existing in Draco, rather than in Ursa Major, because the original temple depicted the night sky at the time of its origin—possibly around 2700 BCE, the era of Imhotep and Pharaoh Djoser.

The carved temple walls contained the seeds of every Egyptian prayer, history lesson, mystery play, and wisdom text. No wonder Naneferkaptah walked about the temples endlessly, literally lost inside the towering pages of enormous stone books. At Karnak, he would see the story of creations played out endlessly in the hypostyle hall, its lotus columns rising up toward heaven. (Please see plate 37 of the color insert.) At Philae, he would have read the stories of the death of Osiris and the magical conception of Horus, all Egyptian mysteries of Isis. At Abydos, he would have found himself inside the oldest mysteries of Osiris and his transformations. At Edfu, he would have found the story of the heroic struggle of Horus and Seth, the battle between light and darkness, order and chaos.

The Temple of Edfu is spectacular—the most complete temple found in ancient Egypt. It is also one of the oldest. Each layer is built upon the sacred grounds of the temple before it, incorporating, as Egyptians often did, the "seed stone" of the previous building. Often the seed stone, as it is in the Temple of Man in Luxor, is the phallus of the god Min, and it rests in the center of the temple, like a penis inserted within a vagina. This parent stone generates the new temple. It grows outward from the central core of the sanctuary.

THE HOUSE OF LIFE

Among the many marvels of preservation at Edfu is one of my favorite rooms—the library room, or house of life. Every temple apparently kept one. At Edfu, we find it tucked away on the right-hand side of the hypostyle hall near the entrance. The architect and scribe goddess Seshet flanks either side of the doorway. (Please see plate 9 of the color insert.) I stand to look at her a moment, her scribe's pen upraised and poised to count upon a papyrus leaf the pharaoh's many years and to write his story. She wears the leopard skin of a high priestess. Upon her human head rests a star with seven petals, inside an upturned set of cow horns. Some authors have suggested that Seshet, the goddess of both astronomy and writing, may indicate contact between humans and celestial beings from the Pleiades, the seven stars that appear inside the horns of the constellation Taurus.

Every temple in ancient Egypt kept a small library room watched over by Seshet. Small libraries containing the festival texts are found in the temples of Isis at Philae, Khnum at Esna, and Montu at Tod, twenty miles south of Luxor. Other libraries were mentioned at Esna, Memphis, Abydos, Koptos, and Akhmim. In Tell el Amarna, the radical monotheist Akhenaten kept a library of rituals and prayers to the sun disc, Aten. Some of these are thought to have found their way into the Old Testament. Professor James B. Pritchard notes in particular the similarities between the Psalm 104 and the Hymn to Aten.[8]

No actual texts were ever found in the Edfu library, but inside the room are two niches where the sacred texts were stored. Hieroglyphs carved on the walls inside the house of life provide a catalog of books that were in use when the existent Temple of Horus was active from 140 to 124 BCE. They are:

- ➤ The books and the great rolls of pure leather that detail the smiting of demons, the repelling of the crocodile, the protection of the hour, the preservation of the barge, and the carrying of the barge
- ➤ The book of bringing out the king in procession
- ➤ The book of conducting the ritual
- ➤ The book of protecting the city, the house, the White Crown, the throne, and the year
- ➤ The book of appeasing Sekhmet
- ➤ The book of driving away lions, repulsing crocodiles, and repelling reptiles
- ➤ Knowing all the secrets of the laboratory
- ➤ Knowing the divine offering in all their details, and all the inventories of the secret forms of the neteru, all the aspects of the associated deities, which are copied daily for the temple, every day, each one after the other, so that the souls of the deities will remain in this place and will not leave this temple—ever
- ➤ The book of the inventory of the temple
- ➤ The book of the capture of enemies
- ➤ The books of all the writings of combat
- ➤ The book of temple conduct
- ➤ Instructions for decorating a wall
- ➤ Instructions for protection of the body
- ➤ The book of magical protection of the king in his palace
- ➤ Spells for repelling the evil eye
- ➤ Knowing the periodic returns of the two heavenly bodies
- ➤ List of all the sacred places and what is in them
- ➤ Every ritual related to the god's leaving his temple on festival days[9]

These are only the books of temple rites listed on the walls. Clement of Alexandria suggests that other books kept in the great house of books may have included many other texts used by lector priests, high priests, and lesser scribes to instruct students on a regular basis. Over the course of their training, student scribes would have copied and recopied hundred of chapters from the so-called books of the dead. Many nobles in the ancient communities bore the title Scribe in the House of Life, or Supervisor of the House of Life.

The sacred texts fell into seven distinct categories:

→ Book of hymns to the gods (1 book)
→ Book accounting the king's life (1 book)
→ Books on astrological matters (4 books)
→ Books on cosmology, geography, construction of temples, lands dedicated to temples, and provisions and utensils of temples (10 books)
→ Books written in hieroglyphic script on education and temple business, including the art of making sacrifices (primarily offerings of first fruits), hymns, prayers, processions, and feasts (10 books)
→ Books written in hieratic script on laws, gods, and priestly training (10 books)
→ Medical books on diseases of the eye and other diseases, organs, drugs, and gynecology (6 books)

Clement of Alexandria unequivocally attributed the authorship of all forty-two of these sacred books to Thoth, or Hermes Trismegistus. We do not know whether these are the same forty-two books that were used in the temples during the Eighteenth Dynasty of Egypt—allegedly the books that were written by Thoth with his own fingers.

I understand the bibliomania of the ancient Egyptian scribe. There are books in my library that I have pored over and pawed to death in my studies. Every ten to fifteen years or so, I have tried to buy replacements for them. An out-of-print book practically sends me into tears. A dutiful Egyptian scribe copied the original until it dissolved, and then he recopied the copies, carefully attributing its original sources.

It was this precise record keeping that informed archaeologists that the great temple to Hathor in Dendera was rebuilt by the Ptolemies according to the original design. The original design was said to be detailed in a three-thousand-year-old text written on leather during the time of the followers of Horus. A copy of that text reportedly was found in ancient times in a crypt inside a coffer presided over by Sixth Dynasty pharaoh Pepi I. That copy specified the plan and layout for the original temple and its astrological ceilings. The Ptolemies dutifully depicted on the zodiacal ceiling of the reconstructed temple the sky exactly as it appeared nearly three thousand years earlier.

We will probably never know if such books as the magical Book of Thoth that Naneferkaptah gripped with the dark claw of his mummified fingers existed. Papyrus crumbles away. Animal skins rot. Even the hieroglyphic inscriptions of stone flake away or are buried in mud. Egypt kept three thousand years of knowledge—or more—but much of it may still lie buried in the sand.

THE LOST TEMPLES OF WISDOM

The temples of Greece were built on Egyptian wisdom and spiritual principles. The ancient temples of Mycenea were said to have been built on Egyptian foundation stones during the time of the early Middle Kingdom of Egypt, and the culture of the temple was taught to them by four Egyptian priestesses of Isis. The oracles, the Orphic rites, the Eleusinian Mysteries—all were patterned on Egyptian principles. The temples themselves throughout the aeons were built on the ruins of previous temples, exact copies of the exacting sciences and cosmologies preserved in stone, for the temples of the neteru were eternal, while the mud houses of the priests and noble families passed away, buried in the floods.

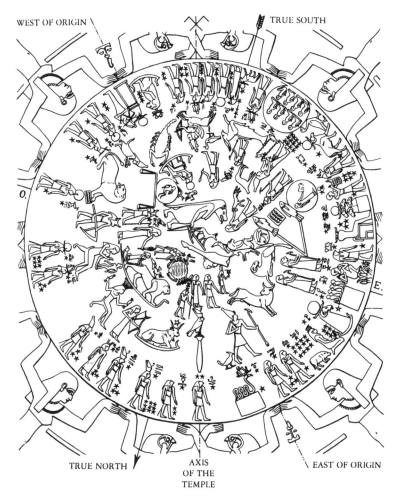

WEST OF ORIGIN

TRUE SOUTH

O.

E.

TRUE NORTH

AXIS
OF THE
TEMPLE

EAST OF ORIGIN

The zodiacal ceiling at the Temple of Hathor at Dendera was installed in the temple during the Ptolemaic era. It is said to represent the founding of Hathor's temple here during the predynastic era. Note that the constellation Draco (the hippo goddess in the center) holds her hand on the pole star. Draco rather than the Thigh, or the Great Bear that we know, was the pole star around 2550 BCE during the Fourth Dynasty of the Old Kingdom. (Illustration by Lucie Lamy, from Sacred Science: The King of Pharaonic Theocracy, *published by Inner Traditions and used with permission)*

In time, the shining limestone casings of the pyramids, which once had gleamed like beacons in the rising sun, were torn from their places to construct new mosques and bridges in Cairo. The Christian, Turk, and Roman invaders saw little value in the ancient Egyptians' spiritual understanding of the higher mysteries—and even less value in the antiquity of their documents.

Even as the Greeks and Romans sought to create the greatest library of knowledge in the world under Ptolemy III, the ancient Egyptian priests kept the origins of their culture and their history to themselves. The Alexandrian philosopher Ammonius Saccus was the Egyptian-born teacher of the Neoplatonist thinkers Origen and Plotinus. His work influenced early Christian thinkers and writers, but his philosophies may have had pagan roots. His family most likely dedicated him as a child to the service of the hidden god Ammon—Amun having been Hellenized into Ammon. True to the form of an ancient Egyptian high priest, Ammonius never wrote down any of his religious philosophies, for they could be used against him as evidence of his paganism. Instead, he allowed himself to be called Christian, but his theology had Gnostic Coptic overtones.

He also never allowed his teachings to be copied down by his students. Even Plotinus, also Egyptian-born but not a Christian, never divulged the whereabouts of his family, even to Porphyry, his student and biographer.[10] The native Egyptian priests remained skeptical of the invaders seeking their wisdom, and rightly so.

Soon after the Christian zealots became prominent in Alexandria, the wisdom texts became a threat. Pope Theophilus specifically banned pagan texts and closed the temples in 391 CE. He destroyed the Serapeum and its contents and turned a blind eye to the murder of Egyptian and Greek philosophers like Hypatia, who engaged in the study of astronomy and math because the information came from pagan sources.

Three hundred years later, the writings of those pagan philosophers were destroyed. In six short months, 400,000 papyrus scrolls and parchments, all of the remaining sacred texts in the Library of Alexandria, three thousand years of high wisdom of Egypt, as well as its many dynastic records—all were burned to heat the bathwaters of caliphs. In

640 CE, when Caliph Omar justified his book burning, he said, "If those books contain the same doctrine as The Koran, they are of no use, since The Koran contains all the necessary truths. If they contain controversy, they should be destroyed."[11]

What could be saved during these dark years may have been tucked into clay jars. These were stored in cachés inside the catacombed, monastic cells that littered the *wadis* and monasteries of Coptic Christian Egypt. Although they are a decidedly Christian sect, many Copts held on to the last remnants of the old ways. The sacred language of their church service bears a striking resemblance to the ancient language in the land of Khem.

In time, the Sphinx lost its nose during the Marmaluk army's artillery practice. Long ago, the ancient beard fell into the sand, was buried and rediscovered, and then parts of it were carted off to Great Britain. Even in the time of Herodutus's travels to Egypt (possibly 454 BCE), the Sphinx must have been swallowed up by drifting sand. (Please see plate 34 of the color insert.) The philosopher recalls a visit to the pyramids of Giza, but nowhere does he mention the Sphinx. As Egypt entered the modern era, it did not take long for the enterprising businessmen who ran the railroads to churn through the burial grounds of many a necropolis, leaving devastation behind as they ripped mummies from their coffins to burn them in the furnace rooms of trains that sped along the Nile Valley. The dense resin derived from the ancient embalming process caused those mummies to burn with an intense energy and heat.

The fragmentary history of Egypt—especially its predynastic history—has been painstakingly re-created from potsherds, stones, and bits of statues. Without the libraries filled with books, which the Greeks and Egyptians meant to safeguard forever, our findings can hardly be entirely accurate.

Nearly two thousand years have passed since the Greeks walked on Egyptian sands and worshipped in Egyptian temples. The ancient Egyptians and their wisdom seem but a dim memory, a magical realm of forgotten magic. In 1798, Napoleon and his soldiers arrived in Egypt.

Yellow sand had drifted into the temples. It rose twenty times the height of a man, nearly reaching the tops of the lotus bud columns that sprouted like stunted stone flowers. Sandstone columns lay in rubble. A towering rose granite obelisk, its glyphs gleaming as if carved yesterday, lay shattered on its side in the sand. Once again the Sphinx crouched in sand up to its neck and stared through the visitors as if they were merely a passing mirage; its eyes intently gazed east into eternity. The stern faces of the pharaohs and gods had been hacked by chisels and hammers, scoured by sand, and eroded by wind and time.

Napoleon held his breath. Everywhere he turned—toward the temples, the river, the palm groves, or the sand—he sensed the presence of ancient mystery. He must have felt this power as tangibly as he could still feel the heat of the Egyptian sun on his skin. Perhaps he felt it more strongly because he could not read the stone inscriptions, but as he gazed upon the images of the rising sun, the birds, the knotted cords, the cattle, he wondered what these stones might reveal if they could speak. At every bend in the river, centuries of art, ancient records, lost histories, and perhaps eternal truths waited to be deciphered. He hired 150 engineers, scientists, mathematicians, naturalists, and artists to record the wonders of a lost civilization.

Napoleon felt awestruck by what he saw in Egypt. On the Giza Plateau, he gathered his soldiers, artists, and scholars and declared with great reverence, "From the summit of yonder pyramids, forty centuries look down upon you." The man who tried to conquer the world found himself overwhelmed by the murmur of whispering sands, which local people say are the muffled voices and chants of the ancients. He confessed to his men that "[t]he Egyptians of old thought like men a hundred feet tall. We in Europe are but Lilliputians."[12]

Still, Egypt itself has a way of keeping its secrets. After spending a night inside the Great Pyramid, Napoleon emerged the next morning, pale, sweating, and visibly shaken—unable to speak of the visions he had witnessed alone during the night. (Please see plate 1 of the color insert.)

Khaemwast and
Si-Osire Journey to Duat

The story of the high priest of Ptah and his son Si-Osire is another of the mystical demotic tales about the fourth son of Ramses the Great, Khaemwast. In this case, the hero of the story is the child named for Osiris, the god who presides over the land of the dead and offers us a look into life after death. The demotic script of this particular story was copied sometime around 200 BCE. It would have been concurrent with the kinds of texts that might have found their way into the Library of Alexandria.

It depicts the Egyptian land of the dead with its traditional journey through the hours and gates of the night as a netherworld (or neter-world) that had some of the elements of the Greek myth of Orpheus and his descent into Hades. In both cases, we see that life there continues after life on this plane ends, but the circumstances we find there are dependent on the actions of life on Earth. The blessed are richly rewarded, and sinners suffer eternal punishment.[1]

Notably, the story of Khaemwast and Si-Osire is very similar to the parable that Jesus tells in Luke 16:19–31 of the rich man and the poor man named Lazarus. In it, a rich man lives in fine purple robes while a poor man lives and dies at his doorstep. Then the rich man in torment in the next life looks up to see Lazarus, the poor man, at the side of Abraham, the patriarch, in heaven. He asks for mercy, but Abraham replies, "Between us and you a great chasm is established to prevent anyone from crossing from our side to yours or from your side to ours." Moreover, Abraham advises the damned man that those who do not listen to the prophets while they were living will not listen to their ghosts.

It is possible that the parable of the rich man and Lazarus, the poor man, which is ascribed to the authors of the so-called Q source, was drawn from the Egyptian wisdom literature that sets forth the story of Khaemwast and Si-Osire. Here is the story.

> *Khaemwast, the high priest of Ptah, son of Ramses the Great and his second wife Isisnofret, lived in Memphis with his wife, Mehusekhe, and their three daughters, but Khaemwast wanted a son.*
>
> *He oversaw the works of builders, sculptors, jewelers, and artists. He built for the gods Ptah, Sokar, Osiris, and Re many architectural wonders in Memphis, Saqqara, and Karnak, and he asked the gods for a son. A magician great in magic, Khaemwast knew all the spells in the Book of Thoth. He had done battle with Nubia's greatest sorcerers and won. He had prepared and celebrated the Heb-Sed Festival with his father, Ramses II, the king. Khaemwast was set to inherit the throne, but still he wanted a son. Even a wise man needed a son to perform the sacred rites for him in the next world.*
>
> *One night as Mehusekhe slept in the temple, the god spoke to her. "Mehusekhe," the god said. "Go tomorrow to the place where your husband bathes. Find the honeydew melon vine that grows there. Take a branch of it with its gourds, grind them into a potion and drink it, then lie beside him that night to receive his fluid. You shall have a son." Mehusekhe did everything she had been told to do in the dream. That night she conceived a child. When Khaemwast learned of her pregnancy, his heart beat in wild happiness. He created a magical spell for Mehusekhe to bind the child in her body for its nine months and hung the amulet around her neck.*
>
> *Prince Khaemwast had a dream of his own. He dreamed that a god spoke to him, saying, "The child that your wife, Mehusekhe, received from you will be a boy. Name him Si-Osire, and he will perform many wonders in Egypt." Khaemwast told Mehusekhe his dream, and she was very*

happy. When the boy was born, Mehusekhe cradled him to her breast, and he drank eagerly. Khaemwast named their firstborn son Si-Osire so that it was on Earth as it had been in their dreams.

When Si-Osire was a year old, people said, "He looks to be two!" When he was two years old, they said, "He looks three!" Khaemwast loved the boy so much he watched over him all day long. Si-Osire grew big and strong. Almost as soon as Khaemwast put the boy in school, Si-Osire surpassed his teacher, the scribe. Soon he was reciting books with the wisest scribes in the house of life at the Temple of Ptah. All who heard the boy called him a wonder.

On the day that Khaemwast was to present his son at the pharaoh's banquet, and while they were at home preparing themselves, they heard the sound of wailing. Khaemwast and Si-Osire looked down into the street where the coffin of a rich man was passing by on its way to the cemetery. The priest of Anubis led the way, and two oxen pulled the sledge. Many mourners followed behind with loud, keening wails. They beat their chests with their fists and scattered dust on their heads. Servants passed by, too, carrying many loaves of bread, cakes, alabaster jars of oil, and many fruits of the field. The scent of myrrh followed them. The gilded coffin in its shrine was inscribed on all sides top to bottom with hieroglyphs and jewels, so greatly honored was the man being buried. As they watched the procession disappear, soon Khaemwast saw a second corpse being carried out of Memphis through the street. This was the body of a poor man, wrapped only in a mat, and no one walked in procession behind him.

"By Ptah the great," said Khaemwast, "see how much happier the rich man is, how the sound of many mourners follows him in his wake, and how silently the poor man is carried to his grave."

The child Si-Osire said, "May it be with you in Duat as it will be with the poor man. May you not go as this rich man into Duat."

The words of Si-Osire startled and saddened Khaemwast. "Is that my son who says this to me?"

"If you wish, father, I will show you the fates of the poor man and the rich man."

Then Si-Osire lightly touched his father's hand, and their two spirits flew off, Si-Osire leading them into the western desert. They entered the mountain, which was black as night, until they found themselves in the fourth hall. Khaemwast observed there several people who were plaiting ropes as quickly as their donkeys chewed them up. Others had many jugs of water and loaves of bread hung above them. They leapt and scrambled, trying to grasp the provisions and bring them down. Even so, many more people dug pits at their feet causing them to sink into the ground without reaching the bread and water.

Si-Osire led Khaemwast into the fifth hall where the noble spirits stood in their ranks while those accused of crimes stood pleading at the entrance to the door. There the pivot of the door to the fifth hall was fixed into the socket of a man's right eye. His loud shrieks, lamentations, and pleading were terrible. At the sixth hall, Khaemwast saw the gods on their regal seats listening to the accusations of servants against their masters during the trials of all who dwelt in Duat.

In the seventh hall, Khaemwast gazed upon the mysterious form of the great god Osiris seated on his golden throne and wearing the white atef crown with its two brilliant white plumes. To his left stood the jackal god Anubis, to his right the ibis god Thoth, and on either side stood the tribunal gods in the underworld. At the center of the room before them all stood the scales. Here the good deeds were weighed against the bad, and so was the fate of a man's life decided. The heart must be balanced by the white feather of truth. Anubis announced the weighing in the scales, and Thoth, the great scribe in the house of life, copied it down. The heart of the one who was found to have more misdeeds than good deeds was fed to Ammit, the devourer, whose belly is the belly of the deepest darkness in the underworld. Body and soul together were devoured and sent into the belly of the beast. This man never breathed again. But for the man found to have done more good on Earth than ill, he was gathered in by the great tribunal gods before Osiris, lord of Duat, and his soul flew forth into the sky like a great winged thing to live forever with the great souls of the Divine. He whose good deeds equaled his misdeeds was not condemned to

Ammit, was not allowed to fly up to the gods, but was made to be a spirit who served Sokar-Osiris in Duat.

Now Khaemwast gazed upon a rich man—a man of high status— clothed in a spotless, white garment of royal linen and standing at the side of Osiris. Khaemwast was quiet, taking in all that he had seen.

Si-Osire stood before Khaemwast. "My father," said the son. "Did you see that rich man in royal linen standing near Osiris? He is the poor man that we saw being carried out from Memphis wrapped in a reed mat and with no one walking behind him. Here, in Duat, his misdeeds were weighed against the good deeds he had done on Earth. Thoth found that over the length of his life and in consideration of his luck on Earth, his goodness was greater than his lack. Thus Osiris gave to him the funerary tributes of that rich man who was carried from Memphis with great honor. This poor man has taken his place among the noble spirits as a man of God who serves Sokar-Osiris and stands beside Osiris.

"When the rich man was taken to the underworld, they weighed his deeds in the balance, and they found his misdeeds more numerous than the good ones. He has been imprisoned in the underworld. He is the man you saw with the pivot of the door affixed in his eye socket so that the door to Duat swings open and shut on his eye. His mouth is forever open in great lamentation. By Osiris, the great god, lord of Duat, when I said to you on Earth, 'May it be with you in Duat as it will be with the poor man. May you not go as this rich man into Duat,' I knew what would happen to him!"

Khaemwast stood in awe of what his son had shown him. Still, he was unsure about one thing. "My son, Si-Osire, you have shown me many marvels in Duat. But tell me, what has happened to those people who plait their ropes while their donkeys chew them up? And why do the provisions of those others hang so far above their heads, and as they reach toward them, others dig pits beneath their feet?"

"In truth, my father Khaemwast," said Si-Osire, "those people whose donkeys chew up the ropes as they plait them were people on Earth who had no luck, who lived under a curse of the gods. They sweated night and

day for their livelihood, while their women robbed them behind their backs, and they found no bread to eat. In Duat, their misdeeds outweighed their good deeds. What happened on Earth happens now in the underworld. So it is also with those whose provisions hang above them. As they scramble to reach their goals, others dig pits at their feet to prevent them from gaining it. On Earth, they were people who had their lives before them, but the gods dug pits under their feet to prevent them from attaining their goals. When they came to the underworld, what had happened to them on Earth was made to happen here when their souls were received in Duat.

"Take it to your heart, my father Khaemwast. He who is beneficent on Earth, to him beneficence is received in the netherworld. And he who is evil, to him evil is ordained. So it is and forever will be. The things that you have seen in the netherworld at Memphis, they happen in all forty-two nomes of the judges of the great god Osiris."

When Si-Osire finished delivering his sermon to his father, Khaemwast the high priest, the son came down from the desert of Memphis. Khaemwast embraced him, holding his son's hand in his hand. "My son Si-Osire, is it a different way we are going down than the way we went up?" But Si-Osire did not answer his father at all.

Khaemwast marveled over all that he had experienced, saying, "My son Si-Osire will become one of the shining ones among all the spirits, a true man of God, and I shall go with him, saying, 'This is my son!'" While he was still full of wonder at all he had seen in Duat, Khaemwast recited incantations from the book of exorcising spirits, and so they returned to Earth. But those great mysteries that he had seen in the other world, things that he could not reveal to any other man on Earth, stayed with him and weighed heavily on him. When Si-Osire reached twelve years of age, no scribe in Memphis could compare with his recitation of spells and his making of magic.

Traveling
through the Dark

A day or two before my mother's death, in a moment of clarity, she said to me, "I'm not afraid of dying. I just don't know how to do it." My mother never let a conundrum stump her. Really, she was a remarkably fearless person who met every challenge with a glint in her eye. I assured her that I knew she would figure out a way to manage it. In his introduction to *The Doors of Perception,* Aldous Huxley wrote that we should judge all things as if we saw them from our deathbed. "If the doors of perception were cleansed, every thing would appear to man as it is—infinite."[1]

It is important to remember that all life experience exists within the mind of God. Death is a process of transformation that is a part of the life experience. It is not the antithesis to life. All these books of the afterlife offer valid ways of approaching spiritual development through tapping into the layers of the subconscious and unconscious mind. The distinction can be made here between levels of awareness with regard to these altered states.

The subconscious mind field may be entered in the same way that one may dive into a river's depth or a dream state. What exists there may be brought up and into the light for further examination. It reflects daily, psychospiritual experience (as it differs from psycho*logical* experience). The unconscious seldom sees the light of day. Most of these contents are mysterious and unknowable to us in our current incarnation.

Yet the unconscious exists, affects our current lives, and is hidden from us for some purpose—and perhaps that purpose is to keep our focus on the spiritual tasks at hand. This information may exist in the realm of our personal and planetary akashic records.

When the current life experience ends and the records are again opened and inscribed, we can see more clearly where we are in our soul's development. The Egyptian books of the afterlife offer us a view of both these levels of life experience. The texts speak to us in the sacred hieroglyphs that are like the language of dreams. Having some idea of how this realm appears while we are alive prepares us for the deep transformative experience of death when it occurs.

When I travel in Egypt, I never get my fill of standing at the entrance to any one of the evocative, vivid, and almost hallucinogenic tombs inscribed with beauty unimaginable and terrible. I feel a kind of awestruck reverence for that dreamscape, imagining how these images might flicker to life in the dark. I understand staring at a page of hieroglyphs and then falling into them, getting lost for hours or days (or was that years?), in hopes of returning with some kernel of wisdom, some inkling of true *ma'aty*.

IN THE BELLY OF ATUM

The first time I stood inside the Egyptian underworld, deep in the bowels of the mountain at the Valley of the Kings, I had traversed long halls and crouched my nearly six-foot frame down to avoid banging my head on the low ceilings. I stepped along a narrow, descending, wooden floor over a pit so deep it seemed to have no end. When we arrived in the final cavern where the stone sarcophagus lay, the Egyptian doorkeepers stationed at the opening of the tomb shaft turned out all the lights. I'd never experienced such total darkness, such cloying air. All that told me I was still alive was the smell of sweat and dust.

Chapter 175 of the Coffin Texts, the funerary writings of the Middle Kingdom era, describes the realm of the dead in dramatic terms. At death the scribe Ani finds himself conversing in the dark with Atum and Thoth. "What manner of country is this to which I have come? There is neither water nor air. . . . It is depth unfathomable; it is black as the blackest night, and men wander helplessly therein. In it a man may not live in quietness of heart, nor may the longings of love be satisfied."[2]

At death the god Osiris finds himself thrust into a similar dark and empty chasm. In Egypt's story of Osiris is the origin of its teachings about suffering, life, death, and eternity. The first man to be born in god's image on Earth becomes the first to die. The enigma is this: all things die—even divine beings. They die in order to transform and to come again, as Osiris or Jesus was said to have done.

Osiris is born into the verdant garden of Earth with its green fields, its red hibiscus, its pomegranates, dates, lotus, wheat, and papyrus. All this beauty and even Osiris himself are destined to pass away. Murdered by his brother, Seth, and hacked to bits, Osiris dies and is buried. He falls into the earth. Coffin Text 1080, found primarily at Deir el Bersha near Hermopolis and dating from the Eighth Dynasty, offers us our first view of what happens to the soul in the afterworld. Osiris finds himself trapped in the coils of an ouroboros, a great serpent that is the enveloping aspect of the god Atum. In later dynasties, this serpent is identified with Apep, or Mehen, aspects of Sethian energy. Here it is the dark aspect of the one God.

Osiris is devoured, "locked in darkness and surrounded by fire" inside the belly of Atum. The Lake of Fire is all consuming, and we are told, its purpose is regenerative.[3] This becomes the first vision of hell as Christians know it, or Jaheem in Islam and Gehenna in the Hebrew traditions.

During the New Kingdom when the great hidden god became known as Amun, versions of this same underworld journey said Osiris had been ensnared in the coils of the Apep serpent. As the negative, dark, or feminine body of the hidden god Amen, his counterpart was called Amentet, another name for the land of the dead. The two serpents of creation in Hermopolis—Amun and Amentet—now represent the hidden world of departed spirits.

To those familiar with the earlier creation myths of Ptah in Memphis, Atum in Heliopolis, and Thoth in Deir el Bersha, the emptiness that followed death was the face of Atum—the deep, unknowable nothingness before any god existed. This is the inert body of Atum before light sprang from the crevice of his lips and time began. At death Osiris returns to the place that existed before he was born, and he finds himself trapped in timelessness. Worse even than having been forgotten, it is as if he had never existed.

ATUM IS THE TOMB

In the dark, rocky desert-land abyss, Osiris cries out pitifully to Atum, begging for release. He tosses and turns in the darkness. He yearns; he aches for all that has vanished. He has lost his beautiful wife. He has lost love. He has lost the green garden of his bright earthly home. More than broken in physical form, he is brokenhearted, barely able to lift his arms or his head.

Chapter 175 of the Book of the Dead provides us with a script of the dialogue between Osiris, the dead, and Atum, the creator. When Osiris asks how the longings of his heart might be satisfied in this place, Atum answers: "I have provided illumination in place of water and air, satisfaction and quiet in place of bread and beer."[4]

This answers the essential question of religion; that is, "What do we get out of our religious beliefs?" The answer is enlightenment (illumination) and peace, what the ancient Egyptians called hotep *and is represented by the hieroglyph for communion—the bread and beer of the Egyptians. This is the peace that accompanies enlightenment. In Buddhist meditation, the place of peace and nothingness may be called the "sweet spot."*

Newly dead, however, Osiris has not come to that kind of acceptance. In this dark, empty place, he battles loneliness and feels completely abandoned. In his bones, he knows now the loneliness that Atum must have felt before the dawn of creation—the great emptiness that lacks companionship, perhaps, one imagines, with nothing but his own tormenting thoughts in the dark. He wanders in emptiness, unloved and lost.

In the tomb of Queen Nefertari, Osiris and Atum are portrayed seated back-to-back in the underworld. The two divinities of the neterworld cannot observe each other in the darkness although they reign side by side.

Osiris: *Shall I behold your face?*

Atum: *I will not allow you to suffer sorrow.*

Osiris tries to bargain with Atum. First, he complains of the injustice of his position, saying that every other god rides in Atum's Boat of Millions of Years, but Atum says that place now belongs to Horus, the son of Osiris, who has inherited his position. Next, Osiris cajoles Atum, saying how good it would be for one god to look upon another, and the god assures him: "My face will look upon your face."

Now wondering, no doubt, when this misery will end, Osiris comes to the critical question: "But how long shall I live?" to which Atum replies, "You will live more than millions of years, an era of millions."

This is not the picture Osiris had in mind about eternal life. Eternal nothingness is not high up on one's bucket list. It is a conundrum because life is transitory and only nothing lasts forever. Osiris's desire to see Atum is a longing for the transitory illusion of a world that cannot be forever. Eternity and life are not synonymous. What then, one wonders?

In response to Osiris's anxiety and fear, Atum tells him the truth: "In the end, I will destroy everything that I have created. Earth will become again part of the primeval ocean like the abyss of waters in their original state. Then I will be what will remain—just I and Osiris—when I have changed myself back into the Old Serpent who knew no man and saw no god."[5]

Earth and the entire cosmos shall pass away. The earthly struggle between Horus and Seth lasts as long as time. The struggle ends when time stops, but then Earth itself will end. At that point, what will the battle between light and dark have mattered?

INSIDE ATUM'S DREAM

One might imagine this life of ours is Atum's dream—a dream from the mind of God, the Great Creator. The light-filled world is God's conscious thought. The underworld also is part of Atum's dream. The unconscious mind, the subterranean being, was created from the many coils of the serpent. These become the *arits*, or halls, in the land of the dead. Eventually, when Osiris and all temporal beings fall out of time and matter, when we are no longer a conscious thought of Atum's, then we fall into the unconscious realm—the subterranean world.

In the end, even consciousness will stop. The great mind will have its final thought. At that time, Atum will withdraw what he has given. It will be as if the world had never been. The ouroboros will swallow himself and his creation.

Might this be the true meaning of the phrase "I and the Father are One"? Then, we might ask, what was the point of the sacrificed god-man Osiris? Horus, the son, inherits Earth and the way of sexual and human regeneration in time. Seth is joined to Re at last, and the god of disruption and death earns enlightenment. But what does Osiris inherit? He inherits what Atum believes is "fair"—"a fate different from all other gods. I have given him the region of the dead."[6]

There is a deep mystery here. Osiris becomes our salvation. Death is the only promise that we have of any future resurrection. I am reminded here of a joke I heard about the two caterpillars looking at a butterfly. One says to the other, "You'll never catch me up in one of those things." We know, of course, that he will go up into one of those things. He will become some fantastical creature he could never possibly have imagined he would become, a winged thing. But first, he has to die. He has to crawl into an inert state, like a mummy in a cocoon of bandages; he has to dissolve into a gelatinous mass and lose any resemblance to his former life before he can be reborn as a butterfly.

Once Osiris appeared in this underworld, we began to catch a glimmer of the way in which his appearance there reconstructed the realm of the dead. Osiris is taken into the body of Mehen, the great serpent who appears in the New Kingdom texts. Once inside the serpent, we see the god traveling through Mehen's darkened belly. The serpentine coils begin to be depicted as segmented spaces, and each space, or coil, becomes identified with one of twelve hours of the night. The coils of the great serpent in the New Kingdom texts developed into spaces whose qualities were identified as the hours of the night.

The land of the dead, the land of spirits where Osiris reigns, becomes the place of spiritual awakening, release, and understanding. Osiris, as he is often depicted, inert and wrapped up inside his shining white mummy cloths, becomes our hope and salvation. He is the only possibility of a future life. When Atum takes Osiris back into himself, Osiris is that resident god spark, an infinitesimal speck of matter that was the former self. It is the germ of a seed of possibility. There will be other creations, and other lives can burst forth out of decay and death. That is a powerful promise.

To die is the only way to be reborn. Osiris is the only hope that Atum has of not collapsing into nothingness himself. Because Atum looks upon the face of Osiris, every god and every goddess seed that issues forth from Atum is dedicated to Osiris. In the land of the dead, the pure departed souls pass into the Hall of Truth to see the glorious face of Osiris and to be renewed. The dead become Osirified. What has been done for Osiris by the great spirit of Atum—to become the spark of his future incarnation—is done for all spiritual beings. In Duat, one receives deep healing and is given life, health, and strength.

THE UNDERWORLD AS A STATE OF CONSCIOUSNESS

In meditation, dreams, or shamanic states, the living spirit can also journey to the land of the gods. At various places and times, Egypt's underworld had different names. The Greeks referred to it as the netherworld, or the world of shades. The Egyptians' conception is closer to gods' world, or *neter*world—a plane of existence beyond this one.

The Egyptian scribes endlessly copied and studied these states of consciousness and unconsciousness through their work with the sacred books of the dead. Through meditation and practice, the scribes came to understand light and shadow. Every day they lived within the realm of the gods and knew that Osiris, being the first death, had prepared the way for us to follow. The true (and lengthy) title of the Book of What Is in Duat tells us why we need to know what awaits us on the other side. "To know the *ba* souls of the Duat, to know what is done, to know the spiritual enlightenment of Re, to know the secret *ba* souls, to know what happens in the hours and their gods, to know what to say to them, to know the gates and the ways in which the great god passes . . . to know the flourishing and the annihilated."[7]

The underworld of the Egyptians may resemble the tomb, but actually it is neither above nor below. Calling it, more precisely, by its Egyptian name of neterworld signifies it as the world of divine beings.[8] While we enter this realm at death, this psychic space can be accessed in life through meditation, shamanic journey, and astral projection. The world we live in is a holograph made of light, sound, and energy vibrations.

Life and death are bound by laws of duality. The invisible space— the astral realm and the unconscious—is created at the same time that the outer, physical world is created. Where there is Earth, sky, and the starry heavens whose emanations we do see, there also are regions akin to Earth, sky, and the starry heavens that we do not see.

The portal to the grave, or the place where the sun sets in the Valley of the Kings, becomes the point of change. Light turns into darkness. We might also think of it in galactic terms as the point where the cosmic cataclysm known as the big bang spews forth its stream of light and matter on one side, or consumes light and matter into a black hole on the other side. At the opening to the grave, the conscious world that we knew in our daylit hours begins to consume itself and turn inside out. The hidden realm of Amentet can be perceived as air on Earth's upper crust, but inside the mountain of the Valley of the Kings, it becomes the phantasmagoria of the inner landscape.

AMUN IN THE UNDERWORLD OF THE NEW KINGDOM

In the creation myth of Thoth in Hermopolis, we saw eight beings floating in the cosmic soup. They were paired oppositions. The priests of Thebes took this idea of the eight beings at Hermopolis and merged it with the idea of the ouroboric serpent of Atum found at Heliopolis. The serpent became a being called Kamutef (the ka of his mother), and it preceded all creation, even the paired opposites. This great sea serpent was the desire nature or *ka* spirit of the Great Mother. It bore some resemblance to Tiamat, the writhing serpent of the Babylonians, or to the Chinese dragon, or to the wyrm in Beowulf. Kamutef, the bull snake of his mother, begat a serpent son, Irta. The three made a kind of underworld trinity: Mother, son, and spirit of the underworld.

This serpent's undulations set up the wave vibrations that created life. As with the serpent of Atum, the coils of Kamutef tried to envelop one in the underworld at life's end. The soul rode the undulations of the great serpent as if riding the cosmic waters in a boat. In particular, the dead were said to sail in the *hennu* boat (🛶) of Re.

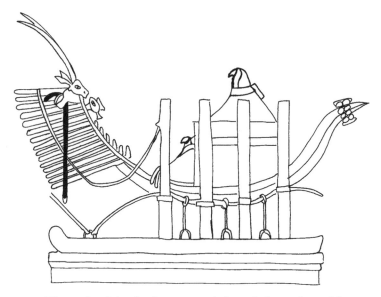

The souls of the dead were towed through the underworld
in the hennu *boat, the solar boat of Re.*

Like the undulations of the ithyphallic god Min, with whom Kamutef is also associated, the image suggests a sexual energy linked to the motif of repeated births. Kamutef kept up a constant cycle of renewal. The serpent power is the rising energy of sexual creation that begets renewal.[9] The ouroboros that eats its tail may also been seen as inserting its tail into its mouth, an image of copulation. Kamutef might be seen as the wriggling sperm, or tadpole energy, swimming in the primordial abyss. As the sperm reaches the ovum, perhaps the light of Re in this case, or what represents the other side of death, the serpentine tail detaches. It merges with the light.

At death, we are told, we detach from our bodies by detaching (breaking free) of the silver cord that has bound our true spiritual essence to this physical form. In other words, whether in life or in death, the snake must shed its skin to grow. What remains at the end of our lives is the serpent. The energy is not lost. It has just transformed, carrying us and our DNA, which is also not lost, to become the seed of rebirth or the stardust that begets other creations.

During ancient harvests in the city of Coptos, the priests walked with the pharaoh into the field to cut the first sheaf of wheat. Together they praised Amun, the hidden god; Min, the god of sexual energy; and Hathor, the mother goddess of the regenerative power of life. They said, "How mysterious is that which is done to her in the darkness."[10]

Amun's magical power began in the fluids of Nun, the cosmic soup. It suggests a magic inherent in the cosmic dust of the universe and in the plasma of all potential life-forms. Amun is the invisible life force coiled up inside the dark. Amun authored the universe and keeps the akashic records. Says Utterance 1146 of the Pyramid Texts: "I am the outflow of the Primeval Flood, he who emerged from the waters. I am the Provider of Attributes, the serpent with its many coils. I am the Scribe of the Divine Book, which says what has been and effects what is yet to be."[11]

BEINGS IN THE UNDERWORLD

At death what we have lost seems forever vanished from sight. The grief that Horus, the son of Osiris, expresses to the Earth god Geb during the ancient Osirian mystery play is palpable to any who has lost a parent. "They have put my father in the earth," he says. "They have made it necessary to bewail him."[12]

Horus, the child of Isis and Osiris, must rule Earth in his father's absence. Yet another son, Anubis, Osiris's firstborn son from his union with Nephthys, joins his father in the afterlife. As Osiris creates a space for the newly departed, Anubis becomes the psychopomp who guides their spirits through the Halls of Osiris.

Many of the hymns and prayers contained in the Book of Coming Forth by Day (Pert em Heru) offer a liturgy that we associate more with a book of common prayer. The underworld images that dance across the walls of Egyptian tombs, however, resemble something more akin to the Tibetan Book of the Dead. Phantasmagoric creatures greet us, drawing us into unfamiliar territories. Their images lend themselves to symbolic interpretation of an unconscious realm.

Apparently the heaviness of flesh creates a kind of amnesia that prevents us from knowing that what we have not faced in life will face us at death. The creatures appear to us as nightmares because we have forgotten the importance of working with synchronism and symbol in our waking life, or listening for messages from the dreamworld. The unconscious often uses frightening images that will not dissipate until at last we grasp their meaning. In a similar way, the Bible recounts Jacob wrestling with an angel (Genesis 32:22–31). The parable suggests that we cannot go further in our spiritual development until we have looked into the face of what has tormented us, saying, "I will not let you go until you bless me."

On the walls of the tomb, the serpent with three heads or the man with his head on backward are images, among others, of our disavowed selves. Their appearance in our nightmares and at death is divinely ordained. We must greet these fears and temptations. We must call them by name. We must know them, because it is through the encounter with them that our consciousness is changed.

At most underworld entrances and in many sarcophagus rooms, the black dogs Anubis and Upuaut appear. While Anubis prepares the human vessel for its entrance into the underworld, Upuaut guards the gateway and opens the way into altered states of being. These jackals appear as openers of the way as early as the First Dynasty of Egypt. The Dogon tribe of Sudan, who probably are linked to Egypt's early ancestors, have a strong connection to the star Sirius, the bright Dog Star, which appears in the constellation Canis Major. They know, for example, that there are actually two stars: Sirius A and Sirius B, which appear to circle each other.[13]

The Canis Major and Canis Minor constellations may repre-

Anubis is guardian of the mysteries of life after death.

sent Anubis and Upuaut, but the Dog Star itself, called Sothis by the Egyptians, is linked to Isis, and the hidden twin star may be linked to Nephthys. According to Egyptian myth, Nephthys may have birthed Anubis, but Isis raised him; thus he is connected to both sister goddesses and to Osiris as his son. The jackal opens the way for Osiris to both enter and exit the underworld. Sothis announces the reemergence of Osiris, as the constellation Orion begins to rise into the sky again during the dog days of August. His reappearance after having been underground for seventy-two days coincides with the seventy-two days of funerary preparation that the priests of Anubis performed for burial.

The dog as messenger from or guardian of the underworld is more than an Egyptian myth. It appears to have some validity in the psychological states of those in the process of dying. I have known many people, my mother included, who, at some time before their death, saw Anubis in the room. When Mother leaned up in her hospital bed and asked, "What's that dog doing here?" I knew her death was around the corner. Whether or not she knew it, I can't say. Anubis was with her for about three weeks.

When my friend Harold Moss, an Egyptian priest of Horus, on a different occasion saw and physically felt the dog, he immediately recognized him as Anubis. Although Harold's death was not immediate, he understood the appearance of Anubis and began preparing himself.

MANSIONS IN THE UNDERWORLD

The land where Osiris reigns has many names. The unconscious has a way of expanding and acquiring new chambers to discover. Certainly Egyptian ideas about the afterlife changed over the course of its three-thousand-year history. During the New Kingdom, Neter-Khert meant the "cemetery," the divine subterranean place, or literally, "the god's possessions." Amenta originally referred to the fifth division of the underworld, or the darkest, most treacherous hour of the night. Amenta was the place one was most likely to become stuck in inertia and never achieve rebirth. In Thebes, it became associated with the hidden land of the gods and with Manu, which simply meant "the western lands." In Saqqara and in the deserts of the Giza Plateau, Restau indicated the passages through the realm of the dead, which were overseen by Osiris. Raymond O. Faulkner defined it as "the place of the dragging." The Egyptian hieroglyph for Restau uses a sign for the ramp that leads to the tomb. On this ramp, the mummy and its shrines and burial furnishings were dragged by sledge to the tomb.[14]

During the time of the Pyramid Texts, and most likely well before it, there came into consciousness the Sekhet-hetep, or the Field of Peace, what the Greeks later called the Elysian Fields. Its first gateway was the Sekhet Iaru, or the Field of Reeds. It most closely resembled life as we know it on this side of Earth. To get there, one crossed the great divide, a river that resembled the Nile or the Milky Way. The river was said to lie "between the thighs of Nut." In the Sixth Dynasty Pyramid Text of Pepi I, Utterance 517 specifically asks for the king to be ferried over into a starry realm to live in joy with the gods forever.[15]

The rebirth of the soul seems linked to the thighs of Nut in that the Milky Way, or "the Cool Region," as Pharaoh Unas called it, was seen as the goddess herself. Where the Milky Way appears to break into two streams is a concave "womblike" area. In this place, the star Deneb appears during winter solstice. The winter solstice celebrates the conception of the divine. The summer solstice heralds the coming flood, which actually occurs nearly nine months later. These linked solstices and the inundation celebrate the renewal of the land, the conception and birth of the holy child, and finally the symbolic birthday of the pharaoh.[16] In the Fifth Dynasty Pyramid of Unas Text, Unas called the ferryman, and in this way, he gained entrance into the Sekhet Iaru.

Geb, the Earth god, first ruled the Sekhet Iaru. By the strength of his will—his gravity, so to speak—he either grasped the souls of the dead and retained them in his body or released them into heaven. In the Pyramid Text of Pepi I, Utterance 512 recounts that the realm of Geb consists of three things: "The Mounds of Horus, the Mounds of Seth and the Sekhet Iaru," or Field of Reeds.[17] During the Fifth Dynasty, the heavenly realms above belonged to the hawk god, Horus, and the subterranean realm below belonged to the serpent god, Seth. The Sekhet Iaru was a point of contact between the two gods.

In psychospiritual states, these realms may represent three states of being: the spiritual, the physical, and the borderland between the two. The way of Horus and the way of Seth are not in opposition; rather, they unify opposites. Heraclitus, perhaps citing the same mystery that gave us "as above, so below," said, "The path up and down is one and the same." Both spiritual and earthly experiences lead toward enlightenment. Death and birth are part of the one mystery. Our true purpose is union with the God who created us as a part of a divine natural world and as a reflection of its divine body.

AKHET AND DUAT

Inside the Pyramid of Unas lie two rooms that suggest two possible domains of the afterlife—Duat and Akhet. Both these realms become more developed in the later Coffin Texts, the Book of Gates, the Book of What Is in Duat, and other books of the dead. Egyptologist James P. Allen suggests that the sarcophagus room is the entrance into and exit from Duat and that the antechamber of the pyramid links with Akhet.[18]

Oriented on an east–west axis, Duat emphasizes the planets and stars at the horizon. This way of rebirth follows a solar, cyclical understanding of living and dying. Oriented toward the northern sky, Akhet represented the shining, radiant world of eternal light. The Pyramid Texts linked Akhet with the Imperishable Stars. Later, Akhet developed into a junction at the horizon between earth and sky, where a portal opens that provides us entrance into "Light Land." This opening into light may appear when the soul separates from the body. In any case, Akhet refers to the "place of becoming spirit," where our consciousness merges with the *akh* of higher mind.

The soul of the deceased travels to Akhet, the starry realm of the Imperishable Stars, by riding on the back of the Serpent in the Sky.

Through speculative astronomer-Egyptologists like Adrian Gilbert, Robert Bauval, and Graham Hancock, we can see that such geophysical structures as the pyramids are arranged in imitation of celestial objects. By observing celestial events, the ancient priest-astronomer perceived propitious moments when cracks between the worlds appeared and the gods came closer. The three pyramids on the Giza Plateau by day mirror the three shining stars in the belt of Orion (Osiris) at night.[19] Solstices and equinoxes marked the spiritual opening and closing of the gateways into divine realms. If changes in the heavens reflect changes on Earth, isn't it possible that our human transformations on Earth are reflected both in heaven and in the environment in which we live? We are discovering more frequently that a change in consciousness indeed does create a change within the physical structure of matter.

DUAT AND THE ENTRANCE INTO OTHER DIMENSIONS

The most commonly understood definition of Duat was the land that existed beyond the entrance to the tomb. Simultaneously, Duat (sometimes Tuat) was that region inside the body of Nut. Within Duat were many mansions, including the Halls of Ma'at. Rising flames guarded the portal into Duat. Serpents of flame guarded further entrances and exits through the halls of the underworld. In Saqqara, between the tomb of Unas and the Heb-Sed Festival courtyard we find a row of rearing cobras. These cobras indicate the great mystery of transformation that took place there—an initiation and opening into realms beyond ordinary reckoning.

The gateway to Duat is the gateway of *dua* or dawn. Dua also means "tomorrow," symbolized as the rise of the morning star, a phrase Egyptologist Alexandre Piankoff has translated as the One of the Morning—⌂✹. Dawn is a crack between worlds, a gateway into the future. It is the concept of the true Stargate. Dua leads to the gods through a fiery, dangerous, and transformative gateway into the plane of spiritual light. Every initiation into the mysteries of God involves a dark night of the soul and a trial by fire before attaining enlightenment or seeing the dawning light.

During the Middle Kingdom, the Coffin Texts deemphasize Akhet. The books of the afterlife focused more on the subterranean elements ruled by Osiris inside the Duat. An Osirian afterlife was offered to everyone; the deceased even referred to himself as "an Osiris." This underworld was filled with threatening beings, traps, and snares that the dead struggled to overcome. The Coffin Texts spells gave the dead protection against these dangers and kept him from "dying a second death."

The Nineteenth Dynasty pharaoh Seti I (1314–1304 BCE), father of Ramses II and grandfather of the high priest magician Khaemwast, elevated these texts to their highest artistic level since the Pyramid Texts. His beautifully executed Temple to Osiris at Abydos employs symbolic architectural design. (Please see plate 35 of the color insert for an image of Seti I.) The portraits inside the seven shrine chapels show obvious reverence for the mystery rites of Osiris depicted on every wall of the temple. In the hypostyle hall of Abydos, sunlight streams through the ceiling to illuminate specific texts on the columns and walls. Seti I offers incense to Osiris in one scene, and makes an offering to Amun Re, the hidden god whose airy attributes include the feathers on his head and the sky blue color of his skin. In a separate scene, the divine family appears as a trinity and includes the seated Osiris, his wife Isis, and their son Horus. In yet another, Sekhmet stands with Seti I.

Seti's tomb in the Valley of the Kings—the longest (three hundred feet), deepest, and most beautiful tomb in the valley—became the model for every tomb that came after it. Every square inch of the tomb has been plastered and brightly painted. From its corridors and side chapels to the astronomical ceilings, the art of the tomb is more than decoration; it is a way of magically conveying spiritual truths that only symbol can impress upon the psyche. Alexandre Piankoff quotes German philosopher Karl Jaspers as saying, "The ideas which man evolves about God are not God himself. Yet the divinity is to be brought to our consciousness with the help of notions [symbols]."[20]

In the tomb of Merenptah, Seti I's grandson, there appear to be seven distinct layers to the tomb design, which includes four corridors, a pit, a pillared hall, an antechamber, and a sarcophagus room. (Seti I's tomb actually extends farther than the sarcophagus room, going down to the water table, a detail we will explore soon.) The seven layers may be linked to the seven portals in the Book of Gates, or to the seven shrines and coffins that contain the mummy and the seven spiritual bodies of the Egyptian tradition, as identified by psychospiritual researcher Robert Masters. Notably there are also seven scorpions who guard Isis, seven Hathors, seven rays of gold from the hieroglyph *nub* 𓇳. When Seth tore his brother Osiris into bits and threw them into the Nile, seven parts floated into Upper Egypt and seven parts into Lower Egypt. Seven was a number of great reverence to the Egyptians.

ENTERING THE TOMB

On the lintel above the doorway to the tomb, the sun god Amun-Re and the beetle god Khepera stand enclosed in the golden orb of the sun. The sun disk is flanked by Isis and Nephthys. Just inside the door, Isis and Nephthys kneel on the hieroglyph for the word *gold,* which depicts a necklace and golden ingots. Nub not only means gold; it also means that which can be molded into form, and it (Nub) was synonymous with the word *master.* One who knows the secret transformative alchemy of Duat indeed is transmuted and becomes a master alchemist as well as master of one's own destiny. He becomes a golden being.

The first two corridors of the tomb contain row upon row of the text known as the Litany of Re, which offers us the Secret of Osiris Becoming Re. In it, we learn how the two *ba* souls embrace each other so that life and death merge, becoming one being known as the One Joined Together, or the Djeba of Osiris-Re. The text begins at the tomb entrance on the left-hand wall and goes down to the end of the second corridor, where it wraps around and runs on the right-hand wall, coming back up the stairs so that the text ends on the wall opposite from where it began. This is but one graphic example of the great turnaround in which a world depicted one way flips and becomes its complementary opposite.

In fact, the entire experience of walking through the worlds of Duat is a bit like Alice falling down the rabbit hole, and if viewed that way, its illogic begins to take on an impressionistic interpretation of the difference between inner life and outer life. In Duat, when the celestial stars drop below the horizon, they are still stars (dua, ⭐), but are seen as a star having been enclosed inside a dark space (Duat, ⊕).

In their book *Heaven's Mirror,* Graham Hancock and Santha Faiia suggests that Duat has specific celestial coordinates connected to the eastern horizon. They note that the Pyramid Texts tell us that Sahu, the Orion constellation that represents Osiris, purifies himself in light on the horizon. Egyptologist Selim Hassan points out that "[t]his is a true observation of nature, and it really appears as though the stars are swallowed up each morning by the increasing glow of the dawn."[21]

The stars continue to exist in Duat as the constellations fall below the western horizon and circle the equator. If we imagine the earth plane encircled by the orbs of sun, moon, and stars, we come to a midway point in the journey where the celestial ones turn upside down—an understandable idea since people standing at polar opposite locales around the globe all stand with their feet affixed by gravity to Earth's center. The star has five appendages (resembling people) in Egyptian art precisely because the starry realm is also the realm of human souls. Thus, if the upside-down five-pointed human stars were seen from a vast distance in space, those above the equatorial plane might look like this ✵; and those below the equatorial plane might look like this ✵. The pentagram becomes a logical expression for the human light and star shine in Duat at the moment of turnaround.

Professor John Darnell, who has spent most of his life teaching at the Yale Egyptological Institute in Egypt, suggests that in Duat when stars drop below the horizon, they continue in an "attitude the inverse of that in which they rose above the opposite horizon."[22] It is an upside-down netherworld. The stars have turned over, and it happens that they will turn over again and right themselves.

In a cosmic sense, this is the hidden energy of Atum, the god of nothingness and first matter, that spews forth life and then sucks life back into itself. Atum is both the big bang and dark matter universe. It is toward Atum that we ride through to the other side of consciousness. Thus the Litany of Re includes all the forms of light—even those that are invisible. In Duat, we find the names and the ways that light vibration can be manifested, molded, and shaped by experience. These names of Re are the alchemical means of turning dark matter into light, or lead into gold, or shaping the denser vibrations of form into the higher vibrations of light.

THE LITANY OF RE

The Litany of Re lists the names of the seventy-four manifestations of divine light, including the Brilliant One, the Hidden One, the Ever Becoming One, the Watcher, the Traveler, and the Wind in the Souls, among many other names or forms that belong to other divine beings such as Geb, Sekhmet, Isis, Horus, and so on. Each is addressed with a prayer, saying, "You are a soul like the second self of Re."[23]

Again, in complementary action, the body of the mummy was declared divine—every part of its flesh taken into the spiritual body of Osiris-Re and made holy. Such divine recognitions include, "His breast is the Becoming One (Kheperi)," "His breast is the Opener of the Ways," "His phallus is Exalted Earth," "His two feet are He Who Passes through the Mysteries," "His toes are the Two Cobras."[24]

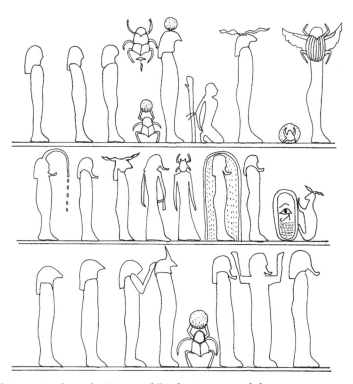

This portion from the Litany of Re depicts some of the seventy-two souls in Duat that are forms of Re.

When one's members become gods, one becomes a god from head to toe. This living body of light is called the Aufu Re. The Litany of Re closed with a coda: "He who reads this book will be purified at the hour of darkness when Re rests in the hidden lands of the west, when Re joins the west of the hidden names. Very true."[25]

THE BOOK OF WHAT IS IN DUAT

After maneuvering two flights of stairs, the third corridor of Seti's tomb begins with scenes from the Book of What Is in Duat. The exquisite bas-relief text splays along these walls, runs above a deeply dug pit, spills over into the chapels dug on either side of the corridor, and even appears in the final sarcophagus chamber. The stairs in every tomb are not inconsequential. Carved into the bedrock, the stairs not only allow access to the deeper regions of the tomb, but this architectural feature also has been used as a symbol of spiritual attainment since the Third Dynasty, when Imhotep built his Step Pyramid for Pharaoh Djoser.

The stairway to heaven, or the ladder as seen in the Pyramid Text of Unas, suggests, among other things, that ascension requires effort. A staircase, especially one as long and steep as this one, must be climbed through effort and force of will. In this situation, having been carried into the underworld, one has to climb out to some degree through one's own volition. The gods will meet us halfway, but we travel by our own efforts the rest of the way. Unas's ladder was held by the gods Horus and Seth, but it was he who had to climb it! The hieroglyph for stairs (reth ⌐⌐), is also the hieroglyph applied to all things that grow, and so it was intended to call to mind the idea of reaching and moving upward, of striving, of growing toward light as plants do. Growth is a matter that comes from within.

Twelve scenes depict the solar journey through the twelve dark, hidden hours of night. The portal to each hour is guarded by a serpent and a goddess. Re travels each night into this land filled with magical entrances, pitfalls, and snares—an upside-down world where one could easily become disoriented. We must learn to right ourselves and recall the purpose of this journey. What draws us onward is the knowledge that there is light at the end of the tunnel. At every entrance, we are becoming the light we seek.

The book's transformative text, its 741 names and images of underworld deities and other details, runs along the floor in three registers. In the middle register, the boat of the sun is conveyed along the waters of the Nun, which represents a collective unconscious rather than a personal one. The boat may be seen as our body, a physical vehicle that has carried us through life. The inner light of Re has always been contained in this shrine. The body (the container) floats along the collective unconscious that runs not only through this physical life but also arises from a mysterious wellspring that we cannot see and returns to a realm of mystery at the end of our life cycle.

The boat carries us out of this life experience as surely as the coffin of Osiris floated down the Nile and was carried out to sea. In dreams, we experience similar transport and vehicles that contain our identities and experiences. The modern dreamscape uses automobiles, airplanes, and trains, but the metaphor remains the same. In ancient times, the Dog Star Sirius, in the form of Isis led the hennu boat that carried Osiris into and out of the underworld. In the night sky below the Dog Star, we find Argo, the constellation of the ship. This is the ship in which Jason and the Argonauts sailed on a similarly fantastical journey through the psyche. Even in the cloying dark of the tomb, the inner light still shines, and the boat is steered along the seas steady as she goes.

Even so, the dead are not without danger. During the fourth hour of the night, the journey takes a dramatic shift. The pit opens beneath us, and from the upper register, the coffin appears to slide down a ramp into the dark space below. Dangerous creatures and supernatural beings, enemies of Osiris and the dead, fill Duat. They are aspects of Seth. Forces of decay, terror, and chaos are led by Apopis, who is an enormous snake with many coils. The light is weak, and the coffin slips into the depths.

Thus the chthonic serpents appear. Some have three heads, or two heads, or heads where tails should be; some have human heads and legs. The boat transforms itself into a two-headed serpent with a snake's head at either prow. Some of our terrors are collective, and some are our own personal dragons to slay. Rather than sailing or floating, the boat has to be towed across a sand bar or an island, and it will take serpent energy to move this boat across the hot desert sand. A key to understanding serpent energy is to consider how snakes move: because of the way serpents' scales are made, they are one of the few creatures that must eternally move forward. It is impossible for a serpent to move backward. In this darkness and silence, there is nothing except the sound of one's own voice speaking to helpers one cannot see, but prayers are there, naming the darkness to overcome it. Faith sustains us, and in such darkness, the conscious mind must continue to call out to name the unconscious.

In this fourth hour, the ibis god Thoth and the hawk god Sokar hold between them the solar Eye of Horus. This darkness represents the blindness that all souls need to admit to in order to overcome it. The eye is the symbol of wholeness and unification. As healers and shamans, Thoth and Sokar assure us that this darkness is part of the healing process. We are being made whole. We are being taught how to see rightly, to see with new eyes. We are mastering the serpent energy of desire, the underbelly of the snake. We are learning that we are creators of our experience.

Here, before we move into the fifth hour, is the portal to which Si-Osire took his father Khaemwast to witness the hinge of the door that was eternally embedded in the wounded eye of the rich man who mistreated others. His blindness to others followed him into Duat. Again the Book of AmDuat reminds us that it is good to learn these lessons and truths about ourselves and the unconscious before we need them. "Whoever knows it is one with right paths."[26]

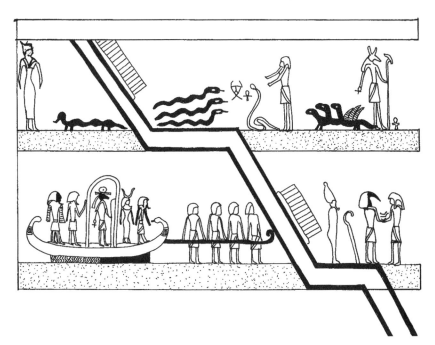

The Fourth Hour of the Night from the Book of What Is in Duat. Here we see the coffin's treacherous slide from the opening of the tomb down into the underworld, a descent that continues into the darkest levels. Note the eye that the god Thoth is offering to the hawk god (bottom right). It will grow in strength through Duat.

THE DARKEST HOURS OF THE NIGHT

The Fifth Hour of Night and the Fifth Pylon of the Book of Gates became the most important texts of the afterlife. They represent one of the darkest hours of the night and the place of deepest inertia. Both books appear in Seti I's tomb. Here Horus escorts Seti into the presence of Osiris. Here the traveler in the underworld comes to a pyramid or mound of earth surrounded by water. Here is the moment of possible regeneration and renewal, if all goes well. It symbolizes Zep Tepi, that moment when the new Earth rises from the primordial floodwaters. The text of the fifth gate/hour on the tomb wall seems unusual. It nearly always appears next to the gate for the twelfth hour, confirming the idea that our entry into eternal life and our return to light hinges on this fifth hour of trial. The boat of Re no longer sails and must be hauled through the underworld. The exceedingly long tow rope held by gods and goddesses must mean something like "the gods are pulling for you."

Inside the cavern of Sokar and enclosed by the twin Earth gods Aker, we find a winged serpent with the head of Osiris at its tail. The feet of Sokar stand upon its back, and the three heads of Re (Harakhty, Re, Atum) appear at its head. They represent the dawn, noon, and evening light. Perhaps they also represent birth, life, and death (completion), or past, present, and future. At this time, one learns that any future life depends upon the reintegration of past life experiences into renewed life. When the spirit is eternal, it becomes essential to "get it right." The soul must gain mastery over its personal blindness. Doing so leads to a glimmer that presages the return of light.

The entire cavern is lit by flames that arise from the mouth of Isis—great magic, indeed. A lake of fire seems to enclose this place, but hieroglyphically, it is both cool water and fire, a union that Eric Hornung and Theodor Abt define as "a blessing or sheer destruction, depending on the attitude of the person toward this other world."[27] In this hour of the night, one's resistance to transformation can have dire consequences.

In the tomb of Seti I, a passageway extends downward and beyond the sarcophagus room into the deepest part of the mountain. In this corridor, the sixth, seventh, and eighth hours of the night occur. The sixth hour represents the midnight hour, the moment of greatest darkness in which transformation occurs. The two eyes of Re appear, and one's vision is restored as well as the possibility of perspective and depth of field, which cannot be accomplished with only one eye. These eyes are depicted as being small, but they will grow in strength. By the eleventh hour, they have become those two strong eyes that peer outside through the false door of the tomb, looking again into the outer world.

By learning to see in the dark, we shall have increased our vision of the tasks required of the spiritual life. The god Thoth offers an ibis to a goddess who holds the pupils of the sun in her hands behind her back. The kind of seeing we are meant to have is that of Sia, the wisdom of the spiritual eyes, rather than the vision of physical eyes. These spiritual eyes are those that guide a man "to his fields," that is, into conscious life. Again, this is a task best performed by the living. Here one reconnects with the ancestors, incorporating the lessons of those who have come before us, gleaning their wisdom, acknowledging their experience as necessary for our own continued, conscious renewal.

The *khat,* or corpse, is bound up inside the body of a five-headed serpent and carried away. It is only an empty container. It is what the container holds that matters. The ouroboric serpent, whose name is Tail in the Mouth, resembles the Old Serpent that encircled Atum in the waters of the Nun just before creation. The serpent encircles the fluid of future life. This is a womb in which something new is being made—perhaps a new life or a new container for spiritual understanding.

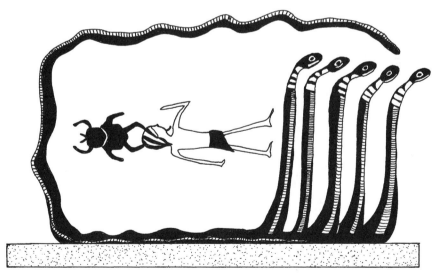

The darkest hour of the night depicts the khat *inside the coils of the five-headed serpent of darkness, but upon his head is the dung beetle Khepera, which even in the darkest hour represents the power of alchemical transformation.*

The Osiris that entered the tomb with Re at sunset now merges at midnight with Atum, the creative principle of the universe. When spiritual knowledge is consciously attached to form, we have the birth of enlightened leaders. Osiris is the ba soul of Re, we are told. The two of them merged become the *djeba,* literally the body-soul.[28] Osiris is the container for the soul of Re, and the work of creating and birthing enlightened leaders conscious of their purposeful regeneration is a part of the mystery of this realm. The child of Khaemwast, Si-Osire, known to us through the ancient Egyptian stories of his magical actions, was depicted as just such a master teacher. His name means "One Osiris-Re," indicating through his name that he was born an enlightened being. He has unified oppositions and incorporated both identities into one body.

We have come now to the hours in the Book of What Is in Duat when the turnaround occurs. As we move upward, returning toward the light again, conscious awareness returns. The hours seven through

During the final hour of the night, death has been conquered. The all-seeing eyes know the two ways of Duat, but more importantly the soul now sees with spiritual eyes what was hidden from view on Earth. At last, the conquered serpent carries the ba soul to eternal life in the skies.

twelve bring us back to the surface, to Akhet and the gate on the eastern horizon. Much happens here, but the hardest part is over. More can be read about these hours in *Knowledge for the Afterlife* by Theodor Abt and Eric Hornung. Suffice it to say that here the darkness has been tapped and an opening has been made through which the light might begin to shine and lead us home.

Si-Osire and
the Ethiopian Magician

The legends of Si-Osire and Khaemwast take place during the reign
of Ramses III (1279–1213 BCE) of the New Kingdom. By this time,
Egypt had already experienced two intermediary periods of chaos and
disruption. These intermediary periods mark the transitions between
the Old Kingdom and the Middle Kingdom and between the Middle
Kingdom and the New Kingdom.

According to the temple scenes in Luxor, Medinet Habu, Abydos,
Karnak, and elsewhere, the pharaoh met his enemies in battle on multiple fronts. The Hittites, the Syrians, and Asiatic tribes from the east
presented challenges as did the Libyans from the west and African
tribes from the south. Ramses II intended to impress the Nubians and
Ethiopians with his might by building a monument at Abu Simbel.
Carved into the side of a mountain, his statues rose sixty-seven feet
high. Inside the darkened inner sanctum, Ramses II appeared seated
as a god with three other omnipotent divinities—Amun, Ra-Harakhty,
and Ptah.

Drought and famine, along with the invasion of the sea peoples,
brought an end to the reign of Ramses and his descendants. There
followed a Third Intermediate period of disruption and chaos that
included split rulership between the north and south. The country
became divided into two distinct regions, and the Libyan and Nubian
rulers variously traded predominance. For the last one hundred years

This eighteenth-century talismanic scroll from Ethiopia depicts a sorcerer using serpent magic. Many healing scrolls, created and used by traditional diviners, include handwritten texts—protective prayers, spell-casting formulas—interspersed with drawn and painted images. The box that forms this figure's nose bears a striking similarity to images of the coffin of Osiris floating above the waters in the underworld and surrounded by the coils of a great serpent.

of the Third Intermediate period, the Nubians reigned from the south. It was not until 664 BCE that Late Kingdom ruler Psamtik I reunited Egypt into its final glory days.

While the tales of Khaemwast assume a historical context, in all probability the text was written several centuries after the fact. It may allude to the conflicts with the Nubian rulers, using the reference to Khaemwast, Ramses the Great's son, as a reminder of true Egyptian magic and power.

On one level, the tale simply assures the listener of the power and influence of Egypt, but the tales of Si-Osire are more than that. Their true themes illuminate the struggle between chaos and order. The world is set aright not simply by magic but by true words of power whose origin comes from a right alignment with the creative power and the will of God.

The tale of Si-Osire and the Ethiopian magician exhibits explicit spiritual knowledge as well as some remarkable psychic feats. These demonstrations include the power of affirmations, spirit communication, dream interpretation, and intuitive gifts, as well as the possibility of remote viewing, astral flight, reincarnation, and the reading of akashic records. In some ways, the twelve-year-old Si-Osire is similar to the story of the boy Jesus, who at age twelve began to teach the learned scholars in the temple of "his father's house" in Jerusalem (Luke 2:39–52). Both precocious children demonstrated a knowledge that comes not from books but from the heart.

Each divine and magical child was born into earthly form to set things aright again through personal sacrifice. As each child commits himself to a higher calling, he knows that this means forsaking his earthly family. The message each must demonstrate to the world at large is this: death can be overcome. Says Si-Osire, "I entered (into earthly form) with the idea of returning to be born in the world to enact magic against the old enemy." Si-Osire accepts the fact of his rebirth or resurrection in the same way that Jesus the Christ showed himself to his disciples as resurrected in spirit, promising to return again.

The Q source of the Luke 2:41–49 gospel probably was written in Greek during the first century CE. The tales of Si-Osire, while they reference the New Kingdom, first appeared in demotic script during the Greco-Roman period (305 BCE–395 CE). It is possible that the Christian Nag Hammadi texts found in Egypt share a common thread with the ancient Egyptian wisdom teachings of Si-Osire.

Here is that ancient story.[1]

One day, soon after Khaemwast had presented Si-Osire to his father, Pharaoh Ramses II, an Ethiopian sorcerer appeared in the court at the royal palace in Memphis. He stood before the princes, the military generals, and the sages, and to each he said, "On my body is a sealed letter for the pharaoh."

The Ethiopian was brought before the pharaoh, at which time he presented his challenge to Egypt. "Is there someone who can read this letter that I have brought to Egypt for the pharaoh? Its contents must be read without opening the seal. If there is no high priest, scribe, or magician in all of Egypt who can do so, I will return to Ethiopia and spread the news of Egypt's weakness all across my country."

The courtiers glanced at each other, embarrassed and confused by the challenge. None could name any place where such a magi existed. "By Ptah," each asked the other, "isn't there one scribe swift of hand and mind who can read the sealed letter? Is it even possible?"

Then the pharaoh said, "Bring my son, the high priest Khaemwast."

When Khaemwast appeared, he bowed low to the pharaoh and offered the king his blessings. The pharaoh said, "My son, an Ethiopian sorcerer has come to my court and demanded to know if there is one holy man in Egypt who can read his letter without breaking its seal. Can it be done?"

Khaemwast was baffled by this request. Although he could think of no such wise man either, he did not want Egypt's incompetence spread about Ethiopia. "Give me ten days and let me see what I can do," he said.

Because he would need some privacy to combat the evil Ethiopian's sorcery against Egypt, the pharaoh set aside a special place for Khaemwast to think and work his magic. Still, the pharaoh was worried. He left the court followed by his troubles that sent him to bed and kept him from drinking and eating. Khaemwast went straight to his apartments having no idea what to do. He, too, buried himself in covers from head to toe. Where could he find such a magician to counter the Ethiopian?

When Mehusekhe, his wife, heard the news, she hurried to the apartments where she found the high priest lying in a heap of bedclothes. She reached out to him, but he was quiet and cold as death. "My husband," she said, "why are you cold and still? Are you sick? Are you brokenhearted?"

"Go away, Mehusekhe," he said. "What grieves me is no matter for a woman."

Mehusekhe sent in Si-Osire, who stood over his father, saying, "My father, why are you depressed? Tell me the troubles that you have bottled up in your heart and I will make them cease."

"Don't bother about the things in my heart, son. You are too young— only twelve years old. Worry about yourself, not me."

"Tell me," persisted Si-Osire, "so that I may lighten your heart."

The high priest thought for a moment before saying, "Son, an Ethiopian sorcerer has come to Egypt carrying a sealed letter around his neck. He demands that an Egyptian magician read the letter without opening it. If no one can be found to do so, then he will humiliate Egypt in the land of Ethiopia. That is why my heart is sad."

When Si-Osire heard this, he laughed for a long time.

The high priest grew angry. "Why are you laughing?"

"I am laughing," said Si-Osire, "because you are berating yourself over such a small matter. Get up, father. I can read the Ethiopian's letter, and I will know what is written there without breaking its seal."

Khaemwast threw off the covers and sat up. "What? Is that the truth?"

Si-Osire told his father to go to the library downstairs and take out any book of his choosing. "I will stay up here in this room and read the book in your hand without even seeing it." Khaemwast hurried to the library and took down book after book. Each book Si-Osire read without having seen it and without Khaemwast having opened it. When Khaemwast returned to his apartments, he was elated. Together the two of them hurried to tell the good news to the pharaoh, who prepared a feast for Khaemwast and his brilliant, magical son.

The next day, the pharaoh gathered his court and ordered the sorcerer of Ethiopia to be brought in with the sealed letter on his body. The sorcerer stood in the middle of the gathering. The boy Si-Osire came out and stood near him. He looked the sorcerer up and down, then said, "You sad man. May Amun strike you! Here you've come from Ethiopia into the beautiful gardens of Osiris, stood at the footstool of the rising sun, Harakhty, and avowed to curse Egypt's shining spirit by trying to humiliate us among your people."

The sorcerer eyed the boy in turn. "I see the inspiration of Amun has come over you. What I have to say is written in this letter. Do not lie about what is written there in front of your king!"

"Nor will you lie," said the boy. At this, the two agreed.

Now a hush fell over the court. When Si-Osire spoke at last, all leaned forward to hear. "The letter hanging about the sorcerer's neck says: Once Pharaoh Menkhepera Si-Amun ruled as a beneficent king and the land overflowed with good things. The king gave back in abundance and built great temples.

"Then one day while the ruler was in Nubia surveying and assessing the crops in the fields of Amun, he overheard three Ethiopian sorcerers conspiring. One said in a loud voice, 'If it weren't for the fact that Amun or the king would kill me, I would cast a spell over Egypt to make its people suffer three days and three nights never seeing any more light than that from a castor oil lamp.'

"Another said, 'If it weren't for the fact that Amun and the king could tear me to pieces, I would cast my magic over Egypt and bring its pharaoh to Ethiopia where I'd have his back beaten with five hundred blows of the stick in front of the viceroy. Then in six hours precisely, I'd send him back to Egypt—beaten and bloody.'

"Said the third, 'Were it not for fear of death, I would seize Egypt with my magic and make the land infertile for three years.'

"When the viceroy heard what the three Ethiopians had said, he ordered them to be brought to his court. He demanded to know who would cast a spell over Egypt and create darkness for three days.

"'It was Hor, the son of the Sow,' they said.

"'Who would use a spell to bring the pharaoh to my court in Nubia, publicly scourge him with five hundred lashes, and promptly return him to Egypt?'

"'It was Hor, the son of the Negress,' they replied.

"'Who would use magic to make the fields of Egypt infertile for three years?'

"'It was Hor, the son of the princess,' they replied.

"The viceroy told Hor, the son of the Negress, 'Put your spell in writing. I swear by Amun and the bull of Meroe that if your work satisfies me, I'll shower you with all good things.'

"Hor, the son of the Negress, made four wax ushabti, said words of power over them, gave them breath and the figures came alive. 'Go to Egypt,' he commanded them. 'Grab the pharaoh and bring him to the palace of the viceroy, then beat him five hundred blows in front of the court before you carry him back to Egypt.'

"The bewitched ushabti went straight to Egypt by night, overpowered the pharaoh, and carried him to the land of the Nubians. Before the viceroy, he was beaten five hundred times with a stick, then returned to Egypt precisely in six hours."

Si-Osire stopped his narration and looked at the Ethiopian sorcerer who stood before the court of Ramses. "Swear by the inspiration of Amun that moves through you. Is the story I am telling truly written in your letter?"

"Every word of it," said the sorcerer. "Continue."

Si-Osire turned to the pharaoh. "After the ushabti had returned Pharaoh Si-Amun to Egypt with his rear end beaten and in pain, the pharaoh lay down in the shrine in the Temple of Horus. When his courtiers arrived in the morning, the pharaoh asked them, 'What happened to Egypt and to me during the night?'

"The courtiers chided him, treating him as if he had lost his mind. 'You are well, oh pharaoh, oh great one. The goddess Isis will ease your troubled mind. We are not sure what you mean, oh pharaoh, oh great lord. Just now you were lying down in front of the shrine of Horus begging for protection.'

"The king rose and showed his courtiers his bruised back side. 'By god, some creatures took me to Nubia last night. Someone beat me with five hundred blows of the stick in front of the viceroy and six hours later I'm back in Egypt.'

"When they saw his beaten hind parts, the courtiers gasped. They called the high priest and librarian, Hor, who was Si-Amun's son by his wife Paneshe. He was a highly learned man. When he came to the palace and took one look at the pharaoh, he said, 'My lord, this is the work of Ethiopian sorcerers. I must use my magic to find them and expel them.'

"'Quickly then!' said the king. 'Save me from Nubia's sorcery this night.'

"The librarian magician Hor, son of Paneshe, returned with his books and amulets to the pharaoh's quarters. Reciting spells, he fastened his amulets to the king's arm. Then Hor sailed to Hermopolis, entered the temple there, made his offerings, and poured libations before Thoth, the great, great, great, great, great, thrice-greatest god and lord of Hermopolis. 'Look favorably on me, Thoth,' he prayed. 'Do not let the Ethiopians humiliate Egypt. You, oh Thoth, possess the magic of writing. You suspended the heavens and made the earth. You established the underworld and placed the gods among the stars. Grant me the wisdom and the means to save pharaoh from these sorceries.'

"That night he slept in the temple. In a dream Thoth said to him, 'Hor, son of Paneshe, librarian of Pharaoh Si-Amun, when morning comes, go to the library of this Temple of Hermopolis. There you will find a closed and sealed box. Open it. Open the next box therein. In that lies a scroll of papyrus, written with my own hand. Copy it and return it to its place. This is the Book of Magic, which has protected me from the impious. It will protect the pharaoh from the sorceries of the Ethiopians.'

"When Hor awoke from his dream, he did everything that he had been told. Hurrying back to the palace, he made for the pharaoh an amulet inscribed with a spell against sorcery. The next day arrived. The enchanted ushabti of Hor, the son of the Negress, returned to Egypt that night and went straight to the place where the pharaoh lay sleeping, but they could not overpower him because of the amulets, so they returned to the viceroy empty-handed.

"The next morning the pharaoh told Hor, the son of Paneshe, everything that he had seen that night—how the Ethiopian sorcerers had turned away, unable to get power over him. Now Hor, son of Paneshe, ordered pure and abundant wax brought to him. He made a group of ushabti and pronounced spells over them. When he breathed on them, they came to life, and he said, 'Go to Nubia tonight. Bring the viceroy back to Egypt to the palace of the pharaoh. After he has been beaten with five hundred blows of the stick, send him back to Nubia within six hours.'

"Then the countersorcery of Hor, son of Paneshe, traveled swiftly to Nubia hidden in the clouds of night. The Egyptian ushabti overpowered the viceroy, carried him back to Egypt, beat him in front of the pharaoh five hundred times; then they returned him home within six hours."

Si-Osire had held his audience rapt with his story. Now the people of Egypt held their breath as they heard him demand an answer from the sorcerer. "The power of Amun is upon you, O wicked sorcerer from Ethiopia. Are the words I have spoken written in your letter?"

The Ethiopian bowed, touching his forehead to the ground. "Every word. Keep reading."

"After the beating," Si-Osire read, "and after they had carried the viceroy home, they lay him down on the floor of the palace. He rose in great pain the next morning. 'They beat me with five hundred blows of the stick before the pharaoh of Egypt,' he complained. He showed his princes his back, and they cried aloud. The viceroy ordered them to bring Hor, son of the Negress, to him. 'May Amun curse you. May the bull of Meroe curse you! You told the Egyptians how we made magic against them. Now how will you save me from the hand of Hor, son of Paneshe?'

"The Ethiopian sorcerer bound an amulet to the viceroy's wrist to save him from Hor, son of Paneshe. The next night when the ushabti of the Egyptians traveled to Nubia, they were able to carry off the viceroy, beat him before the pharaoh five hundred times, then take him back to Nubia, all within six hours. This went on for three days. The Ethiopian sorcerer was unable to save the viceroy from the magic of Hor, son of Paneshe.

"In deep anguish, he ordered Hor, the son of the Negress, to be brought. 'Woe to you, enemy from Ethiopia. Your sorcery is no good. You've humiliated me by the hand of the Egyptians. By Amun and the bull of Meroe, if you can't save me from the astral flight of their magicians, I will have you put to death.'

"'Master,' cried the sorcerer. 'Send me to Egypt to confront this magician. I'll put my hand against his. He will see the scorn I hold for his skill.'

"After the sorcerer was sent away, he went to his mother, the Negress. She warned him, 'If you go to Egypt to do sorcery, be careful. You aren't able to do battle with their magic. Don't let them catch you or you'll never see Ethiopia again.'

"Her son ignored her pleading. 'Besides,' he said, 'there is no way to avoid going. I'll have to use my magic.'

"'In that case,' his mother said, 'should they catch you, we will have agreed on several signs between us. If you fail to return, I will come to you and see if I can save you.'

"They decided that if Hor were to be overcome while his mother was eating, her cup of water would turn to blood, her food would turn the color of flesh, and the sky would turn blood red. With that settled, Hor filled himself and his satchel with every kind of magic he could find, going to all the temples of Amun and every temple along the length of the river all the way down to Memphis. He tried to move about stealthily, but the pharaoh's men caught him and brought him before the angry king.

'Ho! You who use magic against me while the people of Egypt look on, you spell-speaking scribe in the house of life who casts spells and counterspells for the viceroy, bring him to me!' In the corner of the pharaoh's court, the Egyptian magician stood, listening and watching.

"Then Hor, son of Paneshe, called out to the sorcerer. 'Ho! Enemy from Ethiopia, aren't you Hor, the son of the Negress, whom I saved from drowning in the reeds of Re? You and your companion from Ethiopia were gurgling in the water. You were thrown down a hill east of Heliopolis. Do you regret my freeing the pharaoh from your beatings? Have you come to Egypt to battle with magic against me? As Amun is my witness, the gods of Heliopolis and Egypt have brought you here in order to punish you in retaliation.'

"When Hor, son of the Negress, heard the voice of Hor, son of Paneshe, he answered, 'So is that you, to whom I taught the jackal language, who does sorcery against me?' Then the Ethiopian invoked a spell causing fire to erupt in the pharaoh's court. The princes of Egypt gasped and ran to the sacred library, saying, 'Hurry! Do something.'

"Hor, son of Paneshe, invoked a spell that opened the sky causing a southern rain to fall over the flame and extinguish it instantly.

"Again the Ethiopian spoke words of power and caused a dark, roaring cloud to descend upon the court. So strong was the wind and thick was the darkness no one could see his companion at his side. Hor, son of Paneshe, recited his spell to the sky and the evil wind stopped; the darkness cleared.

"Then Hor, the son of the Negress, used his most powerful magical spell, causing a great slab of stone to appear in the sky above the pharaoh's head. It was 200 cubits in length and 50 cubits wide. He commanded it to fall upon the pharaoh and his princes, thereby leaving Egypt without any king. Pharaoh looked at the vault of stone above him, and a cry flew from his gaping mouth and those of his courtiers. Quickly the Egyptian magician, Hor, son of Paneshe, pronounced a magic formula that made a papyrus boat float through the air and attach to the vault of stone. Then it flew off with the stone in tow toward a great pool of water near the courtyard.

"Having been defeated three times, the Ethiopian knew that his magic could not win against the Egyptian's magic. Now he recited a spell to make himself invisible and to transport himself home. Just as quickly, Hor, son of Paneshe, cast a spell revealing the sorcerer's magic tricks and allowing the pharaoh and his court to see the Ethiopian clearly. The sorcerer took the form of a gander and was about to fly off when the spell of Hor, son of Paneshe, caused him to turn back only to find a fowler standing over him with knife in hand. His death was imminent.

"It was then that the signs that the sorcerer had set between himself and his mother came to pass before her. She transported herself to Egypt, taking the form of a goose who flew above the palace squawking and bemoaning the fate of her son. Looking into the sky, Hor, son of Paneshe, *could see the Negress in the guise of a goose, and his spell caused her to fall to the ground on her back. Now a fowler also stood over her with a knife. Quickly she took the form of a simple Ethiopian woman praying, 'Do not kill us, Hor, son of Paneshe. We have failed, but let us go. Transport us back to Ethiopia, and we will leave Egypt alone forever.'*

"Hor, son of Paneshe, declared that he would not remove the spell until they swore never to return to Egypt. The Negress raised her hand and swore not to come back for all eternity. The son of the Negress swore, 'I will not return to Egypt for 1,500 years.' Now the Egyptian magician countered his own spell and gave the mother and her son a boat made of ether to carry them far away, back to their city in Nubia."

Si-Osire finished his recitation of the letter standing before his father, the high priest Khaemwast, before Pharaoh Ramses II, and in front of all the people of Egypt. Khaemwast observed all of it and heard everything. The Ethiopian sorcerer kept his forehead on the ground, but the affair was far from over. Si-Osire addressed the great pharaoh Ramses II and the crowd of people in his court. "This man you see before you is Hor, the son of the Negress. The words that I am reading are written in the amulet he hangs about his neck. He has not repented of that which he did 1,500 years ago and has come back to Egypt again to cast his spells on us.

"By the blessings of Osiris, the Good Being, the lord of the hidden lands of the west, and in whom my spirit rests," said the boy. "I am Hor, son of Paneshe. This man, who stands before you, Pharaoh, found out that the wicked Ethiopian would cast his spells against Egypt again and that there would be no learned magician in Egypt at the time to do battle with him. I prayed before Osiris in Amenti to let me come into the world again to stop the humiliation of Egypt in the lands of Ethiopia and Nubia."

The boy pointed now to the high priest Khaemwast who stood listening and watching. "Osiris brought me back to Earth. When my ba awoke, I flew to Memphis to find this high priest, the son of pharaoh. I grew as a vine growing, and I entered the vine that would become a fruit and a seed with the idea of returning into the body again to be born in the world to enact magic against this old enemy from Ethiopia."

Then the greatest Egyptian magician—Hor, son of Paneshe, in the shape of the boy Si-Osire—pronounced a heka on the man of Ethiopia who stood in the middle of the court. The pharaoh and all of his courtiers watched as a fire encircled the evil sorcerer, then it enveloped him, and finally the fire consumed him.

Si-Osire became a shadow. He dissolved from view before the eyes of the pharaoh and his father, Khaemwast. The pharaoh and his sons marveled at all they had seen that day, saying, "There is no scribe or wise man like Hor, son of Paneshe. And we will never see the likes of him again." But the high priest Khaemwast sobbed open-mouthed when his son Si-Osire had passed away as a shadow. Pharaoh asked for preparations to be made to feed and lodge Khaemwast in the apartments, hoping to comfort him in the loss of his son.

When evening fell Khaemwast entered his apartment with a heavy heart. Mehusekhe lay beside him, and that night they conceived a child, a boy whom they named Wesymenthor. He was a wonderful boy, but still on every occasion Khaemwast, the high priest, never failed to make offerings and libations before the genius of Hor, son of Paneshe.

Articulating the Portals
between Death and Life

In the foggy desert air before dawn, the archaeologists turn over on their cots, relishing the coolness before the blast of the sun. The Arab *fellahin* they employ to explore the Saqqara necropolis begin to roll up their rugs, say their prayers, and light the fire to heat the water for morning coffee. Nearby, atop a pile of rubble that leads to one of the Old Kingdom tombs, a desert hound stands, his tail curved over his back. He eyes the head workman who stops giving orders long enough to observe the pair of golden eyes observing him.

In Egyptian mythology, two jackals were seen as guardians between the worlds. The jackal god Anubis, the most well known jackal, escorted the recent dead into the underworld where the heart was weighed in judgment. If deemed worthy, the spirit was escorted into the Halls of Osiris. The other jackal, Upuaut, was called the Opener of the Way because he led the initiates into the mysteries along darkened corridors toward enlightenment.

On this particular day in 1881, the head watchman saw the jackal outlined in the dim gray light. It loped toward one of the pyramids, which seemed to be no more than a pile of rubble, then the animal stopped and turned to see if the man would follow him. The workman took up the invitation. Occasionally the jackal turned back, stared, and then continued on in a desultory manner. The astonished foreman watched as the jackal looked once again over his shoulder, before it disappeared seemingly down a hole. Could there be a tomb there with its treasure undisturbed?

The workman crawled into a darkened tunnel, and Upuaut indeed had led him straight into a chamber filled with treasure. It was not the gold he hoped for, but the oldest sacred Egyptian spiritual text ever found—the Pyramid Text of Unas. The walls of the sarcophagus room, the antechamber, and the entryway were covered in row upon row of precise, beautiful hieroglyphs. Many of them still bore the green paint that seemed as fresh and new as green stalks of wheat in a field. The cobalt blue vaulted ceiling was spangled with brilliant, individually painted golden stars. It was an image of heavenly proportions.

THE PYRAMID TEXTS

Gaston Maspero and Auguste Mariette were the first of many Egyptologists to examine the Pyramid Texts, which predate the more familiar Egyptian books of the afterlife by more than seven hundred years. Of the five Old Kingdom Pyramid Texts found in the tombs of Saqqara, the text of the Fifth Dynasty pharaoh Unas (2375–2345 BCE) is the oldest.

The appearance of these hieroglyphs is unusual in many respects, primarily because the religious text seems to appear full-blown in the midst of the Old Kingdom. Perhaps the words were a long time coming, developed in an oral tradition over many centuries before they were inscribed. Perhaps they were ancient scripts developed by another culture, and Unas decided that they should be written at last in stone and kept for all time. Perhaps they were part of an overall plan laid down for Saqqara that included the huge jubilee or Heb-Sed initiation complex. Certainly the words are a kind of initiation—whether welcoming the soul into the afterlife or initiating the spirit-infused body into the world. The text forms a kind of dreamscape in which Unas takes on the role of Osiris.

The prominent role Osiris plays here is as Sahu, or the constellation Orion, the hunter, which was already part of the mystery tradition on the Giza Plateau in the initiation rites of the Great Pyramid. The three Giza pyramids, it is now understood, align to the three brightest stars in Orion's belt. (See *The Orion Mystery;* see also plate 1 of the color insert.)

In Utterance 432, a spirit of the dead cries out to the sky goddess Nut:

> *Oh Great One who became sky, you are strong. You are*
> *   mighty.*
> *You fill every place with your beauty.*
> *The whole world lies beneath you. You possess it!*
> *As you enfold earth and all things in your arms, enfold*
> *   me, too.*
> *Make of me an indestructible star in your body.*[1]

That is the quest of all the blessed dead—to return to the heavens from which they came. The Hopi likewise honored the star people, and their *sohu* dancers depicted three stars like those in the belt of Orion. (See possible connection to the Kachina star of the Hopi in *The Orion Zone* by Gary A. David.)

When the three stars appear to lie low on the horizon, both the feast days of the Osirian Mysteries and the Festival of the Two Ladies began. (The two ladies were the two sisters of Osiris, Isis and Nephthys, who uplift Osiris and raise him from the dead.) In Utterance 466, the pharaoh aligns with the *sahu,* or body of light that is Osiris. His spirit awakens with the words: "O king, you are this great star, the companion who traverses the sky with *sah* (a body of light), who navigates the Duat [underworld]. You rise in the eastern sky, being renewed in your due season and rejuvenated in due time."[2]

The Pyramid Texts, at any rate, are unusual for being the first collected spiritual records of the transformations we call life and death. Some of these texts appear nowhere else except in the Pyramid Text of Unas. In that regard, this text is the vision of one man who chose to immortalize his spiritual quest, a journey one might say that is equally as individual a vision of the gods' realm as was Akhenaten's vision of the sun god, Aten. The text is both beautiful and fierce, very much like life itself.

Yet another anomaly occurs. As we have come to understand how the ancient Egyptian theology developed over the three millennia of the culture's existence, this text indicates a dual theological vision. Two theories of the afterlife occur inside the one pyramid. The solar cult of Re in Heliopolis is more engaged with the revitalization of soul and person in the same way that the sun rises each day in its constant and ceaseless becoming. The stellar theology encourages a lineage with the Imperishable Stars, the neteru of the Milky Way, and this way places one inside the eternity of the creative life force.

The two differing theologies may represent a kind of completion, rather than a competition. The way we have read these Pyramid Texts in the past, going in a circular fashion from wall to wall, starting from the outside and working our way in, may not be the correct way to read them. What if they were meant to be read from the inside out, starting with the sarcophagus room with its emphasis on waking up and eating—that is, eating the spiritual food of the Divine. Then one moves into the amazing, lucid, and delicious texts of the antechamber, which I have always envisioned rather like how it must feel to a fetus to be sitting inside the womb of the mother, reading what is written on her belly, getting our instructions before the next assignment, as it were. Finally one moves through the narrow passageway, which is a birth canal. One leaves the dark mysterious, spirit-filled world as we descend into the light of day, into the world of matter.

What interests me as well is the hieroglyphic aspect of the number 4. When we stand inside the Pyramid of Unas's antechamber and read the texts from east to west, as the sun moves, we are reading the Re texts. Think of yourself as situated at true north. The east is to your right; the west is to your left. That is the horizontal bar of the number 4. Now read the text from the north to the south. These northern texts are the celestial details of life with the Imperishable Ones. They directly face the southern texts and the passage out of the chamber, which is low, tight, and cramped. That is the way of incarnation. These paired walls represent the vertical line of the number 4—which bears a similar shape to the ankh ☥, or divine emblem of rebirth. Four is simply a shorthand way of saying that we have united paired oppositions that intentionally work together. Both the stellar and the solar Pyramid Texts record the mystical spiritual impulses of the ancient world in which the pharaoh's spirit affirms in Utterances 273–74: "His lifetime is eternity. His limit is everlastingless."[3]

Experiential Egyptologist Rosemary Clark has said that "[m]agic is the technology of transformation, its primary product being the transformed human being whose innate consciousness has awakened."[4] By carving these beautiful hieroglyphs inside his pyramid, Unas affirmed eternal life for his spirit and for the spirits of those who read and copied these words thereafter. Particular inscriptions refer to the fact that these rites had been used in Heb-Sed Festival ceremonies well before 3000 BCE. For thousands of years, ancient Egyptians chose to be buried in Saqqara near the Pyramid of Djoser complex.

The Pyramid Texts of the Fifth and Sixth Dynasties include 714 invocations and prayers. The Unas pyramid uses only 227 utterances. It is possible that the text, which is sometimes written in first person but at other times written in third person, was intended to be spoken aloud. (Each utterance begins with the words to say.) The text is part of a ritual of transfiguration making the speaker "one of the Imperishable Stars," a shining spirit in the heavens, living among gods. Pharaoh Unas turns toward life and light to nourish him and to help him overthrow the hypnotic powers of darkness that might ensnare him inside this soporific limbo.

Sexual Mysteries in the Pyramid Texts

Inside the antechamber within the belly of Earth, we are likewise inside the belly of sky. Nut, the celestial mother, presents herself as both the beautiful turquoise day-lit sky and the mysterious lapis lazuli of night. The stars were all the souls that dwelt within her, those waiting to be born and also the souls of the dead taken back into her body. The night sky was all the possibilities of earthly manifestation, all that was seen, and all that remains to be seen. Here lies possibility, waiting to inhale the breath of life, and listening to the sound of the mother's heartbeat in the dark.

Imagine the pharaoh sitting in the dark heart of his pyramid, entranced, partaking of the five-thousand-year-old renewal rites of the Heb-Sed Festival. During his initiation, he has received two magical things. One is the placenta, which was saved from his birth. The other was the tekenu (△ ⊜ ꝋ ⌇), a human form lying in a fetal position wrapped within animal skins. To pass through the skin meant to be reborn. (A similar word *tekhni* referred to that which is hidden.)

The texts found in the antechamber probably detailed the central initiation rites of the pharaoh or high priest (*sem* priest) during the Heb-Sed Festival. The pharaoh celebrated his renewal rites during the thirty-year Heb-Sed Festival, and thereafter continued to celebrate it about every seven years. As comfortable as it may feel to be so close to the spirit of Nut, Atum, Osiris, and Isis sitting inside this womb, we can't stay here. Preparations for our appearance, or reappearance, have already been underway. There is work to do.

The story that appears on the walls in the Pyramid of Unas, to a degree, is the story of Everyman, a tale of the soul's sojourn from life to death and death into life. Pharaoh Unas's name literally means "the Being" (*un* ꜱ⃝ ⌇). His namesake is a form of Osiris called Un-nefer (ꜱ⃝ ⌇ ⌅), or the Beautiful Being. All humankind is called *uniu* (ꜱ⃝ ⌇ 𓏤𓏤), or human beings. The hieroglyph *as* (𓏤 𓈖) is a hieroglyphic mark of emphasis, but as with all hieroglyphs, it represents more than one thing. The name of the ancient Egyptian goddess Isis is As-t. The name has been translated to mean the throne, or the lap, of the goddess. As also signifies the tomb. Both the tomb of Osiris and the womb of Isis are places of deep transformation. The pharaonic name alludes to the regenerative sexual imagery taken on by the pharaoh during his coronation.

Utterance 313 written on the entrance wall to the tomb of Unas provides a vivid hieroglyphic story that emphasizes the sexual nature of the womb/tomb motif. Literally it read: "The bolt of Babi is pulled out. The doors of the sky are open. . . . What lets every Horus glide through will also let Unas glide through, over the fire glow, under that which assembles the gods. They make a way for Unas that Unas may pass along it. Unas is a Horus."[5]

Babi, the baboon god, guards the gates into the other worlds. He is not a human consciousness but an animal consciousness, an instinctual kind of awareness. His actions and impulses are primal. The bolt that is drawn back is written with the hieroglyph of the phallus; thus it is more than the bolt of a door. One might say that the phallus of Babi is the key to heaven. One notes that Babi may be related to the word *Babylon,* which meant "gateway of God."

The actual word for the phallus and the door bolt is *seth* ( ). Interestingly, Seth, the murderer of Osiris, condemned his brother to the grave. The sexual act begets mortality. One might say that to be born of a sexual union is to be born in time, and to be born in time is to give oneself over to death. What is the cause of death? Seth. This reminds me of the writing of Earlyne Chaney, psychic and founder of Astara Foundation. In her book *Initiation in the Great Pyramid,* she recalls a moment in her vision quest in which her spirit, in undergoing a death experience, found itself called back to the ecstatic moment of sexual union. It was so beautiful that she had to fight her impulse to jump back into the body of the mother, to be pulled back into karma on a material plane.[6]

The regenerative Babi withdraws from the womb of the sky mother in order to open the portal between worlds. Now, in true hieroglyphic fashion, the text can be read multiple ways: it refers not only to the opening of the doors of the kundalini for the soul's entrance into heaven but also to the opening of the doors of Earth for the soul's entrance into form. The soul seed resides now in the womb.

The Pyramid Text of Unas is not so much a burial text as it is a text of rebirth. The spirit first receives admonitions to arise and go west, in the direction of the sun's motion—that is, the spirit begins his movement into time. Prayers protect the spirit from the chaotic serpents of decay and the eternal darkness he would suffer in traveling east away from the sun. The spirit eats of the spiritual food and offerings that have been given for his sustenance. In the antechamber on the northern wall, his soul is aligned with the circumpolar stars so that he remembers now and ever that he is an eternal spirit—even after death, he is eternal. "Body to earth, soul to sky," says Utterance 474 of the Pyramid Texts.[7]

Lifted up, he floats in his boat upon the waters toward the Fields of Peace. Ferried from this world to the next, he receives his rightful place beside the gods, but he cannot stay here in this place. The texts tell us of his previous struggles during his life on Earth, in the way that Osiris struggled with his brother Seth. It is the way of karma. Battles must be fought in order for the good to triumph.

The spirit moves through the long corridor, the cramped passageway that describes his birth or rebirth. The text and construction of the tomb passage are metaphoric for the cramped birth canal. To traverse it, one must double over, practically crawling out on hands and knees. In Teti's tomb, one has to descend the tunnel backward, backing up into the womb/tomb, so that when one is reborn, it is in the position of the child emerging head and crown first.

On one wall of the Unas corridor is written the story of how Isis births the young Horus, who merges with the pharaoh as the hero of this story. On the other wall is the story of how Neith births Sobek, the crocodile. The upper and lower worlds lie together inside this birth canal that leads into and out of the Pyramid of Unas. The corridor is linked to the star Sirius, which is the celestial Isis. Perhaps the soul is given an opportunity to choose its passage—the heavenly realm or rebirth into human form.

Shamanic States in the Pyramid Text

I have never thought that the Pyramid Text could be interpreted only as funerary. The words also must be interpreted as initiatory—that is, as a text of beginnings. The text works, again, through its simultaneously occurring paired oppositions as a text of two transformations: from life into death and from death into life. The language lends itself to multiple interpretations. The Egyptian scribe made few distinctions between verb tenses. He lived, he lives, and he will live use similar verb constructions. This use of tense makes a spiritual statement about the simultaneity of time.

The passageway from birth to death also runs from death to birth, but more than that, it a passageway between worlds, a conduit into altered states of consciousness. A shaman is one who has died and been reborn. He has a foot in both worlds. All life is a circular passage, a transformation without beginning or end. One may think of Unas as a dead king entering his tomb, as a child entering into incarnation, or as a shaman entering into an altered state. Whatever the case, he travels through the underworld beyond earthly time and into the world of the eternal Divine.

The pharaoh, as the embodiment of Horus and the divine son of Osiris, became the spiritual focal point for the people. As such, he served as high priest in every temple, knew every god, and enacted the divine laws. As a high priest, he must have undertaken extensive spiritual training, initiations, and vision quests. Greg Reeder, a contributing editor to *KMT* magazine, which devotes itself to Egyptological studies, suggests that the many afterlife texts serve the living shaman as a death-in-life initiation ceremony.

From the time of the earliest dynasties to the New Kingdom, these priestly initiation ceremonies moved the high priest initiate through the experience of death. The ancient Egyptian spirit voyage is not dissimiliar to that which occurs in other shamanic cultures wherein the shaman begins his vision quest tightly wrapped in a quilt or in animal skins and is buried.

In ancient Egypt, the living shaman was put into a catatonic state and taken into the tomb for three days. While living, he passed through the stages of death, experiencing the underworld and gaining from it spiritual wisdom. He may have arrived at the tomb pulled on a sledge and already in a state of trance, wrapped tightly inside an animal skin as if he were dead and sitting or lying in a fetal position.

Some temple walls show the tekenu as no more than a dark mass of matter—even a bundle of assorted body parts in a bag. Other illustrations show a face upon the bundle, and still other images depict the tekenu awakening, an arm reaching out in front of its face. The clothed, bundled figure crouched in the fetal position resembles the position of a child folded into the womb—a position similar to that of burial during the predynastic era.[8] Some Egyptologists have suggested that the image is that of a sacrificial victim, but sacrifice of servants and courtiers apparently ended in predynastic times.

While he is in a catatonic state, the tekenu *of Rekhmire is wrapped in an animal skin and left on its bier inside his Eighteenth Dynasty tomb.*

When Rekhmire awakens from his deathlike shamanic state, he was said to have "passed through the skin." During the Eighteenth Dynasty, Rekhmire was a highly ranked individual—the chief vizier of Pharaoh Tuthmosis III.

Tek-nu literally meant to enter into nothingness, into the void, or the Nun, while the word *tekenu* indicated some higher state of awareness, meaning the equivalent of "to pierce the sky." Even as early as the Pyramid Text of Unas, the idea of the tekenu was already in place. Utterance 306 depicts Unas ascending on a ladder to enter the sky. The ascension text describes the pharaoh as having "power upon him," "terror about him," and "magic at his feet."[9]

The scene is reminiscent of the story of Jacob's ladder that appears in Genesis whereupon angels move down from heaven and souls move up while Jacob sleeps upon a stone. Unas sees the souls of heaven (Pe) descending the ladder and the souls of Earth (Nekhen) ascending to Atum. Perhaps in a less dreamlike and more visceral analogy, the text resembles that scene from playwright Tony Kushner's work *Angels in America* in which Prior Walter ascends to heaven in a deathbed hallucination with the "power and terror and magic" about him.

In any case, the tekenu envisions the portals between life and life hereafter. Standing there, as the conduit between heaven and Earth, Unas enters a state likened to death. He has become Osiris. In a vision he speaks to Atum, the god of the beginning and the god of nothingness, saying that he (Unas) is in (or on) Earth like a *duau*. The exact implication is not entirely clear; some have seen it as a "baglike offering" similar to the tekenu and related to the mounds of the Earth god Geb. Piankoff interpreted it to mean "the morning star," as if it were the first star to escape from the halls of Duat and rest low on the horizon in the morning. It may be that the star is linked to another star. Unas simultaneously declares that he is bright as the brightest star, shining as Sirius (Sopdet), the star that heralded the beginning of the year, the rise of the Nile, and the rebirth of the land.

What follows are a few lines of the Utterance 306 resurrection text that seem to address a pivotal theological question: "Has he [Atum] killed you after his heart told him that you should die through him?"[10] In other words, "Didn't your god promise that you were immortal? So how is it that you have died?" The question addressed to Unas as Osiris seems to ponder how the first mortal (and divine) man can die, if he has been told that he is divine.

The key must lie in the phrase *that you should die* through *him*. It has the kind of ring to it that resonates with the statement made by Jesus in John 14:6: "I am the way, the truth, and the life. No one comes to the Father, but *through* me." Life in the physical separates us from the Creator and death ultimately brings us face-to-face with God. We can recall that in John 14:2–4 just above the previous passage, Jesus has said that he is going to prepare a place for others. "In my Father's house are many rooms; if it were not so, I would have told you. I am going there to prepare a place for you. And if I go and prepare a place for you, I will come back and take you to be with me that you also may be where I am. You know the way to the place where I am going."

The role of Osiris is not only to tend the green Earth but also to die and tend the lands beyond Earth, to make a place for souls in transition. That task of preparing a place for others is the work of a shamanic emissary who has entered into the many realms of Duat during his vision quest ritual and has come back to report what the next life holds.

Utterance 306 concludes with this proclamation: "He remains! He remains! The *sma* remains!" The word *sma* has a double meaning, indicating both "sacrifice" and "unification." This spiritual text refers to the atonement (the sense of being at-one-ment) between the spirit of the being called Unas and Atum, the hidden god. He has become an *akh,* a shining spirit that represents communion with the mind of God.

In the following text, Utterance 307, Unas declares himself to be a Heliopolite; that is, he declares himself to be a being of light, a citizen of the ancient city of Heliopolis (Anu). Specifically, he links himself to the mysterious death and rebirth of the phoenix upon its pyre. Those mystery rites were performed in the city of Anu (now Cairo) and were connected to the pyramids on the necropolis at Giza during the Fourth Dynasty. (Only twenty-one miles separates the two ancient cities and burial sites.) While no inscribed initiation or burial text remains in the Giza pyramids, one may assume that the rites Unas mentions in his Pyramid Text were very similar to those taking place in Giza.

Like the phoenix who is consumed by the fire, Unas is reborn from the flame. "My nest is with you Re. I will ascend to the sky," he says.[11] Unas takes the form of a great bird of light rising up toward the Imperishable Stars, beyond the stars of the equator, beyond the realm of the sun and its daily coming and going. He is no longer time-bound; Unas is immortal. Says Utterance 302: "He flies who flies! He flies away from you, O men. He is no longer upon earth, he is in the sky. He rushes at the sky like a heron. He has kissed the sky like a falcon. He has leapt skyward."[12]

I find the last lines of this utterance incredibly poignant. They remind me of a final rush of air when the last breath is released at death. So, too, does the shaman slip away from this world on spirit wings into the next realm.

Unas, as heir to his father-in-law's throne, probably performed the funerary rites for Djedkare Isesi, the previous pharaoh. He may have become initiated into the mysteries at that time or at Djedkare's Heb-Sed Festival held a few years before his death. Unas would have been initiated into the mysteries using this profoundly evocative text and put in charge of the Opening of the Mouth Ceremony after Djedkare died—a role that typically fell to the successor—the eldest son of the pharaoh or the next in line for the throne. (Unas was the husband of Djedkare's royal daughter.)

Unas entered his death-in-life initiations first as a tekenu/sem priest, then as a pharaoh undergoing the Heb-Sed renewal jubilee ceremonies during his thirty-three-year reign, similar jubilee festivals and ceremonies that brought the message of light and eternal life to his people. His last passage through the rites came at his death, of course, a death for which his rituals had well prepared him.

Sacred Eating

Graduates of the Heb-Sed Festival—the pharaoh, firstborn royal children, and the sem priests—are easily recognized as the priestly caste of Egypt. He, or she (as in the Fourth Dynasty princess Nefertiabet, daughter of Khufu and sister of Khafre), will have performed the rite as tekenu, having been devoured by the maw of death, the lioness Sekhmet. (Please see plate 32 of the color insert.) Then, as children of Sekhmet, the priests are reborn in the same way that Re passed through the skin of the sky goddess Nut. The goddess devours them, and the initiate, who is said to have "passed through the skin," is reborn. Because of this rebirth symbolism, the sem priest also wore the sidelock of braided hair, which was the sign of youth and the emblem of Nefertum, the eternally arisen one who is the son of Sekhmet and Ptah.

The burial chamber appears to be the "dining room" of the Divine.

The focal point of it is the stone sacrcophagus, which the Greeks dubbed the sarcophagus, or "sacred eating," in reference to the typical image of the sky goddess Nut on the coffin lid swallowing the sun in the west. The hieroglyphs on the north wall of the sarcophagus chamber provide the menu of foods and other items for the sustenance of the spirit, including milk from the breast of Isis, beer, wine, joints of meat, spices, cakes, breads, and fruits and vegetables, among other things.[13] Unas feasts with Re and Thoth, drinking what they drink and eating what they eat.

The eastern gable of the antechamber provides what is known as the Cannibal Hymn. These Utterances 273–74 represent another example of sacred eating. The text appears only inside the pyramids of Unas and Teti. They have been a tipping point among interpreters of the wisdom texts. Many have seen it as a somewhat gruesome reference to an earlier practice of cannibalism, where after war to the victor go the juicy, fleshy spoils.

> *Sky rains, stars darken,*
> *the vaults of heaven quiver, Earth's bones tremble.*
> *The planets stand still*
> *at seeing Unas rise in his power—*
> *a god who lives on his fathers,*
> *who feeds on his mothers.*[14]

The text goes on to say that Unas eats every divine being that comes to him, "their bellies full of magic. Unas eats their magic and ingests their spirits." Rather than being a text about cannibalism, religious scholar and cultural historian Jeremy Naydler suggests that the spirits of the gods, fathers, and mothers on which Unas feasts are ancestral spirits. In the spirit realm, he has revitalized himself with their energies.[15] Unas dines on spiritual food, eating not of one god but of every god—big ones, middle ones, little ones. He leaves no magic untouched, even scraping his pots with "the thigh bones of old women."

We saw earlier how in healing texts, the wholeness of a weakened individual was attained by ingesting curative properties attributed to divine beings. Here it is no different. Unas invokes—rather than pleading, he commands—the power of the gods to dwell within him. And he demonstrates the power to take those energies and hold them within himself. Unas eats their magic and gulps down their spirits. In this way, he absorbs their powers and magic.

Perhaps it is a tad gruesome, but so is the children's book *Where the Wild Things Are* when the Wild Things call out lovingly to Max, "We'll eat you up, we love you so!" A similar kind of fierce love appears in the liturgy of the communion rite in the Christian mass. The priest consecrates the bread and wine, calling them the body and blood of Christ, saying that this communal feast was given for us and is intended for our consumption. "So to eat the flesh of thy dear son Jesus Christ and to drink his blood . . ."*

Why? One might wonder. The priest then tells us, "So that we may dwell in him and he in us." In that one idea of us eating the life power of another life is the mystery of transubstantiation. That is how the initiate into the mysteries learns to turn death into life. The point of the ritual, whether in Christian or ancient Egyptian terminology, is the same:

"My lifetime is eternity," says Unas.

"I bring you everlasting life," says the sacrificed Christ.

There is no indication that cannibalism was practiced by the dynastic Egyptians. (There may have been a dim predynastic memory of the practice.) The Hymn to Isis refers to the goddess having "made an end to the eating of human flesh."[16] Rather, this Cannibal Hymn by Unas shows us how the pharaoh lives through the powerful, transformative spiritual nature of God through a symbolical ritual eating.

Transubstantiation is magic. Atonement is magic. Sacrifice and

---

*The Prayer of Humble Access, from which this text is quoted, is widely used by many Anglican and Protestant churches. As a communion prayer it was first used and published in 1549 in the First Prayer Book of Edward VI.

renewal of the entire Earth through the death and rebirth of one god (Osiris or Christ) is magic. The Pyramid Texts, seem to tell us that to be born in human form is to die in the highest planes, and to die on Earth is to be born on a higher plane. They seem to say that it is possible for the shamanic king of Egypt, and for the Christ of the Christian mysteries, to make that ascension to heaven while still living, to come back with the news that "being" is about consciousness rather than physical form. After the first death, there is no other.

THE COFFIN TEXTS

After the Pyramid Texts came the Coffin Texts, a transitional work that appeared during the Middle Kingdom Eleventh and Fourteenth Dynasties (between 2080 and 1640 BCE). During this time, the noble men and women who longed for the blessed afterlife, just as their kings and queens had, began to incorporate funerary literature into their burials as well. Many of these inscribed wooden coffins were found in such Middle Egyptian towns as Beni Hassan, Asyut, and Deir el Bersha, the ancient city of Hermopolis that was devoted to the god Thoth.

Most of the 1,185 inscriptions that comprise the Coffin Texts were inscribed in hieratic hand (a more cursive form of hieroglyphs) upon the four sides of the coffins using primarily black ink with red highlights. A few vignettes of specific items were included. Wooden coffins of cedar were hard to come by in the desert. More than likely they came from Lebanon and were a way of linking the dead with Osiris ensnared in his tree of life. The text inscribed both inside and outside the wooden box recalled the resurrection chants of Isis the kite as she hovered around the god.

In these texts, one understands the myth of Osiris as representing both God and Everyman. The story alludes to the way in which Osiris died at the hands of his brother Seth—hacked into pieces and scattered. His body parts were collected, and he became reconstituted (renewed) in the next world. Through the story of how Osiris entered the land of

The Book of Two Ways was inscribed directly on the wooden coffins, and the text ran both inside and outside and around all the edges of the coffin. When additional text was desired, a scroll was tucked into place with the mummy.

the dead, we see with more clarity what happens to the soul after the physical change called death. More details emerge about the trials, the judgment, the confrontations with fear, the passage through darkness, and the final reemergence into a heavenly state of consciousness called enlightenment.

One may see these as inscriptions intended for the dead alone, or one may see them as the ancient scribes did—as documents that show the living how to maneuver through life's obstacles. For if we do not meet these spiritual challenges while we live, they will surely greet us after death. The tale of the rich man in the story of Khaemwast and Si-Osire assures us of that. These Coffin Texts may be the first common text of the sacred document called the Secret of Osiris Becoming Re, a secret document composed for the initiated and enlightened leaders of Egypt written, the wisdom keepers say, in Thoth's own hand.

In the Coffin Texts, Osiris comes to more prominence than he did in the Pyramid Texts. The Book of Two Ways, a major part of these Coffin Texts, tries for the first time to elucidate for the common man the way in which transformation from death to eternal life occurs and how the geography of the other world is arranged.

The Book of Two Ways

This is the first recorded map of the underworld. Chief among the illustrations were detailed maps of the Book of Two Ways and of the Field of Reeds (Sekhet Iaru) or the Field of Peace (Sekhet-hetep), which became equated with the Greek idea of the Elysian Fields where Osiris dwells. Whereas the first inscriptions on ancient coffins were simply two eyes, portals through which the dead could see into the land of the living, by the time of their prominence during the Middle Kingdom, coffins were being inscribed on all four sides, inside and out.

Coffin Text 1072 describes two ways in the underworld known as Restau. "Spell for the ways of this Restau which are on water and land. These ways are here in the opposite direction, each one thereof opposing its companion in the opposite direction. It is those who know them who can find their ways. They are high on the walls of flint."[17]

The two ways on water and on land work as a kind of ancient riddle. One must think in pictures and in hieroglyphic puns in order to visualize it.

The priests of Thoth in Hermopolis probably authored the Book of Two Ways. It was Thoth who first envisioned the world in the cosmic soup as being created in pairs of opposites. The book title probably also obliquely refers to the two ways seen in the Pyramid Text of Unas— that is, the solar way, the way of Re moving from east to west across land, and the stellar way, moving into the eternity of heaven across the celestial waters of the Milky Way. The body of the sky goddess Nut is the fertile kundalini in both contexts. By day, she gives birth to Re in the east and consumes him by swallowing him in the west. At night, then, the soul of Re, which is Osiris, sails along on the life force in the world of the neter, which is the dark night sky inside this goddess's body.

The word *re* is written with an almond-shaped hieroglyph ($\ominus$), usually understood to be the mouth. If we are talking about the two ways of being in relation to the sky goddess Nut, we might be looking at one image that indicates two directions: one *re* opening as the mouth (west) and another *re* opening as a vagina (east). The entrance and the exit are in essence the same when one thinks of the womb of the goddess as the tomb on Earth. Understanding that the entrance to death and life is the same leads to a spiritual illumination. As the Coffin Text Spell 1072 above says, "Those who know them can find their ways."[18]

I am reminded of a dream I had in which I was presented with several doors or portals (another meaning of the word *re* in the hieroglyphs). In the dream, I was told to pick a door, and it didn't matter which one because eventually we have to go through all of them. Note, too, that Re is the god's name, and he is the door of morning and evening.

The Portals and Halls of the Underworld

Primarily, though, the Coffin Texts focused on the detailed judgment scenes. In Coffin Text 1134, the deceased is ferried across the great river, which can be imagined as an underground Nile in the way that the Greeks viewed the River Styx, or as the Milky Way, that is the passage into the spiritual realm. "I have come after I travelled the waters. I moved about until you called, and I passed by the shoulders of Osiris (Orion)."[19] Yet Osiris as Orion is not imperishable. The dead will fall like him, "wrapped up" like a mummy, into the earth. "I am he. I am wrapped-up in darkness."

Having left the plane of earth, the soul must pass through twelve darkened realms that are the twelve hours of the night, or the twelve zodiacal constellations. This realm is filled with serpentine mouths, beings with knives, and ladies of flame that threaten to separate the body and the soul. The intelligent being relies on his words of power and on ownership of all aspects of himself. That is, he is not hacked into pieces as Osiris was hacked into pieces. He has not cut off or disavowed some aspect of himself but has mastered these dark places with his willful, spiritual, magical essence.

Having used the proper words to pass through this realm, he comes to the Hall of Judgment. Here is the first depiction of the emblematic Judgment Day. He must make his confession—or in this case, he states what he has not done—and his heart is weighed against Ma'at, the feather of truth. Those who pass move into the Elysian Fields. And those who fail? Their hearts are devoured by the serpent Apep.

Even so, the justified soul is not finished with its journey. The hereafter, in this case, contains fourteen regions with seven divisions or gateways. The darkened corridors may represent the collective unconscious. Each gate is guarded by three neteru who present challenges. Spell 408 of the Coffin Texts provided the words of power to confront these particular demonic terrors. "I know you. I know your names," says the soul in transition.[20] Having appeased them by knowing their names and the manner of their appearance, the spirit moves on to an idyllic life with his loved ones in the Elysian Fields. Or in some versions, he may spend eternity as a living member among the gods in the solar boat of Re.

In addition to this iconic and extremely important text, there are a multitude of magical transformations (*kheperu,* 🪲) that allow the spirit to take on the forms of whatever he desires. One might see all of these transformations as partaking of the spiritual nature of the natural world. One might become fire, a lotus, grain, a crocodile, or a child, or even (as in Spell 290) "every god into which one might desire to transform."[21] The natural world was a god-filled world, and when this life had passed, one could continue to partake of the divine nature of the spiritual impulse of creation.

To become golden light, pure in spirit like Re, was the goal of Osiris Everyman. In Coffin Text 1029, the transference of energy occurs so that the "Inert One" is awakened. "Raise yourself, O Re. Raise yourself, O you who are in your shrine that you may lap up the winds. May you swallow the vertebrae. May you spit forth the day. May you kiss Ma'at. May the followers go around when the boat travels to Nut. May the Great Ones quiver at your voice. May you count your bones. May you pull together your limbs. May you turn your face to the beautiful West as you come anew every day."[22]

As the soul reaches its complete transformation, it has been both illuminated as Re and it has peered into the void that accompanies the Nun (the abyss) and Amun (the hidden realm). As the Pyramid Texts allude to the Heliopolitans and their cult of the risen phoenix, so do the Coffin Texts allude to the sun worshippers. Coffin Text 1130 provides a final script that proclaims the true powers of Re ("He Whose Names Are Secret," "Lord of the horizon, the Creator who illumines the sky with his own beauty"). The goal of every spell in the Coffin Texts is to return the spirit to light. Re commands all the spirits in heaven, "Make way for this one that he may see Nun and Amun. This one is a mysterious perfect spirit."[23]

The words of power, magic, the skill of his mouth, and his alignment with the creative power of his god have brought him safe thus far. The soul brings his journey of transformation to a conclusion, stating, "I am one skilled at opening portals," and "It has come happily to an end."

THE BOOK OF THE DEAD

The scribe Ani lived his life in the harsh sunlight of the rocky Sahara Desert near the massive mortuary temples and graves of Egypt's first pharaohs Narmer and Aha. More than likely Ani was a lector priest who served the Temple to Osiris in Abydos where he lived and who inscribed the texts inside the darkened tombs in the Valley of the Kings. Ani was a royal scribe in the house of offerings in Abydos, around 1420 BCE. From the beginning, Abydos served an integral part of the mystery cult of Osiris. Here, it is said, Osiris stepped down from heaven to Earth. Here the Great Temple to Osiris was constructed during the First Dynasty. By the Twenty-Sixth Dynasty on this hallowed ground at least ten temples had been built, one on top of the other. Ani would have been a scribe under Pharaoh Amenhotep III, who reestablished the golden age of Egypt.

Ani also may have been a teacher, training younger men in the task of composing, copying, and writing the Pert em Heru, variously translated as the Book of Coming Forth by Day or the Book of Coming into Light. An early translator, Karl Richard Lepsius, dubbed it the Egyptian Book of the Dead, primarily because Egyptologists found the rolled papyrus scrolls tucked under the heads of or near the bodies of mummies. The name stuck.

The book is anything but dead, however; in fact, it exudes vitality and light, assuring the dead and all people that life will continue after this physical form ends. The healing words of power that make the health of a living human being possible are doubly important for those whose earthly lives are in transition. Chapter 44 of the Book of the Dead assures us that after the first death there is no other. "My hiding place is open. The spirit falls headlong into darkness, but the Eye of Horus made me holy, and Upuauti nursed me. I will hide myself among you, O ye Imperishable Stars. My brow is like the brow of Re. My face is open. . . . I know the words of power. In very truth, I am Re himself. . . . I am thy son, O great one, I have seen the hidden things which are thine. I am crowned upon my throne like the king of the gods. I shall not die a second time."[24]

The text draws heavily upon the idea of an eternity lived with Re, and his cyclical pattern of daily regeneration, as well as an eternal life spent in heaven with the Imperishable Stars. By the time the Book of the Dead appeared as the primary text of the New Kingdom, it incorporated for the general public the rituals that had been used previously and exclusively for the pharaohs and nobility during the Pyramid Age and the Coffin Texts of the Middle Kingdom.

In general, the Pert em Heru appears in four distinct segments. The first chapters convey the movement from life into death and descent into the underworld, then follow the origin of the world and of the gods and goddesses and the alignment of the individual. In keeping with the creative impulse that set the world in motion, the spirit of the individual may be reborn daily and cyclically like the sun. In the third section the deceased travels through the day-lit sky in the boat of Re and in the evening boat through the underworld to meet Osiris and be judged. The text completes with the weighing of the heart in the underworld, its vindication and protection, and the final provision of sustenance in the world beyond this one.

This was sacred work with mysterious and hidden knowledge. There was much for the scribe to contemplate, to learn, and to express about the spiritual principles that concern human life on the earth plane and in the next world. The scribe's tasks were transformative rather than menial. It took deep concentration because it taught all of the mysteries of the priesthood of tomb and temple. Life is eternal, and there are just as many challenges in the next realm as there are in this one. How to conduct one's life on Earth and how to be wise enough to meet spiritual challenges was the incredible wisdom legacy that all scribes gained by preparing copies of the Book of the Dead.

Imagine Ani busily training young men—most likely his sons or the sons of friends—to become scribes in the royal court of the pharaoh. He teaches them not only to shape the book's contents but also how to order the text, write in common (demotic) and sacred (hieratic and hieroglyphic) script, and create the precise illustrations of scenes from the next life. He must teach them the correct, transformative words of power that are needed in each situation. The scribe must know which essential texts are so sacred they cannot be changed or written in error. As part of his training, Ani may have asked the scribes to copy over fraying or disintegrating text that had previously been stored in the temple and had fallen into decay. Or perhaps he asked his student scribes to copy this book inserting his name, as they will learn to insert the name of the person for whom the book is being copied in the future.

When it arrived in the British Museum in 1888, the Papyrus of Ani came as one enormous scroll that measured one foot wide and seventy-eight feet in length. It was the largest continuous papyrus ever found, beautifully executed in at least three different hands. The scroll collected the earliest texts of the ancient Egyptian hymns, prayers, and funerary guides to the next life. The scroll numbered 64 chapters, but subsequent finds in later excavations expanded the known text into 192 distinct chapters. No papyrus contains all 192 chapters, so it seems that the person for whom the scroll was intended chose which scenes were needed. Of course, some chapters were considered essential.

One can see that some of the scribes who worked on Ani's papyrus were more adept at keeping the pace of the text moving precisely and rhythmically along the page. Other writers found themselves running out of room and cramped the words to make them fit. Pictorial vignettes were not the norm for papyrus scrolls in 1420 BCE but came into popularity in later dynasties when more common people— those who could read very little—desired some of the same spiritual assistance that pharaohs and noblemen enjoyed. Some of the chapters appear with blank cartouches, Ani's name having been left out. This clearly shows that the papyrus vignettes were drawn first, the text was inscribed later, and then, after purchase by some specific person who commissioned it, the name would be added. In this case, that person was Ani. (Please see plate 14 of the color insert for a copy of Ani's judgment scene.)

The vignettes appear uniformly and beautifully colored, seeming to have been drawn first on the papyrus by a single scribe. The hieratic text was added around the vignette. When the scribe needed more room for the next chapter or vignette, he created a new piece of papyrus and glued it onto the original scroll. That is the beauty of working in papyrus. The natural adhesive quality of the papyrus plant creates an inexhaustible supply of papyri ready to add. Titles for each chapter and for the rubric appear in red ink. The book is a remarkable creation of art.

It is a shame that the British Museum curator E. A. Wallis Budge, in trying to find some way to display the artifact, decided to cut the original scroll into thirty-seven yardstick lengths. Perhaps he made up for his grave error by compiling the one document into his book *The Egyptian Book of the Dead: The Papyrus of Ani*. Budge's Papyrus of Ani contained not only his translation—some charge he translated it poorly—but it also included every hieroglyph found in the papyrus in the order in which it had appeared originally. Because of the scroll's fragility, the original can only be seen in the back room of the British Museum.

Among its mandatory components were "The Opening of the Mouth Ceremony" (Chapter 22) and other chapters like it that were required for the heart and soul of the individual to speak, such as "The Chapter of Not Letting His Heart Be Taken from Him" (Chapter 30) and "The Weighing of the Heart," "The Halls of Ma'at," and "The Negative Confession" (Chapter 125). Ani's papyrus contains versions of the many sacred texts that previously appeared in the Pyramid and Coffin Text compilations—a certain sign that the spiritual underpinnings of Egyptian philosophy continued for two millennia despite changes in political structures and times of civil unrest. The Papyrus of Ani includes some of the essential chapters of protection, transformation, and justification and hymns that are common to all versions of the Book of the Dead.

Opening of the Mouth Ceremony

A number of chapters appear in Ani's lengthy papyrus that relate to the Opening of the Mouth Ceremony. They include "Giving a Mouth to a Man in Duat" (Chapter 21); "Giving a Mouth to the Deceased" (Chapter 22); and "Opening the Mouth of the Deceased in the Underworld" (Chapter 23). In fact, the same Chapter 23 appears twice in the Papyrus of Ani. The repetitions may be in error, but it was no mistake to think that Ani made sure the Opening of the Mouth Ceremony was included.

It was through this process that the *kher hebet* priest, who carried the book scroll, and the *sem* priest, who actually performed the rites and worked his *heka,* provide Ani with the ability to speak, to receive nourishment, and to live on in the next life. That sustenance of bread and beer appears in the incantation in Chapter 148. More than simply carrying the scroll, the kher hebet priest assured that these last rites were performed exactly "according to the book."[25]

Having one's mouth and subsequently opening the mouth would have been essential for any kind of communion ritual, but this is an act of highest creation. The ritual text begins, "My mouth is opened by

The sem *priest performs the Opening of the Mouth Ceremony on an Osirified mummy wearing the* atef *crown. The priest uses the* mestiu, *or adze wand, and wears the skin of a leopard, which signifies his stature as a high priest who has completed his own* tekenu *initiation ceremony.*

Ptah," and in this way, Ani calls upon the energy of the universal life force that has set all things in motion at the beginning of time through speaking it into being. He calls upon the other creator gods: the manifestation of light energy that is Atum and the power and will of the lioness Sekhmet and the magic of Thoth. Aligned with this luminous essence of the divinities, he asserts, "As for any magic spell or any words which may be uttered against me, the gods will rise up against it."[26]

Having his mouth freed of the bonds of Seth (his mummy rags) gave Ani the ability to form the voice vibrations that create the magic of heka in the next realm. Heka works through the proper intonation, among other things. Also in this way, through opening the mouth it was possible to establish a two-way communication between Ani's spirit and the spirit of the gods. In this same way the tekenu in the Pyramid Text was able to communicate with the gods as well as the ancestors about the universal patterns that had been set in place at the dawn of time and their plans for his part in its continuation.

A philosopher-priest and scholar, Richard Reidy reminds his readers that the Opening of the Mouth ritual was one that ancient Egyptian temple priests used in their temples to bring forth the indwelling spirit of a god or goddess into the statue. The statue, he suggests, was not the god but was a habitat where the god might reside. In this same way, the human body was a divinized container for the spirit until such time as it was no longer needed.[27]

To open the mouth of the deceased, the priest touched the lips on the mask of the gilded coffin with three magical instruments. The first was called the ox leg, which may have signified the idea of sacrifice and sacred eating that we first saw in the Cannibal Hymn in the Pyramid Text of Unas. Here the Apis bull was a stand-in for the god Osiris, whose death was the sacrifice that created the realm of the sacred dead. We witness a communion rite here. The book on which this vignette of Ani's was based was said to be so sacred that it appeared in cemeteries that predate Egypt's first kings.

Next came the opening of the mouth and eyes. The instrument used was the *meshtiu* ( ) or adze. Its shape resembles the constellation of the Big Dipper or the Great Bear, which, even in the Pyramid Texts, was considered a destination in the afterlife. One needed to be able to converse with the eternal spirit beings, the Imperishable Ones, who sit in the throne of heaven at the core of the Milky Way.

Following the meshtiu, the priests used a second magical wand that terminated with the ram-head of Amun surmounted by the uraeus cobra. The wand was known as the *ur-hekau,* or the great magic. In the papyrus of Ani, it was depicted as being curved, almost serpentine, but terminating in a ram's head with horns extending out the sides of its head. The horns alluded to the energy of Atum emanating from the mind of the Great Being. It was this that conferred the secret names and the words of power.

Lastly, a flint blade shaped like a fishtail called the *pesesh-kef* was used to strike the statue. The flint knife was used throughout Egypt as early as the predynastic era to cut the umbilical cord of the newborn child. Associated with Isis, the fish had a long connection with the rituals of childbirth and fertility. The gesture may be similar to the gesture of a pontiff (whose mitre is referred to sometimes as a fish hat) touching a child at confirmation to indicate a separation from his previous state of childhood and his renewal and acceptance into adulthood.

In contemplating the Opening the Mouth Ceremony, I have felt drawn to the way in which the hieroglyphs of heaven (⊨) and earth (⌣) become likened to the two upper and lower lips of Ptah, who spoke the world into being. Re, the spiritualized light, is what springs into being, and the soul of the spiritualized man is linked to Re. In that regard, through this Opening the Mouth Ceremony, when the shaman becomes the conduit between the two worlds, he is the tongue of fire. The words of power move between the lips of heaven and earth. The circle of the sun (⊙) is the ouroboros, the serpent biting its tail. Here the above meets the below, and the two lips open and hold between them the seed of light, the essence of self. We are ground and eaten like wheat seeds. Like an Osiris or Jesus, we are sacrificed between the teeth of God, and we nourish him so that "we may dwell in him and he in us."

The Weighing of the Heart

In the vignette of "The Weighing of the Heart," one sees seated in the heavenly realm twelve divine beings, whose names are inscribed beside them. They include Amun, Osiris, Shu, Tefnut, Geb, Nut, Isis, and Nephthys, who are seated together, and Horus, Hathor, and the twin gods Hu and Sia, who represent the ability to speak and the wisdom to know the true words of power.

From the left, the scribe Ani and his beautiful, dark-haired wife enter the Hall of Truth bowing. In a gesture of homage, he crosses his chest with his closed fist. The couple watches as Ani's red heart is placed on the gilded scales of Ma'at to balance against the feather of truth. The birth goddesses, Renenutet and Meskhenet, who have been with Ani and his heart since the beginning, watch this procedure, while Ani's human-headed *ba* soul flies above them.

In chapter 30, Ani, having acquired the power of speech previously, addresses a petition to his own heart, invoking the divine feminine creative spirit. It begins: "My heart, my mother. My heart, my mother. My heart of my becoming!" The text of this speech, known as "Not Letting His Heart Be Taken from Him," often appears inscribed on the talisman of a green scarab beetle. The talisman lay on top of the mummy's actual heart and was tightly bound in the mummy bandages.

Placed thus, Ani had little chance of losing heart during his trial in the neterworld. The temporal heart may be stilled in death, but the heart-soul, which holds the memory of who we truly are, was recognized as the seat of consciousness. The heart can be seen as the vessel that contains not only the memories but also the emotions, the truths about ourselves, the record of deeds and thoughts and desires. If we have a heavy heart, the scales of Ma'at appear out of balance. The idea was for Ani to see his heart as light as a feather balanced against the feather of the goddess Ma'at.

During the Weighing of the Heart Ceremony and his interrogation, he prays that no opposition will be raised against him, that no false words will be uttered against him. The pure of heart know what truth is. The pure of heart can see that everything that is is holy. "You are my *ka* in my body, which unites and strengthens my limbs. You have come forth with me to the beautiful place to which I come" (Chapter XXXb).[28]

Shay, the beneficent god of destiny, stands near the scales of judgment. He represents a kind of guardian angel who has been with us from birth. Shay observes the kneeling Anubis as the jackal god steadies the two pans of the scales. The ibis-headed Thoth observes the weighing with his glittering eye. With his papyrus nib lifted and the scroll held aloft, he prepares to record the true measure of a man. Behind Thoth the drooling goddess Ammit, a hideous creature of the abyss—part crocodile, part lion, part hippopotamus—awaits the result, hoping to

In the underworld, the scribe Ani observes Anubis weighing Ani's heart in the scales of Ma'at. The goddesses Isis and Nephthys, Shay the god of fate, and Ani's own ba *soul observe the outcome.*

devour Ani's heart, to snatch Ani into oblivion if he is judged unworthy of eternal life.

Will Ani's heart be as light as a feather?

In the underworld, this is the season of harvest. In the field of our lives, will we reap what we have sown? Did we follow the laws of ma'at? Were we careful and true in thought, word, and deed? Are we able to look at the harvest and see what gains and losses we made? Thoth announces the result. Ani's heart has been found true, and there is no wickedness in him. He has done no evil, and no evil has befallen anyone by the words that crossed his lips. He has not wasted the temple offerings.

Luckily for Ani, the neteru in heaven proclaim: "He has no sin. There is no accusation against him. . . . Let there be given to him offerings in the presence of Osiris" (Chapter 30b).[29] The text declares that Ani may pass into the Fields of Peace. Ani may partake of a communion of bread and ale, passing into the realm of the neteru.

The Halls of Ma'at

Accompanying the Weighing of the Heart Ceremony is the necessary Chapter 125—perhaps the longest and most important part of the

Osirian Mysteries. Here Ani must make a true assessment of himself before Osiris and the forty-two assessors seated in the Hall of Truth. In what has become known as "The Negative Confession," Ani assures the gods of all that he has not done. For example, Ani says, "I have not stolen the god's offerings."[30] That would have been an easy sin for a priest overseeing temple offerings to have committed. Some might see eating food intended for the *kau* (spirits of the dead) as a minor offense, but, truly, a priest would know that food offered in the temple or to the dead is spiritual food. Taking it would be the equivalent of stealing from the living. He would know in his heart what is properly ma'at and what isn't.

Ani confesses that he has not: blasphemed a god, robbed the poor, maligned a servant to his master, killed or asked another to kill anyone, cheated or falsified, oppressed either his servants or members of his own family, scorned any god, made anyone cry, copulated unlawfully or defiled himself, taken milk from the mouth of a child, kept the gods from their rightful processions, cheated at market, dammed the flowing stream, quenched a needed fire, or trapped game out of season, and so on.

One might compare these essential laws, which first appeared in Ani's particular text some time near 1420 BCE, with those Ten Commandments given to Moses apparently during the same time period. The Hebrew laws represent the same concepts, that is, loving god, loving one's neighbor, honoring the holy days and not lying, not fornicating, not killing or stealing, and so on—all with one notable exception. The Hebrew law proscribed that no other gods than the one creator god be worshipped. This nameless god who could not be described instructed Moses simply to tell his people to call him I Am. The time frame would have been within one hundred years of the monotheistic pharaoh Akhenaten declaring that Aten, the light represented by the disk of the sun, was the one true god of the Egyptians. Ani, who predates Akhenaten, declares before the forty-two named assessors that he is innocent of crimes of the heart.

The Egyptians saw God as multiple, for the nature of the neteru resides in all things. Ani promises to honor all of the neteru duly. I like to think of this as a statement of ecological spirituality. In the Egyptian notion of divine order, we recall that the whole world is the body of the divine. Neter is nature. The river that Ani promises not to dam is the body of the Nile god Hapi. (Please see plate 16 of the color insert.) Ani will honor Hapi. The fire that he will not quench belongs to the goddess Sekhmet. Ani will honor Sekhmet. The god Aker is the god of the mountains and these acres belong to the Divine.

I have always liked this part of Ani's negative confession; call it what it is—an assertion. It as a direct counter to the right-wing belief that God gave us this land and we can do with it what we want. (Ani even says specifically, "Hail, god of Ma'at, I have not laid waste to lands that are plowed," and "Hail, Heart-Laborer who comes from Tebti, I have not polluted the water.")[31] I rather prefer thinking of the world as God's body, and we will do all in our power to preserve its beauty, its goodness, its vitality, its ma'at.

Ani, or any ancient Egyptian, cannot be accused of worshipping false gods. An ancient Egyptian cannot say that God is here, but not there. All life extends from a hidden and unknowable point of origin that the Heliopolitans called Atum. To call out the Divine in individual objects (Hathor the cow or Thoth the ibis) is not to limit the Divine in any way. It is to note and elucidate the particular qualities of the Divine that are active in the world.

Ani's assertions of innocence declare that he has seen and understood the ways in which the power of God works in the world—through the particular qualities of all things. He honors the relationship that humans share with the Divine. He follows a cosmic law, ma'at—the great truth that was laid down at the beginning of time. It is symbolized by the balanced scales in Duat, by the foundation stones that were laid down for the temples of the gods. Ma'at is also the unified balance of opposition. It is not so much night or day that is the victor, but night *and* day, which is the proper order of the world. Therefore it becomes understandable that it is not so much life *or* death, but life *and* death that are the spiritual epicenter of all existence.

All of us receive ma'at at birth, the essential law of order that underpins the spiritual nature of all life. As cocreators made in the image of the Divine, humans are born into perfection that comes from the Creator's hand. At death ma'at (the cosmic principle) is returned to Ma'at (the goddess), to the source of spiritual balance. Ani has not attempted to alter any of the core spiritual truths that were given to him from the day that he was born. He declares, "I live on *ma'at*. I feed on *ma'at*."[32] He has lived a life in accordance with the double law of caring for the Divine and of caring for others as ourselves. The Christ made it plain enough in his statements "Love God" and "Love thy neighbor as thyself."

The big difference in the ancient Egyptian idea of justice and balance, or ma'at, and the Christian tradition that stems from the Decalogue is the concept of personal responsibility. Christians assume that humans are born into sin and must be redeemed by the death of Jesus. Most believe that this life is the sole opportunity for eternal life or damnation. Egyptians believed people were born into the hands of God and that continued right action in accordance with divine truth and natural law kept one spiritually aligned with God. It is up to each of us individually to clean up our messes, clear misunderstandings, seek to do better, and try to align ourselves to the true ma'at and the will of God. The outcome of the weighing of the heart is not necessarily assured. Rosemary Clark suggests that the previous life and the outcome of the scales of ma'at determine whether the soul will experience a return to earthly life (reincarnation) or entrance into the heavenly realms.[33]

Subconscious Archetypes

As he stands before the scales of justice, Ani affirms that here in the Halls of Ma'at he is—as he was in life—"a pure one, washed and fasted." Now Ani addresses the individual assessors by name. "I know you. I know your names," he declares.[34] Some of these beings have names that are linked to a particular moral error that Ani asserts he has not committed. For example, one of my favorite declarations is this one: "Oh, high-of-head who comes from the cave, I have not wanted more than I had."[35]

Could it be that these assessors were at one time a bit of the unconscious that the soul of Ani has faced or now faces? Is the one "high of head" the shadow or the ego who inflated his self-worth? Has the "cave-dweller of the west" ruined everyone else's good time by the sin of his selfish sulking? I find myself musing over the meaning of each assessor's name, as if his name in some way might reflect the psychic disquietude that would follow the deceased who broke the commandments of ma'at. By becoming aware of these assessors and allowing ourselves to be examined by them during our lifetime, by naming the flaws flesh is heir to, we have more likelihood of overcoming the sins that have or will ensnare us.

Many psychologists, including Carl Jung, looked at the archetypes in the Egyptian Book of the Dead, and the similarly written text the Tibetan Book of the Dead, as manifestations of an inner landscape. Perhaps the ancient Egyptians used the teachings in the Pert em Heru as a way of recognizing symbol, using archetype, and restoring a balance to the unconscious. Says Egyptologist Eric Hornung, "[The Egyptians] realized that in sleep and dreams, one experiences these depths as a psychic reality in which one may encounter gods and the deceased alike."[36]

Aside from providing us with a list of what we should not do, Chapter 125 offers simple moral truths to live by, including right speech and action and honoring the dead. Among Ani's "affirmations" are: "I live on *ma'at,* and I feed on *ma'at.* I have done that which was commanded of me and which satisfied the gods. I appeased god by doing his will. I have given bread to the hungry man, water to the thirsty, clothes to the naked, and a boat to the ship-wrecked. I have made offerings to the gods and sacrificed meals for the ancestors (*their shining spirits*)."[37]

Similarly in the Testament of Jacob found in the Apocrypha a person is declared blessed who takes in strangers, gives a drink to the thirsty, or helps those who are alone, in prison, or too weak to help themselves. None of this is beyond the ability of an ordinary individual to perform. Ma'at is human decency and the natural laws of attraction, balance, karma, and reciprocity at work in one's life.

There follow four inquisitions before Ani may enter into the Hall of Osiris and be announced by Thoth. The second examination includes knowing the names of the sacred floor, its halls, doors, and hinges—even the hinge sockets. This brings to mind Khaemwast and Si-Osire's travels into Duat as they passed the man whose heart was not true and who was now trapped with the door hinge in his eye.

From the Fifth Dynasty until the last, the books of the afterlife tried to bring the soul into the life eternal equipped with the knowledge of its words of power and to advise us as to how by thought and action we make our own realities. The soul was prepared to meet the creator and assessor, having lived a life that was in balance and in accordance with ma'at. Having established a lineage to the previous pharaoh and the ancestral souls, one acknowledged a lineage from the divine beings and their companions who first ruled Egypt. The ancestors extended all the way back to the elders of the Ennead of Atum. In this regard, one would be able to perform life functions in the physical realm in a manner that pleased the kas of those Imperishable Ones.

Having been initiated into the solar mysteries of Re, one might perceive now the cosmic order of ingress and egress, of growth and decay, of the cyclical comings and goings in and out of the earthly plane and across the heavens. Attaining enlightenment meant understanding darkness and how an enlightened man, an akhu or shining one, must proceed by his own light. Dark forces exist, but light returns. In just this way, the whole body (called the Aufu Re) is made to exist simultaneously in the flesh, in the mind, in the heart, in the spirit.

Life is about cycles, the smaller daily arcs and the larger arcs that include the circumference of all the ages. It was all deeply interwoven—like the cloth of the goddess Neith that covers the pall of the shrine at death and uplifts the creatures from the depths of the sea at the dawn of creation.

The scribe who worked on writing these books of transformation was doubly blessed. The goal of every soul was to feel prepared for one's death, and the pursuit of spiritual transformation among the living was the ultimate preparation. Scribes were given this possibility of attaining knowledge of the afterlife because they were the wisdom keepers. They kept the feasts, carved and read the temple walls, conducted the ceremonies, and inscribed the Pert em Heru. Chapter 136 describes the benefit of knowing these words of power in advance of death. Rosemary Clark notes the transformation as saying: "As for every initiate for whom this is done while he is among the living, he shall not perish . . . he shall not die again . . . he shall go forth by day as Horus, for he is living."[38]

Can all of these wisdom texts tell us the meaning of life? They must be studied over a lifetime. Each text inscribed in an Egyptian tomb evokes the process of an individual consciousness transforming, growing into a knowledge of the divine light that shines within the obscurity of the flesh. Above the tombs in the Valley of the Kings and Queens hangs the golden image of the solar disk of Re, which encloses Amun and the beetle god Khepera. The goddesses Isis and Nepthys stand in adoration on either side of the golden globe. The goddesses of the double truth (ma'aty)—the light and the dark—guard the doorway. That way lies the darkness, and in the darkness lies the body of Osiris deep in the dark as a seed needing the heat of the sun to awaken and renew.

All these metaphors bring us to the edge of mystery, but they cannot reveal the mystery. Said Greek philosopher Porphyry, "A threshold is a sacred thing."[39]

Temples of Gold, Stone, and Flesh

The treasures of Tutankhamun span one entire wing of the third floor of the Cairo Museum. Howard Carter and Lord Carnavron found it all crammed into four rooms, including magnificent artwork and magical objects tucked between the layers of the shrines, much in the way that they found amulets tucked inside the layers of the mummy. Laying aside a fascination with the golden masks, pectorals, furniture, and jewelry, I have found myself for the last decade going into the Egyptian antiquities museum to stand in front of the shrines of Tutankhamun—two of them in particular. If I could crawl behind the plexiglass cases to see them better, I would. Their dazzling golden surfaces almost make the texts indecipherable at times.

These shrines, and their accompanying linen pall, stone sarcophagi, and gilded wooden coffins, make a fascinating nest of layers in which the mummy itself lies tucked away like a seed. We have already noted the seven corridors and galleries leading into most of the Valley tombs, which were built to resemble the seven pylons through which the soul passed. The Luxor Temple that R. A. Schwaller de Lubicz identified as the Temple of Man is built in layers from its hypostyle hall at the first pylon to the core room that is the holy of holies. Most Egyptian temples are built in layers. The Egyptians also identified layers of spiritual being that compose etheric bodies that cocoon around us and extend out from our physical being.

When Howard Carter disassembled Tutankhamun's burial chamber, he unpacked neatly nested layers that included four golden shrines, a linen pall, a sarcophagus, and three coffins. Most of the burial goods were tucked between the shrines and layers themselves.

All of these layers want to be peeled back in order to understand what lies at the core. These seeds of light waveforms and energy vibrations remind me of the "magnifying transmitter" developed by Nikola Tesla at the turn of the last century. We know it as the Tesla coil, and its basic principle is applied to radios, televisions, and wireless cell towers, which we see everywhere now and which revolutionized the twentieth century. Its principle is the same as that which allows a computer chip inside the Hubble Space Telescope to take an image of the galaxy, amplify it, and send the image back to us through satellite waves of energy moving invisibly over great distances.

Tesla's discovery came from a childhood memory of rolling a fist-sized snowball downhill from the top of a mountain. It suddenly acquired a size as large as a house, creating an avalanche of energy. Through his young adulthood he wondered how the huge energy of an avalanche could come from only a seed of an ice crystal. The Tesla coil now appears ubiquitously in YouTube videos as lightning snapping and electrical volts "singing." Their vibrations create a sound-and-light show. Through the magic of intensifying energy moving through resonant spark gaps, each coil is tuned to the other.

All of his discoveries, Tesla said, were the result of applying a spiritual principle his mother taught him. "The gift of mental power comes from God, Divine Being, and if we concentrate our minds on that truth, we become in tune with this great power. My Mother had taught me to seek all truth in the Bible; therefore I devoted the next few months to the study of this work."[1] The Tesla coil, he said, emerged from his childhood memory and a clue he found in Revelation. He believed that "secrets" could be transmitted through sound vibration. All matter responded to sound. Even Earth, he said, responded to electrical vibrations of definite pitch, just as a tuning fork responds to certain sound waves. In his later years, Tesla envisioned things to come, flying craft that used sound vibrations, for example. Up until the time of his death in 1943, he was working on the amplified energies of what he called a peace ray—others called it a death ray—in which wars were fought without armies or vehicles.[2]

Might it be that the Egyptians had some idea about the ways in which sound vibration affects transformations of form and the transmission of energy? Might that energy be the same vibration that Atum—which Roman philosopher Lucretius first identified as the atom—set in motion across the waters? The vibration of Atum/atom brought forth light and time and space and motion. We know that the ancient Egyptians understood sound well enough to create temples that acted like megaphones. The intonation of prayers inside the sanctuary reverberated through the increasingly larger enclosed chambers so that prayers could be heard in the temple courtyard outside. Certain stones—in particular, the quartzite used to create obelisks and sarcophagi—have properties that enable them to hold sound vibrations set in motion by light rapping or the tone of the human voice.

Inside Tutankhamun's outer shrine, Howard Carter found a linen pall covering a second shrine. There followed a third and fourth shrine, then a red quartzite sarcophagus that held three anthropoid coffins. All of these containers nested within each other like Russian dolls. The third coffin held the youthful golden mask that covered the face of Tutankhamun's mummy. The mummy lay like a seed inside the coffin that then blossomed into the incredible golden beauties of Tutankhamun's treasures. The hieroglyphs and symbols were the seed forms of mental energy that had generated and sustained a culture of spiritual transformation for three thousand years. The elaborate rituals that had accompanied Tutankhamun and all pharaohs to the grave accomplished their intent. Egypt is the seed of every other religion that grew out of the region. It can be found in the Jewish and Christian spiritual traditions, in the hermetic traditions of old Europe and of the early Americas, and even in the philosophical Greek underpinnings of our American culture.

ENTERING THE ROOM OF GOLD

Nearly two thousand years after his burial, King Tut, his treasures, and his religion continue to fascinate us. His golden outer shrine of cedar and oak stood nine feet tall, was gessoed and gilded, and then inlaid with dazzling faience hieroglyphs. The protective *thet* (⚕), or knot of Isis, suggested the fertile womb of the goddess. The ankh (☥) was the sign of eternal life. The *djed* (𓊽), which represented either the spine or the truncated pillar in which Osiris was ensnared, suggested both the stability and the phallic fertility of the god. (Please see plate 21 of the color insert.)

The shrine resembles the tent from which the pharaoh emerged reborn after his shamanic death and rebirth experience during his Heb-Sed Festival at Saqqara. On the outer northern face of the shrine two wide-open eyes (*wadjet*, 𓂀 𓂀) peer out, suggesting the final eleventh hour of the Book of What Is in Duat. These spiritual eyes witness the moment that Osiris rides on the back of the serpent into the starry heaven. On its inner walls one finds the eloquent hymn to Osiris that opens the Egyptian Book of the Dead and two hymns to Re. These were traditional hymns incanted daily as evening vespers for Osiris and matins for Re at the opening of day.

The Hymn to Osiris expresses a particularly moving love for the green and blue world on which we live, personified here as Geb, the Earth god. "You have made this earth with your own hand, and the waters, and the winds, and the vegetation, and all the cattle, and all the feathered fowl, and all the fish, and all the creeping things, and all the wild animals. . . . You have set light over darkness."[3]

The Book of the Divine Cow also appears inscribed inside this shrine. It retells the legend of how Re sent Sekhmet, his lion daughter, to devour humankind after they had grown disobedient. Already the text inside the first shrine recognizes the complementary polarity of Osiris and Re. In essence, the Lord giveth and the Lord taketh away.

The lion goddess played an integral part in the Saqqara Heb-Sed Festival that renewed the pharaoh and the country. The ritual was a physical act with spiritual implications celebrated during the new year festival, also designated as the pharaoh's birthday. Designed to demonstrate the aging king's vitality, the Heb-Sed Festival also reestablished the divinity of the pharaoh, asserting that God, the king, and the land were one.

During this shamanic initiation, the pharaoh experienced his death in a rite of "passing through the skin" of the devouring lion goddess. In other words, Sekhmet had devoured him, and subsequently he was reborn. The ceremonial wearing of the animal skin by the pharaoh as high priest of the mysteries indicates successful completion of this rigorous mystery rite. The king confronted his own death and won. While Tutankhamun was too young and physically weak to have undergone the rigorous rite of a jubilee celebration, this shrine indicates that he knows the ways of rebirth and that he has passed through the skin. Along the edge of the shrine's roof undulates the serpent of wisdom similar to the rearing cobras that decorate the staircase leading to the festival court in Saqqara.

Between the outer and second shrine and spread across a gilded and bronze frame, Howard Carter found a deteriorating, three-thousand-year-old, dark brown linen pall. It must have been exquisite at one time. Decorated with large bronze rosettes, the pall was symbolic of the star-spangled night sky. The pall represents a veil between worlds, a border between life and death. The pall also covers the mystery of our coming into being and may suggest the hymen of the sky goddess Nut, or the amniotic sac of fluid that contains the embryonic, growing, and revitalizing pharaoh. The starry rosettes are the divine souls inside the belly of Nut, including all the heavenly neteru and the souls of the ancestors.

ALCHEMICAL TRANSFORMATIONS

The second shrine is most intriguing. Its sloping roof, slightly peaked above the door, is shaped like the *per ur* (☐), or great house shrine, that shelters the god in his temple. In a similar shrine, the pharaoh sat in public among his people. Here Tutankhamun stands before Osiris and Re-Horakhty. The sister mourners Isis and Nephthys guard the back of the shrine. On the inner roof, which would have been covered by the pall, the goddess Nut spreads her wings of protection over the interior roof of the shrine, just as the goddess inside the coffin lid spreads herself in protection of the mummy. Osiris and Re symbolize the polar opposites of life, which is a little different than saying they represent life and death. It might be more accurate to say that they depict the ebb and flow of life, the circulation of falling and arising energies.

It is no accident that the ancient Library of Alexandria, called the house of life, and the shrines of the pharaoh were built similarly. Both vessels contained the sacred alchemical transformation of base matter into gold. Inside the library, that transformation was turning ignorance into enlightenment. In the sarcophagus, it was turning flesh into spirit.

Constructed in layers much like the shrines, sarcophagi, and coffins that surrounded the body and were guarded by the four goddesses Neith, Selket, Isis, and Nephthys, the Library of Alexandria also has been described as having "an inner body surrounded by four other ones." Those divine beings were Isis, Nephthys, Horus, and Thoth.[4] The sacred texts of the great library were kept inside concentric rings of rooms. Their books were said to be "the emanations of Re," the most holy and secret manuscripts of the ancient Egyptians—the Secret of Osiris Becoming Re. Tutankhamun's shrine is called the Great House because it housed at its core the body of the divinized king. All about the inside and outside of his shrines the magical scripts of transformation held the identical alchemical secrets and demonstrated the ways in which we may turn death into life, lead into gold, and matter into spirit. In other words, this text embodied the magical process of the way in which thoughts were made flesh and words were made spirit.

The heart, the seat of consciousness, is the primary agent of change and renewal. It, and not the brain, generates the illuminating light of consciousness. Thus the shrine contained chapters from the Book of the Dead that protected it from harm in Duat. In other words, in fear and in darkness, in the midst of chaos, one did not want to "lose heart." The heart generated all transformation. The heart scarab guarded the heart of the mummy and became the "engine" of transformation. The inscribed beetle Khepera appeared as the creative heartbeat behind the shrine of the god in the temple. The heart pulls us consciously through all experience, and what it desires changes us. In the underworld, one did not want to lose sight of the power of higher consciousness to quell lower emotional states. These chapters worked with another chapter from the same Book of the Dead that allowed the pharaoh's *ba* soul to begin its transformations in the "Beautiful Amentet," the hidden realms.

OSIRIS BECOMING RE

One panel of Tutankhamun's second shrine shows the god Osiris standing in the center of the panel. His body spans the entire height of the panel as if it were actually the central pillar of a golden temple. In one cycle of the Osirian myth, Isis finds her slain husband trapped within a coffin around which an enormous tree has grown; the tree has become the pillar of a massive temple. The "living" body of Tutankhamun is similarly depicted on the shrine as trapped within his coffin.

Text and images run in three registers on either side corresponding to his head, torso, and feet. The head in the upper register is encircled by the ouroboric serpent Mehen who devours himself. The image brings to mind the waters of chaos that preceded creation. Beside the snake appears the phrase "Adoration. His rays come forth," which

The central panel of Shrine II belonging to Tutankhamun depicts the king as Osiris becoming Re.

refers to Atum's creation of Re from the waters of the Nun.[5] Osiris-Tutankhamun's feet are encircled by a second mehen serpent, also biting its tail, which appears as the serpent in its chthonic form in the neterworld. Inside this ouroboric serpent, we see an image of the sun disk being spat out upon the cosmic waters. Re exists in both places. Apparently this is the first time in ancient history that the image of the ouroboros appears, although the concept of the self-consuming serpent appeared without any drawings in the Pyramid Text of Unas.

Mehen, whose name means "the Enveloper," guards the corpse and is an aspect of Re. On the other hand, the devouring snake Apophis belonged to the brother of Osiris, Seth. Re is both light and time, which coexist and came into being when his name was spoken by Atum at Heliopolis, or Ptah at Memphis. The mehen serpent undulated as the water that received the first word and rippled out across space at the beginning of time. At the end of time, according to the legend, when Atum folds back on itself, he will become again "the Old Serpent who knew no man and saw no god."[6]

According to some, Mehen represents a longer arc of time than the daily twenty-four hours or the yearly 365 days that Re represents. The images express the central idea that within death lies the mystery of potentiality, the mystery of coming again. Within the circle of time that consumes itself, the head of Osiris remains as the seed of a possible future. The three circles together (head, torso, and feet), along with the image of Re at the core, are reminiscent of the hieroglyphs that represent eternity—⧆ ☉ ⧆ (heh).

Within the torso of Osiris dwells the ba of Re. John C. Darnell sees this large figure of Tutankhamun as Osiris, as an illustration of the mysterious union of Re and Osiris, depicted as a giant god, his head high in heaven and his feet in the caverns of Earth.[7] His length might be said to cover the expanse of all time, his head in the beginning and his feet in the end. One epithet of the being was "He who hides the hours." Piankoff suggests that the figure exists outside time as we know it.[8] What we see in the upper register is Osiris within the serpent that is

Re, and in the lower register, we see Re within the serpent coil of Osiris. Each is the seed of the other. The Asian principles of yin and yang contain the seed of the other.

In the upper right-hand register, eight beings appear, described as "the gods in their caverns . . . their bodies in darkness." These deities stand in the darkness of their coffins. Says the text: "Their bodies are in complete darkness when Re passes by. . . . His rays penetrate into their cavern."[9] In the upper left stand manifestations of Re "who created his names out of his members." They may be the differentiated forms of those beings to the right that have been called forth by Re and transformed. Many resemble the human, cat, lion, and ram forms that appear on the opposite panel.[10]

LIFE PROCESSES DEPICTED BY THE SONS OF HORUS

In the lower left-hand register, another cluster of eight beings appear. Four of them are the mummified sons of Horus in their jackal, hawk, ram (rather than baboon), and human forms. The other four are the awakened forms of the sons of Horus. The awakened ones face the scarabs of "becoming." Although they exist in the underworld and their processes are hidden, these beings are transforming through the light of Re. Imset is the human-headed guardian of the liver; Hapi is the baboon-headed guardian of the lungs; Duamutef is the jackal-headed guardian of the stomach; and Qebhsenuf is the ram-headed guardian of the intestines.

Esoterically, says Rosemary Clark, these four sons of Horus represent "the processes by which the natural world moves through the human form and stabilize its function."[11] These sons of Horus helped to process the "fluid of life." The liver as depicted as Imset controls the production of bile. Bilious persons were said to be victims of their anger. Hapi who controlled the lungs provides the revitalizing Osiris the ability to breathe in and out the rejuvenating light and air of Re; thus Hapi might be said to control one's inspiration. The stomach controlled by

Duamutef and the intestines controlled by Qebhsenuf allow us to first make use of those experiences that feed us and then eliminate those experiences from the past that hinder us. These fluid processes release the emotions that hinder transformation from the lower level emotions to spiritual understanding. The four enlivened sons of Horus were called the Becoming Ones.

In the lower left register, two beings, Osiris and an unnamed being—perhaps a future or possible self?—lie inside their coffins in the Place of Annihilation. The coffins lie within three undulating coils of the human-headed serpent that surrounds them. The coils mirror the number of shrines that remain to be opened. The text tells us that these two forms indicate that "the heart of Osiris is in his House of Hearts."[12]

This is Osiris in his place of transformation. We are told that Earth has thrown open the doors to Duat for him, and Osiris may open his eyes. In the House of Hearts, this is the dawning of conscious under-standing of the tasks that lie ahead, the true magical Coming Forth by Day. Yet the text refers to one boat moving upstream and another mov-ing downstream. Apparently the way of earthly reincarnation is in the boat moving south, or upstream. Perhaps this text obliquely refers to the choices that Unas made inside his pyramid, whether to return to Earth or join the Imperishable Stars.

THE UNCONSCIOUS AND THE CONSCIOUS ACTIONS

The middle register is inscribed with Chapter 27 of the Egyptian Book of the Dead, which was the essential chapter of preserving the heart in Duat. The text addresses the being "who created the heart of a man out of his deeds without his being aware of what you are doing."[13]

The text specifically addresses he who has acted without self-awareness. Rather than have his heart speak against him, he asks that "the Great God speaks through his members, he who has sent his heart out of his body." It would seem that the text alludes again to the mehen serpents that surround the head and surround the feet. Perhaps consciousness and unconsciousness are both ways of becoming. The obvious choice is for enlightenment and absolution. If he invokes the Great God who then speaks through him, he appeals to his upper nature to rectify the errors of the unconscious.

Two awakened beings guard the coffins and the mound of hands that lie buried beside them. Hands were an Egyptian way of counting the enemy war dead, but here we have four left hands and an arm that seems to carry them forward. Rather than representing captives, they may be the feminine (receptive) hands of the god Amun. These hands uplifted by the ram god's horns may belong to the sons of Horus who have been regenerating and working through the emotional realms of the unconscious in the darkness. Re is said to light up this region "with his voice," so that its inhabitants may breathe—an image somewhat akin to the dead rising at the sound and vibration of Gabriel's horn.

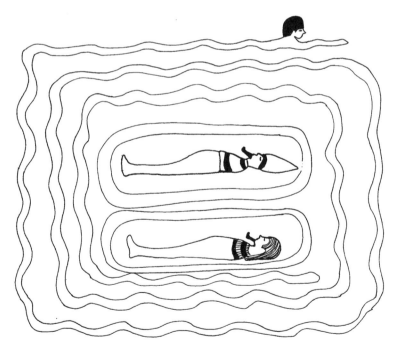

The undulating and spiraling human-headed serpent coils about the bodies that lie in darkness. It represents both the inertia of death and the mystery of transformation that takes place even in the pit of the tomb.

In the middle register, seven figures appear with their arms raised above their heads in adoration of Osiris. The ba Re faces them with its arms upraised, as if all were greeting each other with the familiar phrase *namaste:* the god in me sees the god in you. They lift a rope above their heads and draw out the presence of the shining spirit within. The rope is not a circle. It is a single line indicative of a process of being within the realm of time.

The sixth hour in the Book of Caverns appears in tombs during the Ramesside period. A portion of that text provides a final bit of information that may apply to the unification of Osiris with Re. It returns to the idea of the mehen serpents that surround the god. "Oh Osiris, great deity, whose head is in the darkness and whose hinder parts are in darkness, his corpse has traversed the neterworld, and his *ba* is exalted upon his images."[14]

The beginning and end of time (the head and feet of Osiris-Re) appear occluded from us. It is only within, inside the present moment of Re (symbolized by the soul inside the solar disc inside the belly of Osiris), that the indwelling spirit of the divine can create true "enlightenment."

The belly of Osiris appears pregnant with himself, and the ba soul of Re is the solar child. He is called the one "who binds his seed with his body in order to create his seed within his mysterious self."[15] Just as the sparks of Re and Osiris exist within each other, so does the spark of Atum exist as Re, the principle of all life.

REBORN IN MANIFOLD RAYS OF LIGHT

The panel on the other side of the second shrine seems disorienting at first. Two enormous arms appear to break through the vault of heaven and reach down. Between them emerge three characters—two upside-down Apis bulls and Osiris, who appears to fall from the sky. At the bottom of the shrine, two bodiless arms thrust out of the ground. Osiris is noticeably absent here. It seems that down is up and up is down, except that at the steadying center, the two pairs of arms appear to grasp the sun disk between them and steady it. The golden orb contains the ba of Atum.

Serpent energies surround the entire image. They arise from both heaven and the underworld. The three following registers also depict heavenly and earthly cobras spitting fire energy toward the Osirified man. On the ground in the middle register, the arm of a mummified man lying belly to earth emerges from his cocoon in order to touch the soul of Atum being held by the two pairs of arms. This may indicate the function of the *tekenu* in the shamanic Heb-Sed ritual. Having died, the king now reaches out from his cloak of death toward the light of God.

These beautiful arms denote the ancient birthing ritual. A mother was tended by midwives who supported her in an elevated birthing chair. The child was born upside down, falling head first into the loving arms of the midwife goddess. Osiris goes head down into this world to be reborn. The Salt Papyrus 825 depicts a similar image of a man upside down entering the neterworld. Not only is it an image for birth; it is also the position in which the dead were carried in their coffins into the tomb, their heads piercing the veil between worlds. Even though the process is uncomfortable and scary, "He who goes head down into the netherworld," according to the Salt Papyrus, "also raises heaven."[16] This death and birth image on the second shrine of Tutankhamun depicts the dark hour of inversion before our rebirth, which according to the Book of the Dead "will set the stars aright."

The tricky rebirth is accomplished by focusing on the ba, the divine soul that exists within the spiritual light. That soul is not upside down. Fear turns us upside down. On a physical level, that fear may be linked to the thought of dying and being carried head first into the tomb. Metaphorically, the god Osiris fell face down beneath the horizon when the stars of Orion disappeared in the west for seventy-two days before Orion's reappearance at dawn on the opposite horizon.

On a spiritual level, the real fear is in going about our lives head down and never feeling "lifted up," never taking the action necessary to

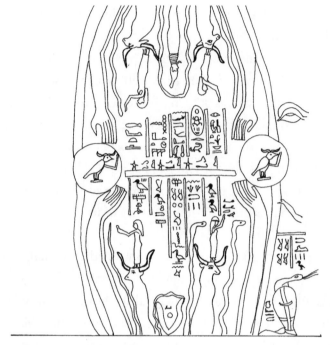

Osiris enters the tomb head down in the same way that a baby emerges from the womb head down. The arms of his sky mother Nut reach out to hold him secure on both horizons.

become enlightened. Even the weak and enshrouded Osiris, wrapped up inside his mummy rags, must reach toward the light to get his bearings. Failing to make conscious life changes because we fear the big turnaround leads us down a destructive and disorienting path.

ACTIVATING THE CHAKRAS

Light vibrations create changes in form and consciousness. The forms of Osiris on this panel receive the life-giving energy of the reared, fire-spitting cobra, a goddess great of magic. Here is Isis depicted as a serpent performing her most awe-inspiring feat—the raising of the dead. The star on her head indicates that she is the rising star Sirius that inaugurates the renewal festival at the opening of the year and precedes the resurrection of Osiris. This is the same serpent energy appearing as the uraeus on the pharaoh's crown. The wise serpent provides direct knowledge (Sia) of the vital life force. A star also appears above Osiris's head and then streams starlight consciousness into the forehead of one figure and above the heads of the subsequent figures.

Six groups of seven figures each appear in three rows. The text for each group reads: "The rays of Re enter their bodies. He calls to their souls."[17] The accompanying texts tell us little about the function of the different qualities of light—solar, lunar, and star light. The fire spewed from the serpent mouths is also a mystery. We are told only "I am Re in his manifestations." In other words, "I am a light form." We may need to infer meaning from the symbols. The rays that emerge from the star light, moonlight, sunlight, or serpent fire vary in number, origin, and direction. But the rays do seem to indicate something specific that is now lost to us.

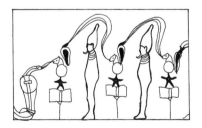

In the three registers of the Second Shrine of Tutankhamun, stellar, lunar (moon with legs), and solar energies stream toward the mummiform beings. These depict the awakening spirit of life communing with its ba soul. Kundalini serpent energies enliven and surround the mummy with hekau.

Clues in the surrounding text give little guidance. Yet the energy strikes the figures in various locations on the body that may seem familiar to those acquainted with yogic practice. There is the possibility that there was some cross-fertilization of Eastern and Western concepts occurring between Egypt and the Indus Valley. Yogic practice in India and Egyptian mystical traditions appear simultaneously in situ around 3000 BCE. This particular shrine predates the writing about yoga in the Rig Veda's earliest reference by approximately six hundred years.

It may be that this panel represents an early implicit, rather than explicit, understanding of the Kriya yogic tradition. The rays depicted in this panel show energies streaming into various bodies, striking various chakra centers, which author Ray Grasse, in his article "Astrology and the Chakras" in *The Waking Dream,* describes as "storage bins" for karma and life experiences.[18] The Tutankhamun text seems to confirm that we carry the energy of our life experience with us. Indeed, "These rays penetrate their bodies," the text says. "He calls their souls. It is indeed they who enter after their souls."[19]

In the upper register, six images of Osiris stand before their human-headed ba souls. The cobra goddess rears and spits fire energy into the forehead, or third eye, of the first Osiris. The text reads, "His head lighting up; thy being around him."[20] While Darnell sees this as a sign of protection, and it probably is, it also appears as a succinct statement of yogic awareness. A five-pointed star appears over his head, and the transformative energy radiates out in three waves. The serpent has awakened the star energy of the *sahasrara,* or crown chakra of the first figure. This center connects the enlightened one with transcendent energy that is the Jewel in the Lotus in the Buddhic tradition.[21] It is the energy of those who have attained mastery.

Three rays from the star created above the head of the first figure activate the third eye and crown chakras of the preceding figures. These beings are energized for the benefit of the ba souls that arise and hover before them. Grasse suggests that in the Eastern mystical tradition, the heart of the third eye, or *ajna* chakra, exists as a five-pointed star.[22] The

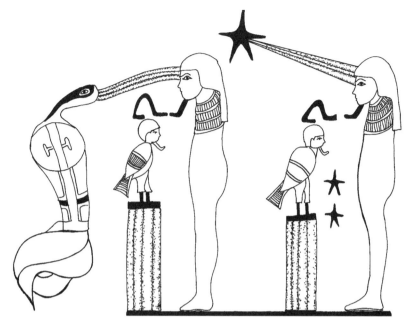

The energy of the wadjet *cobra energizes the third eye and crown chakras of* Tutankhamun. *In life, the pharaoh wore upon his head the uraeus, which was the awakened cobra energy that penetrated the third eye and provided him with spiritual guidance and leadership.*

portal between personal and transpersonal divinity can be found here.

In *The Waking Dream,* Grasse draws a connection between these three chakras and the three upper realms of the Kabbalastic Tree of Life and the trinity of sun, moon, and star in certain yogic traditions.[23] I believe that the three light rays depicted here are emblematic of the three aspects of divine light—the solar beings Khepera, Re, and Atum. They may be the sides of a Great Pyramid that is astronomically aligned to the heavenly bodies. The rays may also represent the trinity of the most highly developed spiritual bodies—the *ka,* the *ba,* and the *khu.*

Four rays of earth energies uplift the ba. The soul awakens and is enlivened through this process. These rays may express the way in which the body and its functions respond to changing experiences as the physical self moves toward a more spiritual self. The rays may represent the four sons of Horus related to the lungs, stomach, small intestines, and liver. As previously discussed, these organs operate for the benefit of the ba soul and contain the karmic record of our earthly existence.[24]

On the right side of the panel in the upper register, six decapitated forms and their floating heads appear before the cat god Mau, an aspect of Re. The cat sits on the back of a serpent in whose coils are seven orbs. Six floating heads surmounted by stars appear to rise on orbs of light connected by three rays of energy to the orbs in the serpentine form beneath Earth. That energy emanates from the wheels of light along the back of a chthonic serpent; the energy radiates into the orbs above. The idea may represent the lunar energy of Osiris in the way that the moon's full light reflects the light of the "hidden" sun on the other side of Earth. This energy indicates the root chakra receiving Earth energies.

The headless bodies receive four rays of lunar energy that stream into their body cavities. The moon—signified by an orb that appears with legs—refers to the moon god Khonsu, known as the Wanderer. The moon energies may be activating the lesser-known *chandra* chakra, which is linked with the back of the head. Both the chandra and the ajna centers, which are lunar and solar receptors respectively, are linked to the pineal gland. As an aspect of moon energy the chandra center reflects a spiritual awareness that contains the memory of earthly experience.

 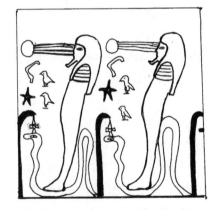

Lunar energy, depicted by the moon disk wandering through the sky on two legs, streams down into the body. Starlight and solar energy also penetrate the crown chakra and third eye (Shrine II of Tutankhamun).

The symbols suggest that form may be spiritualized through earthly experience and that experience is carried with us into higher realms. Energy streaming in both directions suggests a union of Osiris as corpse with the spirit of Re. It also suggests the union of moon and sun, for Osiris is a lunar god as Re is a solar god. The nightly union of moon and sun is witnessed as sunlight illumines the moon that illuminates Earth. Heaven and Earth feed each other.

In the third grouping, six Osirified beings stand as if riding on six undulating serpents. Re's light energizes the third eye of these mummies with such strength that it seems to rock them back on their heels. The serpent energy here is much stronger; the serpents are above ground and rearing. Fire energy streams from the top of their heads into Earth. The six figures stand inside the coils of the serpent Mehen. It is he who carries the energy of Re through its night journey. As early as 3000 BCE, clay Mehen games were used. The serpent appears coiled around itself like an ouroboros. One game used several lion-headed pieces, like the images that appear in the second register, to move about the board.

In the middle register two mummies lie prone, wrapped tightly in linen cloths. A head emerges from each cocoon and one arm reaches out. From the soles of their feet, nine lines of energy radiate upward. From this energy a serpent rises surmounted by a solar disc on legs. The light now appears to stream into the mouths of ten feline figures. While their arms are still tightly swathed, these felines move about on human legs. They seem to be energized with *heka* and words of power. The activation of the *vishudda*, or throat, chakra in yogic traditions stimulates the thyroid gland and connotes the power of communication and self-expression.

Ears, of course, matter when communicating. Listening is as important as speaking. While the voice is needed to project magical words of power, there is a simultaneous need to listen to the voice of the Divine. Four of these creatures exhibit rounded ears like lions, while the six felines in the second group have pointed ears like cats. The lion is linked to the Heb-Sed Festival, as well as to the Sphinx as pharaonic lion. The lion's roar strongly connects to the strength of the commanding voice vibration of the pharaoh. Aker, the double god of Earth, also appears as two lions seated back-to-back with the sun disk resting between their haunches. The name for lion imitated the sound of a roar, *rere,* and was the doubled name of the sun god. The long-eared cat was Mau, who was Re in serpent-taming cat form, probably a wild version of what became the domesticated Egyptian cat.

In addition, in each section solar discs appear to walk on legs—right side up and upside down. The sailing ships of Re appear before each lion at the navel chakra. The words say, "To come forth in the boat of Re."[25] We may infer by these legs that one may choose to go upstream or downstream, to sail in the heavens or to sail in the underworld. Of course, we are told, "The rays of Re penetrate their bodies." The ships are linked with the power of will, indicated by the *manipura,* or navel, chakra, and the commands that come forth from Re appear at the vishudda, or throat, chakra. Together they symbolize the active doing and the active speaking that is an essential ingredient in the transmutation of energy. He has completely aligned himself with right action through the solar principle.

Here the pharaoh is called by name, Tut-ankh-aten: the bodily son of the sun. The shrines of Tutankhamun do not deny the boy king's previous alignment with the solar traditions that his father Akhenaten established. Having become king and returned to the tradition of Amun-Re, however, his shrines do "rightly" realign him with the tradition of Osiris becoming Re.

In the lower left register, the fire-spitting cobra stands before a "totem pole" that includes a boat's sail and mast, a star, and a solar disk terminating in a lion's head on the left side and a spitting cobra on the right. The fire energy streams in three rays from the mouth of the serpent to the lion and from the lion to the serpent. All of this energy is projected in vibrations that move in undulating waves across each form of Osiris. It is difficult to parse out exactly what each represents. The celestial energies—solar, lunar, fire, and even the unseen wind—are activated on the earthly plane. The energy moves in ways that create unified oppositions (Re and Osiris, solar and lunar, cat and lion/ serpent). The head and crown are wrapped in the auric field. Perhaps Osiris sails through the stars.

The middle terrestrial register depicts Amun-Re, the ram god, contained within Duat and hidden in form. Six ram beings face the lion god who stands upon the serpent in a pose similar to the cat whose paws dominate the serpent in the celestial register. The slithering serpent may represent the subterranean waters of Earth. A series of stars surmount a solar disk, and their three energy rays stream onto the ground. All of the names of the Amun rams—such as Uplifted Face or Uplifted Shadow—connote the idea of being raised up within the horns. This is the language of hope.

Six goddesses appear in the final grouping on the bottom register. They open their palms to the ground, and from them energy streams forth, a protypical image of the astrological sign Aquarius. Combined stellar and solar light from above flows into their mouths, representing what appears to be a kind of trance channeling of oracular energy. Or perhaps it is divine energy that is swallowed and taken in.

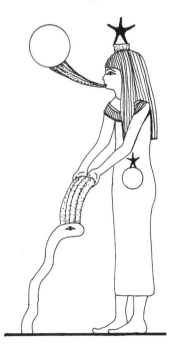

Light activates the throat chakra (via the Opening of the Mouth Ceremony) and the creative, regenerative solar plexus chakra. As the energies stream in, they are transmuted and poured out through an alchemical process of transformation of lower matter into higher forms.

These energies move through them and pour out through their hands and fingertips. The energy falls in four rays onto a serpent that arises from the depths, as the legend says, "before the double horizon." With this energy, each goddess tames the snake whose name is Evil Face, a symbol of the dark, misused power. The serpent in this case may be the underworld form of Seth or Apophis, the enemy of Osiris.

Within the womb of each goddess, a star sits atop a globe of light. Here is the expansive, creative energy of the *svandisthana,* or solar plexus, chakra, the center of creativity and regeneration. In ancient Egypt, the rebirth of the pharaoh and of the world arrives with the rising river. It comes forth at the rise of the star Sirius, or Isis. This image might remind us of the impregnation of the goddess with the holy child: a sacred event that occurs in Egypt during the darkest night of the year—the point at which the sun's rays are weakest and the length of the daylight is shortest. During the winter solstice, one can look into the night sky and find the star Deneb inside the body of the sky goddess Nut who appears as the Milky Way. One can actually see her cloudy white body bending over Earth, her hands in the west and her feet in the east. At the point where the galactic cloud breaks into two streams, which are the goddess's legs, there appears a concave area. This is the womb of the celestial goddess. There, on December 21, the star Deneb rests, a soul awaiting birth. The six goddesses of this frame have such names as She Who Adores, She Who Lights Up, and so on.

I have just read backward the images in all three registers of the exterior right panel of the second shrine. In reality, the hieroglyphs were written right to left, rather than left to right. My backward process, however, has allowed me time to linger over the images. Looking across the three registers, we might be able to see this entire panel as a sort of comic strip of rebirth. Each register represents a trimester of the creative process that begins in the lower right-hand corner with the goddess who represents inception, through the development of the layers of form and the layers of spirit as they become attached to us. At the final panel in the upper left-hand area, we see that the body has been formed and the emotional states have been established. In the end, the ba soul awaits its instructions that stream down into the body from the light that is beyond Light.

One might see the true meaning of the secret phrase that opens the door to the mysteries as being the perfect enunciation of a secret phrase in the sacred language. The key is that it is every word that we have spoken. The vibrations of our words of power—the effect those words have on us and on those around us, these daily words and acts that surround us in our daily waking lives—have set in motion the vibration necessary to unlock the key to the mysteries. Death is the culmination of life experience. It is the final exam.

And then the great turnaround arrives, and morning breaks. The full-length panel at the left, running top to bottom, represents our birth. Divine hands from above lift down the encapsulated ba of Re into the receiving hands of Earth. In nine months, or three trimesters later, the divine king is reborn during the Hed-Sed Festival. He is the son born of the god Atum and the womb of the goddess. He is the embodiment of the divine Re here on Earth coming forth during the new year.

Says Re in Chapter 17 of the Pert em Heru, "I am Re of the setting sun, now rising up! . . . I am yesterday and I know tomorrow. . . . I am the phoenix in Heliopolis. I alone am the keeper of all the personal history within the book of that which is and that which shall be."[26]

At death when a person reaches this point of understanding, he is able to cross from this realm into the next life without fear. When a person reaches this point in life, he has become not only self-actualized and self-determined but also a vessel for the Divine.

Over each shrine, the goddess Nut stretches out full length to cover us, spreading her wings and taking us into her golden body. In a way, the feathers represent the multiform way in which light streams down from above us and envelops us. Imagine the beat of wings, the sound of

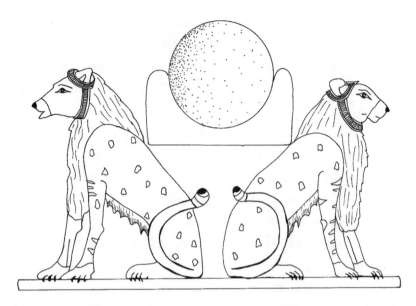

The Aker lions represent the eternal solar energies on the eastern and western horizons. The light of Re shines upon the eternal present. Say the lions: "I am Yesterday and I know Tomorrow."

the ba soul or the wings of the goddess Mut, as she in her vulture form comes down upon us to take us into her body at death or to birth us inside the egg of the world. All is sound and color. All is vibration. All is thought emanating from the divine mind.

Osiris Is the Seed

It is mid-October now, the end of the growing season. And it is the beginning of the ancient Egyptian festival of the Osirian Mysteries—a time that saw Isis and Nephthys mourning Osiris. I go to my garden with a slower step and a little more sadness. The verdant summer is gone from us. The vines have withered on their cane poles, and the dried beans rattle inside their mottled, twisted pods whenever the wind blows. I snap them from the stringy vine and rub them between my palms until the husks fall away. I save the seed, putting the beans in sealed bags to store or give to friends. We could feed a nation if we all remembered how to live this way.

As evening settles over the bronzed hills, all around me the chimney swifts dive, whirl, dive again, dance, then fold their wings and fall into the darkness. Their chirrups in the dusk are a comfort. Soon winter will be upon us. Soon they will be gone. My husband and I will stand in the yard in our coats, staring up at the moonless sky, listening to the stars in Orion's belt sizzle.

In October, we prepare our garden for the spring, spreading sheep manure and straw where the Egyptians would have fertilized their ground with the black soil left from the Nile's annual inundation. We pull dead plants and vines, and I feel compelled to get down on one knee and whisper my thanksgiving to this beautiful Earth of ours that gave us such a life-sustaining garden during the summer.

The Nile inundation mirrored cosmic creation when the all comingled in a watery abyss until a hillock of earth arose. After the floods subsided, the replenished soil of Egypt emerged as fresh and new as if for the first time. The growing season did not depend upon rainfall but rather upon irrigation after the waters began to recede. The fertile sowing season in Egypt began during the month of Khoiak (mid-October to mid-November). Preparing the ground well and planting in the proper season assured survival of the crops, the people, and the land. Most of the fecundity festivals dedicated to Osiris and to the ithyphallic god Min occurred during this month. Both gods symbolized the seed bursting forth in green shoots and the ability of the male to fertilize the female.

At the same time in the sky, a miraculous rising was occurring as the constellation Orion, pushed by the star Sirius to lift its head from the floodwaters, rose in the sky until at last it stood upright. All of these phenomena manifested as one cosmic rejuvenation.

Many harvest celebrations worldwide—most of which occur in autumn—have their origins in the sowing and sorrowing festivals that commemorate the dying and resurrecting god. In both festivals, Osiris is the seed. In the season of harvest (May in ancient Egypt and October here and elsewhere in the Northern Hemisphere), all of the fruits and crops are harvested from the fields. The seed was saved until such time that Orion rose again and the food returned. As in the myth of Osiris's harvest, the Egyptian festivals also included wine, women, and song.

Then, like a chill wind, a change befalls him. Death, disguised as a brother, finds and seizes Osiris. In the myth his brother Set ensnares Osiris in a coffin and throws him into the Nile. In the sky, the stars tell that same story; that is, the constellation Orion dips below the horizon and disappears from sight. In the myth, he is found by Isis who attempts to resurrect him, but his body is again found by Set who hacks his brother to pieces. After his second death, his fourteen pieces, his corporeal matter, is scattered throughout Egypt—an act that "seeds" the future temples of Egypt. Seven cities of Upper Egypt claim seven pieces of his body; seven appear in Lower Egypt. At each site, legend says, Isis and Nephthys found a part of him—his eyes, a finger, a neck bone, a thigh bone, and so on. Each part was wrapped, mummified, and buried as if it were the whole. Each burial site became a temple to the living god Osiris. The fragment became holy, and the temple became the unified, living god.

Thereafter, Osiris would always be "re-membered" because his sister goddesses created a memorial festival through which, for three millennia, the Egyptians participated to give thanks to and pay homage to Osiris.

OSIRIAN MYSTERY TRADITIONS

Once a year, members of the nomes of Egypt where Osiris had been scattered came together as a community to celebrate the Osirian Mysteries. Its rites for remembering and feeding the dead were similar to the South American and Central American Day of the Dead festivals, the Celtic Samhain festival, and the Eleusinian Mysteries of Demeter and Persephone in Greece—except in Egypt, it lasted for an entire month. Two temples were the major centers for the Osirian Mysteries: Abydos in Upper Egypt commemorated his death, while Busiris in Lower Egypt celebrated his resurrection during winter solstice rites.

The festivals began on the first day of Khoiak in public ceremonies. The earth was turned with a hoe during a festival called the Hacking of the Earth. The preparation took twelve days. The activity assured that all came together as a community to till the soil, create the irrigation canals, and build the *shadduf* that would water the land, but more importantly, they came together to help each other. In this way, older community members taught the younger generation customs of worship and farming. Modern-day Egyptians still celebrate the agricultural feast of Sham el Nessim on the winter solstice by planting wheat, lentils, and other seeds to usher in the new year. The sprouting of the seed signifies rebirth, and Egyptians will wish each other *sana kfuwfra,* literally "green year."[1]

I have watched my rural community bind together for the large tasks of planting, cultivating, and harvesting each season—jobs too large for a single man, or even a single family. One farmer helps another harrow, plant, cultivate, and pick, each taking turns in the other's field. Planting together is a beneficent communal act—a value that may be disappearing all too quickly as urban life expands unless we learn to create sustainable community gardens in our cities, neighborhoods, and schools. Seeds remind us that for every end, there arises a new beginning. They remind us that when we care for and nurture what we love, it grows to sustain us.

The core of the Osirian Mysteries began midmonth and lasted ten days from the twelfth to the twenty-first. Most Egyptians participated in a public mystery play. Priestesses embodying Isis and Nephthys keened and mourned the dead Osiris, following a burial sledge to the grave. Still other priestesses processed through the temple carrying winnowing baskets that contained the seed gathered from the last harvest of the previous year. It was said that in just such baskets Isis and Nephthys had gathered the severed limbs of Osiris. Lector priests intoned transfiguration rituals from the sacred texts. High priests from each of the forty-two nomes carried canopic jars that contained the relics of Osiris that were gathered into a single body.

On the twelfth day of the month, two black cows were yoked together to a plow made of tamarisk and a ploughshare of black copper. Behind his father at the plow, a boy scattered the seed, following in his father's tracks. First, the fields of barley were sowed, then the flax, and then the spelt. As the boy and his father worked, they recited hymns to Osiris. A donkey followed the boy through the field, tramping down the seed.

Each animal or plant had a ritual aspect. The two black cows symbolized Isis and Nephthys who go together to weep for Osiris. The ass was Seth, who having murdered Osiris now stomped him firmly into the ground. The durable wood of the plow came from the tamarisk tree that grew up around the body of Osiris at Byblos. The flax became the linen of his funeral pall.

The twelfth day of the month was also the time at which the Orionid meteor showers occurred, which we can still see in mid-October. The meteor shower resembles scattered seed falling from the body of the constellation of Orion, which is the *sahu,* or light body of Osiris. The seeds were essential Osirian symbols. Spelt, a high-protein wheat, and barley were staples of the Egyptian diet. From spelt came bread, and from the barley came beer. This sacred food and drink came to represent spiritual gifts manifested from the body of Osiris. Within the sprouting seed, the soul of the god returned to life. Images of the creative energies that arise from the god can be found in temple carvings at Philae, Abydos, Dendera, and in all of the temples where Osiris was honored. Osiris may lie inert on his bier, yet we know that he lives because we can see the fecund, sexual energy that lifts his phallus like a stalk among the vegetation that grows out of his body.

Seeds signify the beginning and the end of life, the essential alpha and omega. It contains all the potentiality of the future and all the wisdom garnered from the past. The practice of agriculture was essential wisdom that came from Isis and Osiris, both of whom, it was said, devoted their energies to teaching humankind the ways of civilization in order to assure an abundant future. Knowing how to gather, sort, plant, nurture, harvest, and store meant learning to attune to the mysterious, regenerative life force.

Seed is a metaphor for illumination. Hidden in the dark, fecund earth, the seed waits, germinating through the nurturing warmth and rain until it bursts forth and flourishes, growing by the power of light. In just such ways, the subconscious mind, watered in love and with meditation, begins to grow in the conscious mind until it achieves full union in the light as a perfected mind, the garden of supraconsciousness. Change is prerequisite, however. A seed in the soil must die to its current form. To provide nourishment for the seedling, it must be willing to relinquish its shape and become something new and different. Nothing remains as it was. To grow a new spirit that lives as one with the Divine, the human ego that separates us from God and each other must be dissolved.

The central resurrection rites to the Osirian Mysteries were conducted in private temple initiations. One Dendera ritual in the Temple of Hathor lasted nearly half the month. It involved presenting seeds before the naked goddess, and then placing the seeds on a cloth moistened with water. The grain was divided and distributed into four golden vessels. A golden mold in the shape of Osiris was created and filled with alluvial dirt. In another stone sarcophagus, soil was placed and watered for eight days. Then the spelt, having been exposed for one day to the sun, was placed inside the sarcophagus and in the Osirian form. It was covered with reeds. Nile water was poured over it. Ten days later, the reeds were removed and the water drained. Now the grain effigy of Osiris was carried to the tomb, placed in a coffin, and entombed on the last day of the month.

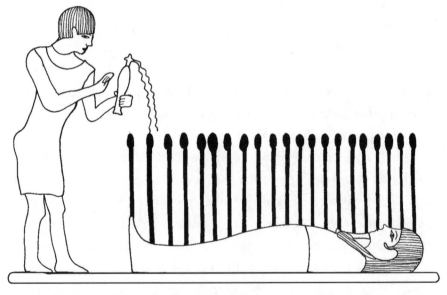

Inside Tutankhamun's Treasury Room, a mummiform of Osiris filled with Nile soil and seed was found. The seeds had already begun to sprout. They symbolized the life force of Egypt's Green Man that surges forth even in the dark recesses of the tomb.

Similar grain mummies have been found in the tombs of the pharaohs. Inside a room built in the Third Dynasty beneath the Step Pyramid at Saqqara, archaeologists have found and radiocarbon-dated 4,500-year-old seeds that were buried with the pharaoh Djoser. Tutankhamun's tomb had a seed bed in the shape of Osiris as the god Nepri, lord of vegetation. His name means "the one who lives, having died." Even in Tut's sealed tomb, the plants had sprouted. They were the sign that the soul of the dead had transformed. Utterance 219 of the Pyramid Text links pharaoh Unas and Osiris: "In your name of Dweller of Orion, with your season in the sky and your season on Earth: O, Osiris, turn your face and look on this King Unas, for your seed, which issued from you is good."[2]

The sprouting seed and the resurrected soul of Osiris apply to all. The dormant potential in every one of us may be the *ka* of Osiris in need of waking.

During Greco-Roman times, the public participated in the Osirian Mysteries as lavishly dressed spectators who witnessed the murder of Osiris, who was locked inside the jeweled casket and cast into the sea. These same participants returned as the army of Horus who fought a mock battle with Seth and his men. Through the mystery play one experienced a ritualized death that symbolized the murder of Osiris. The dramatic appearance of the coffin reminded people of the terrible fate that befell Osiris—in the midst of life and gaiety, death arrived. The ensuing battle represented the defeat of the dark forces of Seth by the might of the heroic god Horus.

For initiates, the mystery culminated in contemplation of one's own death—mysteries that were never spoken aloud, were never recorded on the temple walls, and were only alluded to in later times. They may have been similar to initiation rituals enacted by the Golden Dawn, the Rosicrucians, and the Masons and Knights Templar, all of whom attribute their mysteries to an Egyptian origin. When the spiritualist minister and founder of Astara Foundation Earlyne Chaney began to explain her understanding as an initiate of the mysteries, she said, "To the postulant of the Mysteries the 'dead' referred to souls entombed in the physical form. . . . To be 'resurrected from the dead' meant that the superstructure could be raised to transcend that of the lower personality."[3]

We all have Osirian events in our lives and feel a need to understand loss and renewal on both a psychological and a spiritual level. Yet, we are more than the actions of our bodies and minds. We are spirits having a human experience. We are the way that the Divine can understand matter and its consciousness by seeing what matters to us and how we act and react to loss and return. Humans are the hands of God, the conduits for change. Every change is a loss of one thing in order to gain another. Time is an Osirian experience of aging, of summer turning into fall then winter, of dying plants and dried seeds. It is all a falling away. I can remember standing at the Osirion at Abydos ten days after my mother had passed and tangibly, physically feeling her leave the world and me. I felt her simultaneous regret and exhilaration. Life is a coffin.

Regardless of the degree of initiation, spiritual celebrations and communion still have a profound psychic effect on the individual. The mysteries always call upon us to turn inward and to face the unknown with strength. There was an outer ceremony for nearly every Egyptian, but there was an inner articulation of the mystery for only a few. That's not surprising. Religion is probably the most misunderstood concept of all—primarily because religion is a subcategory of a larger concept, which is spirituality and unity with the Divine.

Herodotus recalls a solstice ceremony in which a bull, a symbol of Osiris called the Good Being, was sacrificed and its carcass stuffed with flour cakes, honey, raisins, figs, incense, myrrh, and other herbs. It roasted over a fire as the priests of Osiris poured oil over it and on the flames to keep the fire going. Afterward, they ate the ox.[4] The ritually sacred body and fluid of the bull of Osiris has become the bread and wine given to all. Anglicans and Catholics might find a resonance with the Eucharistic sacrifice of Christ. The seed is the container of the mystery. Knowing that the god had died, the god was risen, and the god would come again is the essence of the mystery tradition.

In death initiations, one contacts the sorrowful mysteries, but the joyful mysteries lie beneath them. The sarcophagus in which the body is placed bears upon its coffin lid the image of the sky goddess bending over the dead. Literally the word *sarcophagus* means "sacred eating." At the end of the day, the goddess ingests the sun, and it travels through her dark body in the same way that the soul of light is swallowed by death and returns to its source. There, in the dark and stillness, one gestates a new life. The tomb is the womb of the goddess—an entrance and exit. In the words of the hierophant Hermes Trismegestus, "There where everything ends, all begins eternally."[5]

Such was the way of mystery initiations performed under the veil of night. Moving beyond the dark night of the soul, one may burst forth into ecstatic states of poetry, illumination, and wisdom. It is the darkness that provides new meaning to the light.

COMMUNION AND THE SEEDS OF PEACE

The dark soil filled with seed and the body filled with bread and beer are both dedicated to Osiris. Both symbolize the same fecund and rejuvenating power. While the large public mysteries took place less frequently, the priests of the temple performed the same Eucharistic rite weekly in the temple for the benefit of the neteru and at the graves of community members for the benefit of the ancestors. As the seed is watered in the golden trough, so is the seed of the mummy given drink poured on the ground so that it might flourish. Pouring water, the ancient Egyptian priest says, "Your body will live by means of the libation. It is being rejuvenated in your mystery."[6]

At the grave lay a stone in the shape of the *hotep* hieroglyph, which depicts a reed mat unrolled with the offerings on top of it. On it were placed the physical offerings of the reed mat, the bread, and the beer. The *hotep* hieroglyph (⟚) meant "peace," as in "rest in peace." Perhaps that is what the Christian liturgy refers to when it invokes "the peace that passeth understanding."

This symbol of peace also is similar to the expression of embracing one another and sharing the peace. The gesture builds the community of enlightened people who understand that this is more than a hand extended in friendship; it is fellowship. It is becoming alive within each other. In other words, *namaste:* the god in me sees the god in you.

While this communion gathers the members of its congregation and makes them one, more importantly it establishes an expression of love and bonding between the Divine and the individual. "Every offering is a gift between the recipient and the receiver," German Egyptologist Jan Assmann writes. No shadow arises between one's footsteps and the will of God. The living masters who carry this wisdom in their DNA see that all people are one body. Offering rituals were not supplications to the gods. They were not, as Assmann says, "communion between the human and the divine, but rather as an interaction between deities."[7]

That is another way to say, "The Father and I are One."

Chapter 148 of the Book of the Dead was the Egyptian consecration of the sacred elements. Standing before the doorway to the tomb, the sacraments are lifted up. Osiris and Re have been united. Each exists in the embrace of the other. The lector priest, true of voice, reads: "Homage to you, Re, who is the lord, the lord of truth, the only one, the lord of eternity and maker of infinity. I have come before you, lord Re; I have made the seven cows and their bull to flourish. You who have gifts of bread and beer for the glorified spirits, may you give also to my soul with you."[8]

The food of the dead was not simply food. It was God being brought to the grave and offered. It is a human gesture of awareness that consciousness, which is the body of God, exists inside a single broken piece of bread that is the host for the God in all of us. On a physical level, *Tchefa* (𓋴 𓏱 𓏰) was the liquid and food offerings. On another level, it was the body and blood of the Divine. *Tchef* was one of Re's bodies, *Tchefet* was the goddess who lives in the Elysian Fields, and *tchefen* was all life lived joyfully, linking our ancestors and the child to come.

There was a second kind of bread that did not exist on a physical plane. It was called *paut,* and it was written as a hieroglyph of birds in flight, 🦅⌒—the winged *ba* souls rising up beyond matter. Paut was the name for the Ennead, or the nine great gods from whom everything in the universe was made. All these gods and goddesses appear as aspects of Re-Atum. Paut was the life force constantly moving between seen and unseen worlds, a magical process called transubstantiation—an active principle that is always in the process of being made.

There was a third kind of sacred bread and this was *bennu* (🦅). It was the great sacrifice. It was the phoenix, the kernel of the soul tucked inside the body of a grain, crushed and broken and burning in the light. It was full consciousness. It was a lifetime of experience, and it was nothing at all. *Ben* is that which is begotten and passes away, and *ben-ben* (𓊪 〰 𓊪 〰 △), was the bier, the name of the pillar atop which the phoenix made his nest, fanned the spark of fire with his wings, and consumed himself in the flames.

These offerings of bread and libations were made before the Eyes of Horus, in the "sight of God," as it were. Every Egyptian offering included offerings of the Eyes of Horus. Just as the Eye of Horus was blinded by hatred and healed by the love of the goddess, so must the wounded part within us be restored and made whole. Being mortal is a wound. Death in mortal form is the sacrifice we must make to release the life-sustaining force that is spirit and return it as an offering back to the Divine.

Give us this day our daily bread, we pray. Bread is the essence of human life. There are no cultures that do not eat bread. As the W. S. Merwin poem of the same name says: "Each face in the street is a slice of bread, wandering on, searching."[9] From the fire of Re and the heat of transformation, we are the bread of the world, the body of the Divine that feeds and sustains each other, the world, and the Creator who made us.

The Eye of Horus assures that God exists in even the smallest part of every human being. We and the dead are all part of the Divine coming together. The Eye of Horus contained a mathematical concept in which the fragments that make up the eye—its pupil, its eyebrow, and so on—individually signified particular fractions. (Please see plate 19 of the color insert.) The Eye offering was meant to return us to wholeness, to bridge the separation of spirit and matter, to bridge the separation between life and death, to bridge the separation between each other. The ladder to heaven is lifted up by both Horus and Seth, and on it Osiris ascends. Together they reinforced the idea of pulling together all the severed parts of Osiris and of ourselves, all the disowned and disavowed bits that cloud consciousness and separate us from the light that we so long to become.

The weekly communion rituals that sustained the ancestors were not a ritual to make the deceased *like* Osiris but to make him Osiris. Coffin Text 330 provides us with the secret meaning of the seed, which dies in the earth and returns whole, its power multiplied. Here the ba soul of the deceased speaks with Osiris and with the natural world.

> *Whether I live or die I am Osiris. I enter in and*
> *reappear through you.*
> *I decay in you, I grow in you. I fall down in you, I*
> *fall upon my side.*
> *The gods are living in me for I live and grow in the*
> *grain that sustains the ancestors.*
> *I cover the earth, and whether I live or die, I am*
> *barley. I am not destroyed.*
> *I have entered the order (ma'at). I rely upon the*
> *order. I become master of the order. I emerge in*
> *the order.*
> *I make my form distinct. I am the Lord of the*
> *chennet (granary of Memphis).*
> *I have entered into the order. I have reached its*
> *limits.*[10]

BEING: THE BODY OF GOD

The unification of Osiris with Re, as well as Re's unification with all of the other neteru who grew out of Atum's first word, is *ma'at*. That impulse that caused the waters to vibrate and the light to flare out when all that was enfolded inside the body of Atum—that breath of life that created Re—is the ma'at. It is the law of transubstantiation. This becomes that, because at one time, this and that were the same thing, lying side by side. They were not even two molecules in one undifferentiated cell. They were one being. That was Osiris and Re together on the first day, and that is Re and Osiris on the last. All of spirit cloaked in matter is the Aufu Re, literally the flesh of light.

Says the Litany of Re:

> *I am entirely a god.*
> *No limb of mine is without god.*
> *I enter as a god*
> *And I exit as a god.*
> *The gods have transformed themselves into my body.*[11]

It matters less that we know which god "rules" which part of the divine self. It is more important to recognize that all of our human parts are parts of God. Complete integration of the self with God is the essence of the divine ecstatic poetry of Rumi in which the human soul longs for merger with the beloved. The ultimate becoming is the recognition that no separation has ever existed, only the illusion of it.

The swifts that nested in our chimney all summer long have flown away in the last week. The altered quality of light pierced their pineal gland and sent them swirling counterclockwise one day up out of the chimney and down south to a rain forest in Brazil. I used to watch them swirl and move as one body, like a dark sheet flapping in the breeze as they came together to dip and dive above the chimney. They moved so rapidly. How did they know when to fold their wings and dive, and how did they do it so well without bumping into each other? The swifts were moving as one body. Bees do it, and birds and fish and cells moving around at breakneck speed inside our bodies do it. It seems random, eccentric. It isn't.

Physicist Alain Aspect discovered that electrons communicate with each other whether ten feet apart or ten billion miles apart. He discovered that each subatomic particle knows what the other particle is doing.[12] The cells in our body know instinctively what their role is in the organism and how to play it, just as the birds know when it is their turn to fly down the chimney or soar off to Brazil. When Aspect discovered this, he broke apart Einstein's theory of relativity. Suddenly there was something that could communicate faster than the speed of light. It could do this because the information was not traveling at all. It simply existed, each seed of the whole inside every other, forming one sentient being.

Fellow physicist David Bohm explained the universe as a gigantic and splendidly detailed hologram. He saw the whole in every part and determined that as much as we try to dissect it to figure out how it works, all we come away with are smaller and smaller wholes. There are no pieces to pull apart or put together. He concluded that reality did not exist, that it was an illusion. (Perhaps it is a projection by Atum.)[13] He realized that the separation between particles, or people for that matter, is an illusion. There are no signals being passed back and forth. The birds, the cells, the people on this planet are all extensions of the same living being. We have to love our neighbors as ourselves because—well—they are.

I've come back to the idea of the hieroglyph for Re—a dot within a circle, ☉. It is one moment in time and it is every moment in time, a circle is its first vibration out into space, but it is also the container for the All-ness at its core. It is the spark of light at the center of life that is Re. It is spiritualized man surrounded by all his spiritual bodies inside the body of god, which is every aspect of the natural world, seen or unseen. It is the bodies of god. It is the seed stone in the temple. It is the god within his shrine inside that temple. It is the mummy in his coffin inside his cavern within the rooms of Duat. It is Osiris in the arms of Re.

Aufu Re is the energy of the universe. It is the mind of god and its seed thought that created the universe in a brilliant flash of consciousness that is a thousand points of light. It is the flower of life, the rays of consciousness, unfolding and closing. It is the spark inside the ash inside the nest of the phoenix. It is the bread of life. And it is nothing at all.

Glossary

ab: the heart, the seat of consciousness

abtu: the fish associated with Isis that pulled the solar boat through the underworld

ajna: Sanskrit word for the third eye chakra

akhet: the horizon

akhu: the shining spirit, the higher self that connects to the god spark

Amenta: the hidden world in the afterlife

ankh: hieroglyphic sign symbolizing life

arit: a hall in the underworld, one of the seven halls whose doorways are guarded by gatekeepers

atef: the pharaoh's white crown surmounted by a gold disk and trimmed with ostrich feathers

aufu: the physical body of flesh that also contains all of the spiritual bodies

ba: the immortal soul, depicted as a bird with a human head

ben-ben: the sacred stone at Heliopolis that represented the primeval mound that emerged from the waters of chaos at the beginning of time; the shape of obelisks and pyramids may have evolved from this stone

bennu: the phoenix, a mythical bird that builds its pyre on the ben-ben stone, dies, and is reborn from the ashes

caduceus: the staff of Thoth, as physician, with two entwined snakes and two wings at the top

canopic jars: a set of jars that contained some of the internal organs removed from the deceased during mummification

chandra: Sanskrit word for the chakra that contains the memory of earthly experience

cippi: a magical stela with healing powers that depicted Isis protecting her son Horus

Coptic: language descended from ancient Egyptian and used as the liturgical language of the Coptic church

demotic script: an everyday seventh-century-BCE form of ancient Egyptian writing used in the Late Egyptian and Greco-Roman periods

djeba: the united being, specifically refers to the merged entities Osiris and Re

djed: the column of Osiris, sometimes referred to as the spine of Osiris or as a representation of the truncated Tree of Life in which he was ensnared in Byblos

dua: twilight

Duat: the nighttime of the underworld found within the tomb

Ennead: a group of nine gods that represent the entire cycle of all the gods and goddesses

Heb-Sed Festival: this "jubilee" festival celebrated the prowess and renewal of the pharaoh; the festival occurred at regular intervals, specifically at the thirtieth year of reign

heka: magic, words of power

hennu boat: the solar boat that sails at dawn or dusk to and from the neterworld, first described in the Pyramid Text of Unas

hieratic: shorthand form of hieroglyphic writing that was an intermediary step to demotic writing

hieroglyph: the oldest and most pictographic form of ancient Egyptian writing

hotep: peace, the offering of food and drink in the afterlife

Imperishable Ones: the stars, which never set, were seen as eternal souls that never die, specifically ancestral souls and gods located in the night sky of the Northern Hemisphere

ished tree: the Tree of Life on whose leaves Thoth wrote in shining letters

ka: the spirit double of a living person shaped at birth that receives offerings in the afterlife to sustain its life

Kemet: literally the Black Land, ancient Egyptian name for Egypt; refers to the dark soil fertilized by the Nile

khaibit: the shadow; one of the spiritual bodies

khat: the physical container; the body and all its sinews, bones, and organs

khepera: the hieroglyph for transformation and change; also the dung beetle as the aspect of divine transformation

kher ab: a lector priest

khu: *see* akhu

kundalini: latent energy believed to lie coiled at the base of the spine

ma'at: truth, cosmic order, balance, law

ma'aty: the double truth, the interlinked oppositions

manipura: Sanskrit word for the navel chakra

Manu: the western lands, the place where the sun sets; the entrance to the tomb

Mehen: the serpent in the underworld often depicted as eating its tail; also a game played in ancient Egypt

meskhet boat: the boat that sailed to the stars of the northern sky, especially to the Great Bear or Big Dipper constellation where the eternal souls (Imperishable Ones) lived

mys or mes: child of a god; the mystery of birth

necropolis: Greek word meaning "city of the dead" or cemetery

nefer: beautiful

neter: a god or a goddess, a divine being

Neter-Khert: the name for what exists below the god, i.e. the necropolis

neteru: more than one god or goddess

neterworld: the divine world, which may be understood as the underworld of the dead but includes the world of the gods and goddesses in any circumstance

Nun: the nothingness; also the god of the celestial waters, the abyss

ogdoad: the eight divine beings that arose in the cosmic waters through the creative work of Thoth

ostraca: limestone flake or fragment of pottery used for practicing writing

ouroboros: the serpent that eats its tail and indicates infinity or eternity; *see also* Mehen

paut: completion, the nine great gods from which everything in the universe was made

per: literally, a container for anything

per áa: the pharaoh, literally the physical container for the spirit of god

per ankh: the library, also called the house of life

pert: seed, or the season—Pert—for sowing seed

Pert em Heru: the ancient name for what we call the Egyptian Book of the Dead, but to the ancient Egyptian it was more precisely the Book of Coming into Light

per ur: the sanctuary, or holy of holies, often called the Great House

ren: the sacred name

Restau: a place in the necropolis that represents the entrance into the tomb; literally, it was where the body was dragged up an incline to the tomb in Saqqara

sahasrara: the crown chakra, which is described in the Sanskrit tradition as having a thousand multicolored petals

sahu: the shining, golden, or illuminated body, similar to the aura or halo around divinized beings

Sekhet Iaru: the Field of Reeds

Sekhet-hetep: the Field of Peace, or the Elysian Fields

sekhem: the power or will linked to the lion goddess Sekhmet

sem priest: a high priest who wore a lion skin robe, usually the pharaoh or his stand-in

senet: an ancient game similar to Parcheesi that was also a map of the underworld; the object of the game was to reach "home" first, without falling into the pit and, thus, being sent back to the beginning

seshet: a mystery, specifically linked to the written word

shadduf: a pivoted pole with a bucket at one end and a counterweight at the other, used to raise water

stela: an inscribed stone dedicated to someone or commemorating an event

svandisthana: Sanskrit word for the solar plexus chakra, the center of creativity

tchefa: food offering of any kind

tekenu: a sacrificial victim, or one lying in a fetal position wrapped within animal skins

thet: the buckle of Isis, a sign of fertility and abundance; life blood

ur-hekau: great of magic, skilled at words of power

uraeus: the fire-spitting cobra emblem worn by the pharaoh as part of his headdress and indicating the power of the third eye

ushabti: a servant figurine that performed work for the deceased in the afterlife

vishudda: Sanskrit word for the throat chakra

wab priest: a purified servant in the god's temple; one who is "washed and fasted"

wadjet: name of the cobra goddess who serves the pharaoh and appears at his third eye; also the name of the healing Eye of Horus

waz scepter: the forked staff of the pharaoh surmounted by the head of a jackal or the Seth animal

Zep Tepi: literally the First Time, indicating the moment of creation and the inundation of the Nile

Notes

INTRODUCTION TO THE WORK: OPEN SESAME!

1. Generally attributed to Johannes Eckhart, *Meister Eckhart's Sermons.* Found in Roberts, *Prayers from Around the World,* 251.
2. Hornung, *The Secret Lore of Egypt,* 16.
3. Rilke, *Selected Poems of Rainer Maria Rilke,* 151.

COSMOGENESIS: STORIES OF HOW THE WORLD BEGAN

1. Piankoff, *Litany of Re,* 32.
2. Freke and Gandy, *The Hermetica,* 19.
3. Freke, *The Illustrated Book of Sacred Scriptures,* 16–19.
4. Ellis, *Dreams of Isis,* 37.
5. Freke and Gandy, *The Hermetica,* 5.
6. Richardson and Walker-John, *Inner Guide to Egypt,* 6.
7. Michael, *The Alchemy of Sacred Living,* 23.
8. Pinch, *Egyptian Mythology,* 170.
9. Definition by Frederick Page in Keats, *Letters of John Keats,* 53.
10. Ellis, *Awakening Osiris,* 162.
11. Ibid., 65.
12. Clark, *Myth and Symbol in Ancient Egypt,* 61.
13. Author translation based on Lamy, *Egyptian Mysteries,* 9.
14. Ellis, *Awakening Osiris,* 101.
15. Lamy, *Egyptian Mysteries,* 8.
16. Breasted, *Ancient Records of Egypt,* vol. 2, 323.
17. Carus, *On the Nature of Things,* vol. 1, 51.
18. Richardson and Walker-John, *Inner Guide to Egypt,* 47.
19. Lamy, *Egyptian Mysteries,* 79.

20. Piankoff, *Litany of Re*, 39.

21. Malkowski, *Before the Pharaohs*, 215.

CREATION AND EVOLVING STATES OF CONSCIOUSNESS

1. Clark, *Sacred Tradition in Ancient Egypt*, 81.

2. Author translation based on Lichtheim, *Ancient Egyptian Literature*, vol. 1, 169.

3. Lichtheim, *Ancient Egyptian Literature*, vol. 1, 74.

4. Author translation based on Budge, *The Egyptian Book of the Dead*, 453.

5. Clark, *Myth and Symbol in Ancient Egypt*, 78.

6. Frankfort, *Ancient Egyptian Religion*, 97.

7. Clark, *Myth and Symbol in Ancient Egypt*, 56.

8. Frankfort, *Ancient Egyptian Religion*, 97.

9. Ibid., 98–99.

10. Clark, *Myth and Symbol in Ancient Egypt*, 249.

11. Budge, *Legends of the Gods*, 49.

12. Jacq, *Egyptian Magic*, 19.

THE MAGIC OF MAGIC: WORDS OF POWER

1. Frankfort, *Ancient Egyptian Religion*, 29.

2. Faulkner, *The Ancient Egyptian Pyramid Texts*, 225.

3. Jacq, *Egyptian Magic*, 4.

4. Faulkner, *The Ancient Egyptian Pyramid Texts*, 160.

5. Ritner, *The Mechanics of Ancient Egyptian Magical Practice*, 17.

6. Jacq, *Egyptian Magic*, 21.

7. Clark, *Myth and Symbol in Ancient Egypt*, 77.

8. Hornung, *Conceptions of God*, 89.

9. Gospel of Thomas 50 in Meyer, *The Nag Hammadi Library*, 43.

10. Lawlor in Schwaller de Lubicz, *The Temple of Man*, 9.

11. Richardson and Walker-John, *Inner Guide to Egypt*, 19.

12. Lamy, *Egyptian Mysteries*, 78.

13. John Anthony West quoted in Malkowski, *Before the Pharaohs*, 238.

14. Jayne, *The Healing Gods in Ancient Civilizations*, 25.

15. Schwaller de Lubicz, *Sacred Science*, 167.

16. Budge, *The Egyptian Book of the Dead*, 355.

17. Morenz, *Egyptian Religion*, 154.

18. Faulkner, *The Ancient Egyptian Pyramid Texts*, 70.

19. Ellis, *Awakening Osiris*, 43.

20. Cott, *Search for Omm Sety,* 92.

21. Author translation after Piankoff, *The Pyramid of Unas,* 39.

22. Hornung, *Conceptions of God,* 209.

23. Eckankar website: www.eckankar.org/glossary.html.

24. Faulkner, *The Ancient Egyptian Coffin Texts,* vol. 3, 108.

25. Author translation after Piankoff, *The Pyramid of Unas,* 29.

26. Faulkner, *The Ancient Egyptian Coffin Texts,* vol. 1, 249.

27. Cott, *Search for Omm Sety,* 217.

28. Faulkner, *The Ancient Egyptian Pyramid Texts,* 66.

29. Boylan, *Thoth,* 121.

30. Hornung, *Idea into Image,* 95.

31. Faulkner, *The Ancient Egyptian Coffin Texts,* vol. 3, 7.

32. Ibid., 177.

33. Ibid.

ISIS AND HER WORDS OF POWER

1. Campbell, *The Hero with a Thousand Faces,* 3.

2. Borghouts, *Ancient Egyptian Magical Texts,* 20.

PRACTICAL MAGIC FOR EGYPTIAN HEALERS

1. Masters, *The Goddess Sekhmet,* 28.

2. Budge, *Legends of the Gods,* 409.

3. Breasted, *The Edwin Smith Surgical Papyrus,* vol. 1, xv.

4. Breasted, *A History of Egypt from the Earliest Times to the Persian Conquest,* 112–13.

5. Meyer, *The Nag Hammadi Library,* 374.

6. Luckert, *Egyptian Light and Hebrew Fire,* 112.

7. Borghouts, *Ancient Egyptian Magical Texts,* 1.

8. Romer, *Ancient Lives,* 68.

9. Forrest, *Isis Magic,* 79.

10. Betz, *The Greek Magical Papyri in Translation,* 264.

11. Sauneron, *The Priests of Ancient Egypt,* 5.

12. Breasted, *The Edwin Smith Surgical Papyrus,* v.1, 313.

13. Ibid., 451.

14. Ibid., 430.

15. Forrest, *Offering to Isis,* 121.

16. Borghouts, *Ancient Egyptian Magical Texts,* 39.

17. Cline and and Rubalcaba, *The Ancient Egyptian World,* 72.

18. Eddy, *Science and Health with Key to the Scriptures,* 468.

19. Pinch, *Magic in Ancient Egypt,* 142.

20. Bennett and Crowley, *Magic and Mysteries of Ancient Egypt,* 133.

21. van den Dungen, "The Adoration of Re."

22. Watterson, *Gods of Ancient Egypt,* 78.

23. Lichtheim, *Ancient Egyptian Literature,* vol. 1, 37.

24. Gardiner, *Theban Ostraca,* C1: 13–15.

25. "Aretalogy of Isis," in Meyer, *The Ancient Mysteries,* 172.

ISIS AND HER SCORPIONS

1. Murray, *Legends of Ancient Egypt,* 27–29.

2. Jacq, *Egyptian Magic,* 19.

SHOCK AND AWE: MAGICAL SPELLS FOR PROTECTION

1. Hawass, *Valley of the Golden Mummies,* 210.

2. Strudwick, *Texts from the Pyramid Age,* 264.

3. Ibid., 253.

4. Rabinowitz, *Isle of Fire,* 132.

5. Ibid., 132.

6. Cott, *Search for Omm Sety,* 92.

7. Jacq, *Egyptian Magic,* 5.

8. Hornung, *Conceptions of God,* 207.

9. Lorenzi, "Vanished Persian Army Said Found in Desert."

10. Ritner, *Mechanics,* 41.

11. Brier, *Ancient Egyptian Magic,* 228–29.

12. Ibid., 265.

13. Griffith and Thompson, *The Demotic Magical Papyrus of London and Leyden,* 47.

14. Ibid., 34.

15. Ibid., 37.

16. Ibid., 39.

17. Assmann, *Death and Salvation in Ancient Egypt,* 148.

18. Hawass, *Silent Images,* 89.

19. Breasted, *Ancient Records of Egypt,* vol. 2, 89.

20. Ibid., 96.

21. Kousoulis, "Nine Measures of Magic Part 3."

22. Borghouts, *Ancient Egyptian Magical Texts*, 20.

23. Ibid.

24. Cottrell, *Queens of the Pharaohs*, 49.

25. Budge, *Egyptian Magic*, 91–95.

26. Ibid., 73–77.

27. Lichtheim, *Ancient Egyptian Literature*, vol. 2, 182–83.

28. Budge, *Egyptian Magic*, 67–70.

KHAEMWAST AND NANEFERKAPTAH: YEARNING FOR SECRET KNOWLEDGE

1. Lichtheim, *Ancient Egyptian Literature*, vol. 3, 128.

THE LEARNED EGYPTIANS

1. Budge, *Egyptian Magic*, 144.

2. Hauck, *The Emerald Tablet, passim.*

3. Mead, *Thrice Greatest Hermes*, 267.

4. Sauneron, *The Priests of Ancient Egypt*, 110–13.

5. "Asclepium," in Meyer, *The Nag Hammadi Library*, 21–29.

6. Sauneron, *The Priests of Ancient Egypt*, 113–14.

7. Ibid.

8. Pritchard and Fleming, *The Ancient Near East*, 324.

9. Sauneron, *The Priests of Ancient Egypt*, 135.

10. Luckert, *Egyptian Light and Hebrew Fire*, 261–62.

11. MacLeod, *The Library of Alexandria*, 10.

12. West, *The Traveler's Key to Ancient Egypt*, 40.

KHAEMWAST AND SI-OSIRE JOURNEY TO DUAT

1. Lichtheim, *Ancient Egyptian Literature*, vol. 3, 126.

TRAVELING THROUGH THE DARK

1. Huxley, *The Doors of Perception*, 5.

2. Budge, *The Egyptian Book of the Dead*, 77.

3. Hornung, *The Ancient Egyptian Books of the Afterlife*, 11.

4. Clark, *Myth and Symbol in Ancient Egypt*, 139.

5. Ibid., 139–40.

6. Ibid.

7. West, *The Traveler's Key to Ancient Egypt*, 283–84.

8. Richardson and Walker-John, *Inner Guide to Egypt*, 30.

9. Hart, *A Dictionary of Egyptian Gods and Goddesses*, 21.

10. James, *Myths and Ritual in the Ancient Near East*, 115.

11. Clark, *Myth and Symbol in Ancient Egypt*, 50.

12. Frankfort, *Ancient Egyptian Religion*, 187.

13. Scranton, *The Cosmological Origins of Myth and Symbol*, 128.

14. Budge, *The Egyptian Book of the Dead*, cxxxiv–vii.

15. Faulkner, *The Ancient Egyptian Pyramid Texts*, 191.

16. Ellis, *Feasts of Light*, 140.

17. Allen and Der Manuelian, *The Ancient Egyptian Pyramid Texts*, 180.

18. Ibid., 66.

19. Bauval and Gilbert, *The Orion Mystery, passim*.

20. Piankoff, *Litany of Re*, 6.

21. Hancock and Faiia, *Heaven's Mirror*, 82.

22. Darnell, *The Enigmatic Netherworld of the Solar-Osirian Unity*, 428.

23. Piankoff, *Litany of Re*, 12.

24. Piankoff, *Mythological Papyri*, 7–8.

25. Piankoff, *Litany of Re*, 43.

26. Abt and Hornung, *Knowledge for the Afterlife*, 58–59.

27. Ibid., 72.

28. Piankoff, *Litany of Re*, 12.

SI-OSIRE AND THE ETHIOPIAN MAGICIAN

1. Lichtheim, *Ancient Egyptian Literature*, vol. 3, 142–51.

ARTICULATING THE PORTALS BETWEEN DEATH AND LIFE

1. Author translation based on Piankoff, *The Pyramid of Unas*.

2. Faulkner, *The Ancient Egyptian Pyramid Texts*, 155.

3. Ibid., 82.

4. Clark, *The Sacred Tradition in Ancient Egypt*, 264.

5. Author translation based on Piankoff, *The Pyramid of Unas*.

6. Chaney, *Initiation in the Great Pyramid*, 183–84.

7. Frankfort, *Ancient Egyptian Religion*, 100.

8. Reeder, "A Rite of Passage."

9. Faulkner, *The Ancient Egyptian Pyramid Texts*, 94.

10. Piankoff, *The Pyramid of Unas*, 24.

11. Faulkner, *The Ancient Egyptian Pyramid Texts*, 92.

12. Author translation based on Piankoff, *The Pyramid of Unas*.

13. Piankoff, *The Pyramid of Unas*, 75–99.

14. Lichtheim, *Ancient Egyptian Literature*, vol. 1, 36.

15. Naydler, *Shamanic Wisdom in the Pyramid Texts*, 286.

16. "Aretalogy of Isis," in Meyer, *Ancient Mysteries*, 173.

17. Lesko, *The Ancient Egyptian Book of Two Ways*, 80.

18. Ibid.

19. Ibid., 27.

20. Faulkner, *The Ancient Egyptian Coffin Texts*, vol. 2, 60.

21. Ibid., vol. 1, 217.

22. Lesko, *The Ancient Egyptian Book of Two Ways*, 11.

23. Ibid., 130–31.

24. Budge, *The Egyptian Book of the Dead*, 57.

25. Reidy, *Eternal Egypt*, 290–91.

26. Faulkner, *The Egyptian Book of the Dead*, 48.

27. Reidy, *Eternal Egypt*, 292.

28. Budge, *The Egyptian Book of the Dead*, 309.

29. Ibid., 258.

30. Ibid., 31.

31. Ibid., 200.

32. Ibid., 204–5.

33. Clark, *The Sacred Tradition in Ancient Egypt*, 300.

34. Lichtheim, *Ancient Egyptian Literature*, vol. 2, 128.

35. Ibid., 128.

36. Hornung, *Idea into Image*, 95.

37. Budge, *The Egyptian Book of the Dead*, 205.

38. Clark, *The Sacred Tradition in Ancient Egypt*, 389.

39. Lamy, *Egyptian Mysteries*, 26.

TEMPLES OF GOLD, STONE, AND FLESH

1. Tesla, *My Inventions*, 69.

2. Seifer, *Wizard*, 451.

3. Budge, *The Egyptian Book of the Dead*, 60–61.

4. El-Abbadi and Fathallah, *What Happened to the Ancient Library of Alexandria?*, 43.

5. Piankoff, *The Shrines of Tut-Ankh-Amon*, 120.

6. Clark, *Myth and Symbol in Ancient Egypt*, 140.

7. Darnell, *The Enigmatic Netherworld,* 389.

8. Piankoff, *The Shrines of Tut-Ankh-Amon,* 94.

9. Ibid., 123.

10. Ibid., 122.

11. Clark, *The Sacred Tradition in Ancient Egypt,* 107.

12. Piankoff, *The Shrines of Tut-Ankh-Amon,* 125.

13. Ibid., 122.

14. Darnell, *The Enigmatic Netherworld,* 381.

15. Ibid., 383.

16. Ibid., 427–28.

17. Piankoff, *The Shrines of Tut-Ankh-Amon,* 128–31.

18. Grasse, *The Waking Dream,* 294.

19. Piankoff, *The Shrines of Tut-Ankh-Amon,* 128.

20. Darnell, *The Enigmatic Netherworld,* 459.

21. Grasse, *The Waking Dream,* 208.

22. Ibid.

23. Ibid., 241.

24. For a larger discussion of the metaphysical aspects of the four sons of Horus and their yogic traditions, see Isha Schwaller de Lubicz, *The Opening of the Way.*

25. Piankoff, *The Shrines of Tut-Ankh-Amon,* 128.

26. Budge, *The Egyptian Book of the Dead,* 29–31.

OSIRIS IS THE SEED

1. Ellis, *Feasts of Light,* 67.

2. Author translation after Piankoff, *The Pyramid of Unas,* 67.

3. Chaney, *Initiation in the Great Pyramid,* 81.

4. Rawlinson, *The History of Herodotus,* vol. 2, 72.

5. Cavalli, *Embodying Osiris,* 189.

6. Assmann, *The Search for God in Ancient Egypt,* 48.

7. Ibid., 49.

8. Budge, *The Egyptian Book of the Dead,* 366.

9. Merwin, *The Second Four Books of Poems,* 46.

10. Clark, *Myth and Symbol in Ancient Egypt,* 142.

11. Piankoff, *Litany of Re,* 39.

12. Talbot, *The Holographic Universe,* 52–53.

13. Ibid., 31.

Bibliography

Abt, Theodor, and Erik Hornung. *Knowledge for the Afterlife: The Egyptian Amduat; A Quest for Immortality*. Zurich, Switzerland: Living Human Heritage, 2003.

Allen, James P. *Genesis in Egypt: The Philosophy of Ancient Egyptian Creation Accounts*. San Antonio, Tex.: Van Siclen Books, 1995.

———. "Reading a Pyramid." In *Hommages à Jean Leclant*, edited by Catherine Berger, Gisele Clerc, and Nicholas Grimal, 5–28. Cairo: Institut Français de Archéologie Orientale le Caire, Bibliotheque d'Étude 106/1, 1994.

Allen, James P., and Peter Der Manuelian. *The Ancient Egyptian Pyramid Texts*. Leiden, Netherlands: E. J. Brill, 2005.

Andrews, Carol. *The Amulets of Ancient Egypt*. Austin, Tex.: University of Texas Press, 1998.

Assmann, Jan. *Death and Salvation in Ancient Egypt*. Translated by David Lorton. Ithaca, N.Y.: Cornell University Press, 2001.

———. *Moses the Egyptian: The Memory of Egypt in Western Monotheism*. New Haven, Conn.: Harvard University Press, 1998.

———. *The Search for God in Ancient Egypt*. Translated by David Lorton. Ithaca, N.Y.: Cornell University Press, 2001.

Bauval, Robert, and Adrian Gilbert. *The Orion Mystery: Unlocking the Secrets of the Pyramids*. New York: Three Rivers Press, 1994.

Blavatsky, H. P. *The Secret Doctrine: The Synthesis of Science, Religion, and Philosophy*. 2 vols. Wheaton, Ill.: Theosophical University Press, 1999.

Bennett, James, and Vivianne Crowley. *Magic and Mysteries of Ancient Egypt*. New York: Sterling Publications, 2001.

Betz, Hans Dieter. *The Greek Magical Papyri in Translation: Including the Demotic Spells.* Vol. 1, *Texts.* 2nd ed. Chicago: University of Chicago Press, 1992.

Borghouts, J. F. *Ancient Egyptian Magical Texts.* Leiden, Netherlands: E. J. Brill, 1978.

Boylan, Patrick. *Thoth: The Hermes of Egypt.* London: Oxford University Press, 1922.

Breasted, James. *Ancient Records of Egypt.* 5 vols. Chicago: University of Chicago Press, 1907.

———. *The Edwin Smith Surgical Papyrus.* 2 vols. Chicago: University of Chicago Press, 1930.

———. *A History of Egypt from the Earliest Times to the Persian Conquest.* New York: Charles Scribner's Sons, 1905.

Brier, Bob. *Ancient Egyptian Magic.* New York: Quill, 1981.

Budge, E. A. Wallis. *The Egyptian Book of the Dead: The Papyrus of Ani in the British Museum.* New York: Dover, 1967.

———. *Egyptian Magic.* Mineola, N.Y.: Dover Publications, 1971.

———. *Legends of the Gods.* London: Kegan Paul, Trench and Trübner, 1912.

Campbell, Joseph. *The Hero with a Thousand Faces.* 2nd ed. Princeton, N.J.: Princeton University Press, 1968.

Carus, T. Lucretius. *On the Nature of Things.* 2 vols. Translated by Thomas Creech. London: J. Mathews for G. Sawbridge, 1894.

Cavalli, Thomas. *Embodying Osiris: The Secrets of Alchemical Transformation.* Wheaton, Ill.: Quest Books, 2010.

Chaney, Earlyne. *Initiation in the Great Pyramid.* Upland, Calif.: Astara Foundation, 1987.

Clark, Rosemary. *Sacred Magic of Ancient Egypt: The Spiritual Practice Restored.* St. Paul, Minn.: Llewellyn Publications, 2003.

———. *The Sacred Tradition in Ancient Egypt: The Esoteric Wisdom Revealed.* St. Paul, Minn.: Llewellyn, 2000.

Clark, R. T. Rundle. *Myth and Symbol in Ancient Egypt.* Reprint, New York: Thames & Hudson, 1991.

Cline, Eric H., and Jill Rubalcaba. *The Ancient Egyptian World.* New York: Oxford University Press, 2005.

Cott, Jonathan. *Search for Omm Sety.* Garden City, N.J: Doubleday, 1987.

Cottrell, Leonard. *Queens of the Pharaohs.* New York: Macmillan. 1969.

Darnell, John Coleman. *The Enigmatic Netherworld of the Solar-Osirian Unity:*

Cryptographic Compositions in the Tombs of Tutankhamun, Ramses VI and Ramsesses IX. Paulusverlag Fribourg, Switzerland: Academic Press Fribourg, 2004.

David, Gary A. *The Orion Zone: Ancient Star Cities of the American Southwest.* Kempton, Ill.: Adventures Unlimited Press, 2007.

Eddy, Mary Baker. *Science and Health with Key to the Scriptures.* Boston: The Christian Science Board of Directors, 2000.

El-Abbadi, Mostafa, and Omnia Mouner Fathallah. *What Happened to the Ancient Library of Alexandria?* Leiden, Netherlands: E. J. Brill, 2008.

Ellis, Normandi. *Awakening Osiris: The Egyptian Book of the Dead.* Newburyport, Mass.: Phanes Press, 1988. Reprint, Boston: Red Wheel/ Weiser, 2009.

———. *Dreams of Isis: A Woman's Spiritual Sojourn.* Wheaton, Ill.: Quest Books, 1995.

———. *Feasts of Light: Celebrations for the Seasons of Life Based on the Egyptian Goddess Mysteries.* Wheaton, Ill.: Quest Books, 1999.

Faulkner, Raymond O. *The Ancient Egyptian Coffin Texts.* 3 vols. Warminster, U.K.: Aris & Phillips, 1973–78.

———. *The Egyptian Book of the Dead: The Book of Going Forth by Day.* San Francisco: Chronicle Books, 1994.

———. *The Ancient Egyptian Pyramid Texts.* Oxford, U.K.: Oxford University Press, 1969.

Forman, Werner, and Stephen Quirke. *Hieroglyphs and the Afterlife.* Norman, Okla.: University of Oklahoma, 1996.

Forrest, M. Isadora. *Isis Magic.* St. Paul, Minn.: Llewellyn, 2001.

———. *Offering to Isis: Knowing the Goddess through Her Sacred Symbols.* St. Paul, Minn.: Llewellyn, 2005.

Frankfort, Henri. *Ancient Egyptian Religion.* New York: Harper Torchbooks, 1948.

———. *Kingship and the Gods.* Chicago: Oriental Institute of the University of Chicago Press, 1978.

Freke, Timothy. *The Illustrated Book of Sacred Scriptures.* Wheaton, Ill.: Quest Books, 1998.

Freke, Timothy, and Peter Gandy. *The Hermetica: The Lost Wisdom of the Pharaohs.* New York: Jeremy P. Tarcher/Penguin, 1999.

Gardiner, Alan H. *Egyptian Grammar.* 3rd ed. London: Griffith Institute, Oxford University Press, 1957.

——. *Theban Ostraca: Hieratic Texts*. London: Oxford University Press, 1913.

Gee, John. "Prophets, Initiation and the Egyptian Temple." *Journal of the Society for the Study of Egyptian Antiquities* 21 (2004): 97–107.

Grant, Frederick C. *Hellenistic Religions: The Age of Syncretism*. New York: Macmillian Publishing, 1953.

Grasse, Ray. *The Waking Dream: Unlocking the Symbolic Language of Our Lives*. Wheaton, Ill.: Quest Books, 1996.

Griffith, Francis Llewellyn, and Herbert Thompson, eds. *The Demotic Magical Papyrus of London and Leyden*. Vol. 1. London: H. Grevel & Co., 1904.

Guthrie, Kenneth Sylvan, and David Fiedler, eds. *The Pythagorean Sourcebook and Library: An Anthology of Ancient Writings Which Relate to Pythagoras and Pythagorean Philosophy*. Grand Rapids, Mich.: Phanes Press, 1987.

Hancock, Graham, and Santha Faiia. *Heaven's Mirror: Quest for the Lost Civilization*. New York: Random House, 1998.

Harris, Eleanor. *Ancient Egyptian Divination and Magic*. York Beach, Maine: RedWheel/Weiser Books, 1998.

Hart, George. *A Dictionary of Egyptian Gods and Goddesses*. New York: Methuen, 1986.

Hauck, Dennis. *The Emerald Tablet: Alchemy for Personal Transformation*. New York: Penguin/Arkana, 1999.

Hawass, Zahi. *Silent Images: Women in Pharaonic Egypt*. Cairo: American University in Cairo Press, 2009.

——. *Valley of the Golden Mummies*. Cairo: American University Press in Cairo, 2000.

Hornung, Erik. *The Ancient Egyptian Books of the Afterlife*. Translated by David Lorton. Ithaca, N.Y.: Cornell University Press, 1999.

——. *Conceptions of God in Ancient Egypt*. Translated by John Baines. Ithaca, N.Y.: Cornell University Press, 1982.

——. *Idea into Image: Essays on Ancient Egyptian Thought*. Translated by Elizabeth Bredeck. New York: Timken Publishers, 1992.

——. *The Secret Lore of Egypt: Its Impact on the West*. Translated by David Lorton. Ithaca, N.Y.: Cornell University Press, 2001.

Houston, Jean. *The Passion of Isis and Osiris*. New York: Ballantine Books, 1995.

Huxley, Aldous. *The Doors of Perception*. New York: Harper & Row, 1954.

Ions, Veronica. *Egyptian Mythology*. London: Hamlyn Publishing Group, 1968.

Jacq, Christian. *Egyptian Magic*. Translated by Janet Davis. Chicago: Bolchazy-Carducci Publishers, 1985.

James, E. O. *Myths and Ritual in the Ancient Near East.* New York: Praeger, 1965.

Jayne, Walter Addison. *The Healing Gods in Ancient Civilizations.* New York: University Books, 1962.

Keats, John. *Letters of John Keats.* Edited by Frederick Page. London: Oxford University Press, 1965.

Kousoulis, Panagiotis. "Nine Measures of Magic Part 3: 'Overthrowing Apophis': Egyptian Ritual in Practice." *Ancient Egypt Magazine* 2, no. 3 (November–December 2001): 28–35.

Lamy, Lucie. *Egyptian Mysteries: New Light on Ancient Spiritual Knowledge.* New York: Crossroad Publishing, 1981.

LaViolette, Paul A. *Genesis of the Cosmos: The Ancient Science of Continuous Creation.* Rochester, Vt.: Bear & Company, 1995.

Lesko, Leonard H. *The Ancient Egyptian Book of Two Ways.* Berkeley: University of California Press, 1972.

Lichtheim, Miriam. *Ancient Egyptian Literature.* 3 vols. Berkeley: University of California Press, 1973–80.

Lorenzi, Rosella. "Vanished Persian Army Said Found in Desert." *Discovery News,* November 8, 2009. http://news.discovery.com/history/camby-ses-army-remains-sahara.htm.

Luck, Georg. *Arcana Mundi: Magic and the Occult in the Greek and Roman Worlds.* Baltimore, Md.: Johns Hopkins University Press, 1985.

Luckert, Karl W. *Egyptian Light and Hebrew Fire: Theological and Philosophical Roots of Christendom in Evolutionary Perspective.* Albany, N.Y.: State University of New York Press, 1991.

MacLeod, Roy. *The Library of Alexandria: Center of Learning in the Ancient World.* Rev. ed. New York: St. Martin's Press, 2005.

Malkowski, Edward F. *Before the Pharaohs: Egypt's Mysterious Prehistory.* Rochester, Vt.: Bear & Company, 2006.

Manley, Bill, ed. *The Seventy Great Mysteries of Ancient Egypt.* London: Thames & Hudson, 2003.

Massey, Gerald. *Ancient Egypt: Light of the World.* Reprint, New York: Cosimo, 2007.

Masters, Robert. *The Goddess Sekhmet: The Way of the Five Bodies.* Warwick, N.Y.: Amity House, 1988.

Mead, G. R. S. *Thrice Greatest Hermes: Studies in Hellenistic Theosophy and Gnosis.* Reprint, York Beach, Maine: Red Wheel/Weiser, 1992.

Merwin, W. S. *The Second Four Books of Poems*. Port Townsend, Wash.: Copper Canyon Press, 1993.

Meyer, Marvin W., ed. *The Ancient Mysteries: A Sourcebook*. San Francisco: Harper & Row, 1987.

———. *The Nag Hammadi Library*. 3rd ed. New York: Harper & Row, 1988.

Michael, Emory J. *The Alchemy of Sacred Living: Creating a Culture of Light*. Prescott, Ariz.: Mountain Rose Publishing, 1998.

Morenz, Siegried. *Egyptian Religion*. Translated by Ann E. Keep. Ithaca, N.Y.: Cornell University Press, 1973.

Moss, Harold. *Words from a Silent Man*. Notus, Idaho: Paul Shoemaker, 1997.

Murray, Margaret Alice. *Legends of Ancient Egypt*. London: John Murray Publishers, 1913.

Naydler, Jeremy. *Shamanic Wisdom in the Pyramid Texts: The Mystical Tradition of Ancient Egypt*. Rochester, Vt.: Inner Traditions, 2005.

———. *Temple of the Cosmos: The Ancient Egyptian Experience of the Sacred*. Rochester, Vt.: Inner Traditions, 1996.

Neumann, Erich. *The Origins and History of Consciousness*. Bollingen Series XLII. Princeton, N.J.: Princeton University Press, 1974.

Piankoff, Alexandre. *The Litany of Re*. Bollingen Series XL-4. New York: Pantheon Books, 1964.

———. *Mythological Papyri*. New York: Pantheon Books, 1957.

———. *The Pyramid of Unas*. Bollingen Series XL-5. Princeton, N.J.: Princeton University Press, 1968.

———. *The Shrines of Tut-Ankh-Amon*. Edited by N. Rambova. Bollingen Series XL. New York: Harpertorch Books, 1995.

Pinch, Geraldine. *Egyptian Mythology: A Guide to the Gods, Goddesses, and Traditions of Ancient Egypt*. New York: Oxford University Press, 2004.

———. *Magic in Ancient Egypt*. Austin, Tex.: University of Texas Press, 1994.

Pritchard, James B., and Daniel E. Fleming. *The Ancient Near East: An Anthology of Texts and Pictures*. Princeton, N.J.: Princeton University Press, 2010.

Rabinowitz, Jacob. *Isle of Fire*. West Orange, N.J.: Invisible Books, 2004.

Rawlinson, George, ed. *The History of Herodotus*. 4 vols. London: John Murray Publishers, 1858.

Reeder, Greg. "A Rite of Passage: The Enigmatic Tekenu in Ancient Egyptian Funerary Ritual." *KMT: A Modern Journal of Ancient Egypt* 5 no. 3 (Fall 1994): 53–59.

Reidy, Richard. *Eternal Egypt.* Bloomington, Ind.: iUniverse, 2010.

Rice, Michael. *Who's Who in Ancient Egypt.* London: Routledge, 1999.

Richardson, Alan, and Billie Walker-John. *The Inner Guide to Egypt: A Mystical Journey Through Time & Consciousness.* Foreword by Dolores Ashcroft-Nowicki. Woodbury, Minn.: Llewellyn, 2010.

Rilke, Rainer Maria. *Selected Poems of Rainer Maria Rilke.* Translated by Robert Bly. New York: Harper Perennial, 1981.

Ritner, Robert K. *The Mechanics of Ancient Egyptian Magical Practice.* Reprint, Chicago: Oriental Institute of the University of Chicago, 1997.

Roberts, Elizabeth, and Elias Amidon. *Earth Prayers from Around the World: 365 Prayers, Poems, and Invocations for Honoring the Earth.* New York: HarperOne, 1991.

Romer, John. *Ancient Lives: Daily Life in Egypt of the Pharaohs.* New York: Henry Holt & Company, 1990.

Sauneron, Serge. *The Priests of Ancient Egypt.* Ithaca, N.Y.: Cornell University Press, 2000.

Schwaller de Lubicz, Isha. *The Opening of the Way: A Practical Guide to the Wisdom Teachings of Ancient Egypt.* Rochester, Vt.: Inner Traditions, 1979.

Schwaller de Lubicz, R. A. *Sacred Science: The King of Pharaonic Theocracy.* Rochester, Vt.: Inner Traditions, 1982.

———. *Symbol and the Symbolic: Egypt, Science and the Evolution of Consciousness.* Brookline, Mass.: Autumn Press, 1978.

———. *The Temple of Man.* Preface by Robert Lawlor. Rochester, Vt.: Inner Traditions, 1998.

Scranton, Laird. *The Cosmological Origins of Myth and Symbol: From the Dogon and Ancient Egypt to India, Tibet and China.* Rochester, Vt.: Inner Traditions, 2010.

Seifer, Marc J. *Wizard: The Life and Times of Nikola Tesla; Biography of a Genius.* Secaucus, N.J.: Citadel Press, 2001.

Sellers, Jane. *The Death of Gods in Ancient Egypt.* Middlesex, U.K.: Penguin Books, 1992.

Seton-Williams, M. V. *Egyptian Legends and Stories.* New York: Barnes & Noble, 1988.

Strudwick, Nigel C. *Texts from the Pyramid Age: Writings from the Ancient World.* Leiden, Netherlands: E. J. Brill, 2005.

Talbot, Michael. *The Holographic Universe.* New York: HarperCollins, 1991.

Temple, Robert K. G. *The Sirius Mystery.* Rochester, Vt.: Inner Traditions, 1987.

Tesla, Nikola. *My Inventions: The Autobiography of Nikola Tesla*. Williston, Vt.: Hart Brothers Publishing, 1982.

Three Initiates. *The Kybalion: A Study of the Hermetic Philosophy of Ancient Egypt and Greece*. New York: Jeremy Tarcher/Penguin Books, 2008.

Traunecker, Claude, and David Lorton. *The Gods of Egypt*. Ithaca, N.Y.: Cornell University Press, 2001.

van den Dungen, Wim. "The Adoration of Re: Hymn to the Rising Sun." December 14, 2010. www.maat.sofiatopia.org/adoration_of_Re.htm.

Veggi, Anton, and Alison Davidson. *The Book of Doors: An Alchemical Oracle from Ancient Egypt*. Rochester, Vt.: Destiny Books, 1995.

Wainwright, Gordon A. *The Sky Religion in Ancient Egypt*. Westport, Conn.: Greenwood Press, 1971.

Watterson, Barbara. *Gods of Ancient Egypt*. Surrey, U.K.: Bramley Books, 1996.

West, John Anthony. *Serpent in the Sky: The High Wisdom of Ancient Egypt*. Wheaton, Ill.: Quest Books, 1993.

———. *The Traveler's Key to Ancient Egypt: A Guide to the Sacred Places of Ancient Egypt*. Rev. ed. Wheaton, Ill.: Quest Books, 1995.

Wilkinson, Richard. *Symbol and Magic in Egyptian Art*. London: Thames & Hudson, 1994.

Willoughby, Harold. *Pagan Regeneration: A Study of Mystery Initiations in the Graeco Roman World*. Chicago: University of Chicago Press, 1929.

Wilson, Colin. *From Atlantis to the Sphinx: Recovering the Lost Wisdom of the Ancient World*. York Beach, Maine: Red Wheel/Weiser, 1996.

Index

Page numbers in *italics* refer to illustrations.